The Chinese Economy and its Challenges

The remarkable transformation of the Chinese economy in terms of its structure and growth has drawn unprecedented attention from academics, policy makers and businessmen alike. In the past four decades, China swiftly transformed from a centrally-planned to a market-oriented economy, with an economic size just behind the US and ahead of Japan. Amid commendations for China's economic success offering valuable reform and growth lessons to other developing countries, underlying challenges have been emerging, which constitute long-term risks in shaking China's sustainable success. These challenges encompass a wide range of sectors and issues such as the rural-urban divide, state monopoly, policy loans in the banking sector, lack of skilled and sophisticated workers, environmental degradation etc.

This book unveils the risks and challenges embedded in China's spectacular economic success and demonstrates that effective handling of these challenges is vital for China to avoid falling into the "middle-income trap". It is elucidated that feasible solutions are available to accommodate these risks and the clue of success lies in the willingness and ability of China's central leaders to implement further reforms. This book is a valuable reference for undergraduate and postgraduate students, academics, and public and business policy makers who are concerned about the current status and future development of the Chinese economy.

Charles C.L. Kwong is Dean and Professor of Economics, School of Arts and Social Sciences at The Open University of Hong Kong, where he concurrently serves as Director of the Public and Social Policy Research Centre. His research interest focuses on topics pertaining to institutional changes, economic development and the political economy of China. He publishes widely in international journals, and he is a regular media commentator on issues related to the Chinese economy.

Routledge Contemporary China Series

For more information about this series, please visit: https://www.routledge.com/Routledge-Contemporary-China-Series/book-series/SE0768

The Chinese Economy and its Challenges

Transformation of a Rising Economic Power

Charles C.L. Kwong

Routledge
Taylor & Francis Group

LONDON AND NEW YORK

First published 2020 by Routledge

2 Park Square, Milton Park, Abingdon, Oxon OX14 4RN
605 Third Avenue, New York, NY 10017

Routledge is an imprint of the Taylor & Francis Group, an informa business

First issued in paperback 2022

Publisher's Note

The publisher has gone to great lengths to ensure the quality of this reprint
but points out that some imperfections in the original copies may be apparent.

British Library Cataloguing-in-Publication Data
A catalogue record for this book is available from the British Library

Library of Congress Cataloging-in-Publication Data
Names: Kwong, Charles C. L., author.
Title: The Chinese economy and its challenges : transformation of a
   rising economic power / Charles C.L. Kwong.
Description: Milton Park, Abingdon, Oxon ; New York, NY :
   Routledge, 2020. | Series: Routledge contemporary China series |
   Includes bibliographical references and index.
Identifiers: LCCN 2019044837 (print) | LCCN 2019044838
   (ebook)
Subjects: LCSH: China—Economic conditions—1949– | China—
   Economic policy—1949–
Classification: LCC HC427 .K87 2020 (print) | LCC HC427 (ebook) |
   DDC 330.951—dc23
LC record available at https://lccn.loc.gov/2019044837
LC ebook record available at https://lccn.loc.gov/2019044838

ISBN: 978-1-138-78501-4 (hbk)
ISBN: 978-1-03-233735-7 (pbk)
DOI: 10.4324/9781351051224

Typeset in Galliard
by Apex CoVantage, LLC

For my parents, whom I think of every day.

For my wife Sindy and my children Hayden and Hailey, who furnish my life with real meaning.

Contents

Tables

Introduction

China's rise is beyond question a defining phenomenon of the global economy in the 21st century. China, just behind the US, had surpassed Japan as the second-largest economy in the world, with a nominal GDP of US$5.8 trillion and US$5.474 trillion for China and Japan at the end of 2010 respectively (BBC News 2011). It is estimated that China's GDP will reach the level of the US in 2025.[1] In financial dimension, China's stock market capitalisation climbed to US$4.48 trillion, which marginally exceeded Japan's US$4.46 trillion at the end of 2014 (Bloomberg 2014), bearing in mind China's very short history of stock markets.[2] In 2014, China attracted US$128 billion of foreign direct investment (FDI), overtaking the US's US$86 billion to become the world's number one destination for FDI (BBC News 2015). At the turn of the century, China's overseas direct investment (ODI) was only US$6.9 billion. However, since the adoption of the "going out" policy in 2003, China's ODI surged to US$102.9 billion in 2014 and has become one of the top five global investors since 2010 (Zhu and Leung 2015; Shambaugh 2013: 174, 177), which strengthens China's global footprint and influence.

Domestically, China's economic success is equally remarkable. With its average annual growth rate reaching 8–9 percent since the inception of economic reform in the late 1970s, China has lifted about 500 million people out of poverty (The World Bank 2015) and reached a level of upper-middle-income economy, with per capita GNI (Gross National Income) of US$7,400 in 2014 (The World Bank 2016). The average annual growth rate of China's household consumption was 7.7 percent in 1978–2011 and 8.1 percent in 1990–2011. Household consumption in 1990–2011 demonstrated an accelerating trend. Comparing to other BRICS countries,[3] India recorded 5.2 and 5.9 percent while Brazil registered 3.3 and 3.7 percent for the same periods respectively (Ross 2013). Life expectancy, a reflection of quality of medical and health services, rose from 65.84 in 1978 to 76.6 in 2018.[4] Adult literacy rate in China exhibited even more spectacular growth from 77.8 percent in 1990 to about 95.5 percent in 2015,[5] which was the highest among the developing countries in Asia and the Pacific region (UNESCO Institute for Statistics 2012: 13).

Notwithstanding, the impressive accomplishments can be viewed from a contrary perspective. China's GDP growth tapered off from 10.4 percent in 2010 to

6.6 percent in 2018 (NBSC 2014; Trading Economics 2019). China's economy has entered a phase of post high-growth period. Even when China catches up with US's GDP in 2025, China's per capita GDP will only be 24.5 percent of the US.[6] Though China's stock market capitalisation surpassed Japan, the percentage of direct financing[7] stayed at a low level of about 45 percent in 2013 even compared to other developing countries such as Indonesia and India, which reached a level up to 60 to 70 percent (Borst 2014). The underdeveloped direct financing in China is primarily caused by the fact that the stock market has been mainly serving the state-owned enterprises (SOEs) so far and has limited access to private enterprises (PEs) though PEs contributed about 60 percent of China's GDP and 80 percent of urban employment (Guluzade 2019). The stock market has failed to channel funds to the growth engine, the private sector of the economy. Further, China's ODI has been accelerating over the past decade, but it remains a recent phenomenon. Its global stock (2.3 percent) was still relatively small when compared to other advanced economies such as Japan (4.5 percent) and the US (22 percent) in 2013. More importantly, the figure of China's ODI is likely to be overestimated by round-tripping, that is: China's ODI goes mostly to Hong Kong (60 percent), and tax havens and the funds are later reinvested in China in order to enjoy preferential FDI treatment and other advantages. It is estimated that approximately 40 percent of China's ODI to Hong Kong has been channeled back to China as inbound FDI (Garcia-Herrero, Le and Casanova 2015: 5–6).

Spectacular growth in household income and consumption is unprecedented, but its rising income and consumption disparity have reached a worrying level. The Gini Coefficient, a measure of income disparity, reached its historic high of 0.491 in 2008 and then started to decline. The coefficient hit a record low of 0.462 in 2015, but it exhibited a rebound in 2016 and 2017.[8] Over the past decade, China's Gini Coefficient has been persistently higher than the alarming level of 0.4, which can probably lead to social problems and jeopardise long term economic growth. In addition, though China has already been an upper-middle-income economy, its Human Development Index (HDI)[9] was ranked 90 among 188 countries in 2014 (Human Development Report 2015), which indicates China's human development is still lagging behind its rapid income growth. In terms of labour productivity, China maintained a strong average annual growth rate of 12 percent for the period 2003–2007, but the growth rates fell substantially to 9 percent for the period 2008–2012. From a comparative perspective, China's labour productivity was only 17 percent of that of America, 23.9 percent of Japan and 23 percent of Germany.[10]

The previous contrary views have been common among China's observers. Both views actually truly reflect the accomplishments and challenges facing the Chinese economy. The differences lie in the varied focus of the analyses. The primary purpose of this book is not to examine whether an optimistic or a pessimistic view is more valid for the Chinese economy in the future. Instead, this book seeks to examine what bottlenecks and pressing problems China must overcome in order to sustain its economic growth and expanding influence in the global economy in the coming decades. Of primary importance is not its spectacular success over the past decades. The real and practical concerns facing China are the challenges ahead that hinder China's long term growth and development. Without overcoming these hurdles, China will face heightened risks of falling into the middle income trap encountered by the Latin American countries in the 1980s. This book is structured as outlined in the following.

Chapter 1 reviews the background of economic reform inaugurated in the late 1970s and highlights the initial success in the 1980s, which was mainly attributable to the institutional reforms that allowed market to play a greater role in allocating resources and providing incentives for individuals and firms to produce and invest. It then analyses the rising challenges since the 1990s, including slowdown of rural development, rising production costs, declining labour productivity, mounting non-performing loans in the banking sector and so on. Chapter 2 examines the initial success of the rural economy and then scrutinises the sluggish growth of the countryside since the mid-1990s by arguing that the rural problems stem from slow growth in rural industry, local government fiscal constraints and underdevelopment of rural finance. Without solving the rural problems, rural-urban disparity and its associated problems will persist. Chapter 3 focuses on the increasing number of China's SOEs that have been ranked among the top 500 enterprises in the world in terms of assets value. However, taking into the account the monopoly status granted by the state and the favourable credit environment provided by the state-owned commercial banks (SOCBs), SOEs do not seem to outperform private enterprises. This chapter will also evaluate how a substantial state sector has constrained the growth of private enterprises which are the growth engine of the Chinese economy. Chapter 4 propounds that the commercialisation of state banks in 1994 aimed at enhancing efficiency of the banking sector by making state banks operate according to market disciplines. However, evidence shows that SOCBs are still dominated by state policy direction and a de facto commercial banking system is still remote. This chapter examines how a state-dominated banking sector can threaten the macroeconomic stability, impede the development of the private sector, and lower the efficiency of loanable funds utilisation.

After the first four chapters on domestic economy, Chapter 5 analyses China's integration into the global economy. In the early stage of economic reform, China relied on foreign capital and technology, combined with its low labour and land costs, to establish its industrial base and finally evolve into a competitive "global factory". With more than three decades of trade surplus with major trade partners such as the US and EU, China's huge foreign exchange reserve has enabled her to become the largest creditor to the US. China has gradually become a stabiliser in the global financial market, in particular during the global financial crisis in 2008. China's increasing capital outflow to Asia and Africa further ascertains its rising role in the international capital market and ODI. In the midst of its changing role, China's attractiveness in capturing capital inflow is hindered by rising production costs, keen competition from other emerging economies and increasing economic tension between China and the Western countries, in particular the US.

Chapter 6 and 7 examine two critical issues that affect China's sustained growth and competitiveness in the long run. Chapter 6 demonstrates the significance of human capital investment in China. In parallel with China's spectacular economic rise, its labour costs have soared to a level that is just behind Japan, Singapore, Hong Kong, South Korea, Taiwan and Malaysia. Its competitive edge on labour cost has gradually faded away. However, China's workers are still facing a human capital gap with their Western counterparts, which obstructs its path to high value-added production. Only about 13 percent of China's labour force reached tertiary education level. China's Human Capital Index[11] was ranked 64 among 124 countries in 2015. Its ranking is even lower than those of Vietnam, Sri Lanka, Peru and Colombia (World Economic Forum 2015). To break away from the human capital bottleneck, prompt and substantial investment in education and on-the-job training is of primary importance. Adequate and appropriate human capital is a precondition for China to transform its growth model from capital-driven to quality-driven, which relies on high value-added goods and services. Chapter 7 argues that credit and capital-driven growth over the past decades has enable China to maintain impressive growth during the reform era. However, the rising credit-GDP ratio in recent years has rung the alarm that the seemingly workable growth model has gradually been losing its momentum when more credits are need to generate one unit of GDP (i.e., output). Another main pillar of China's growth model is the reliance on low costs of labour and natural resources, but this comparative advantage has been undermined by neighbouring emerging economies such as Vietnam, India and Bangladesh. China needs to re-engineer its growth model to avoid falling into the middle-income trap. The concluding chapter summarises the main findings and arguments of the preceding chapters and highlights the significance of a productivity-led growth model for China's sustained growth in the long run. As an ending note, it argues that, aside from maintaining economic growth, inclusive growth and environmental protection are two pivotal determinants of people's livelihood.

Notes

1 This estimate is based on the assumption of China's real GDP growth at 6.5 percent per annum with an inflation rate of 3 percent while US's real GDP grows at 2.25 percent with an inflation rate of 1.8 percent. For a more detailed discussion on the estimate, see "Chinese and American GDP Forecasts", *The Economist*, 22 August 2014. Available at: www.economist.com/blogs/graphicdetail/2014/08/chinese-and-american-gdp-forecasts (Accessed on 2 February 2016)

2 Shanghai Stock Exchange and Shenzhen Stock Exchange were founded on 26 November and 1 December 1990 respectively.

3 The BRICS countries refer to the fast-growing emerging economies including Brazil, Russia, India, China and South Africa.

4 Data from www.indexmundi.com/facts/china/life-expectancy-at-birth (Accessed on 10 June 2019) and https://knoema.com/atlas/China/topics/Demographics/Population-forecast/Life-expectancy (Accessed on 10 June 2019)

5 Adult literacy rate is defined as the percentage of population aged 15 and above who are able to read and write, along with understanding a short, simple statement

about one's everyday life. For details, see United Nations (2008). China's literacy rate in 2015 was an estimated figure.

6 It is calculated based on the population projection of 1,411 million and 345 million for China and US in 2015. See The World Bank (2016) "Population Estimates and Projections". Available at: http://datatopics.worldbank.org/hnp/popestimates (Accessed on 14 February 2016).

7 Direct financing refers to the corporations that raise funds directly from the capital market, such as stock and bond markets, instead of going through financial intermediaries such as commercial banks.

8 Please refer to the concluding chapter for a more detailed discussion of China's income disparity.

9 HDI is an integrated measure of human development, which takes into account the growth of household income, education attainment and life expectancy.

10 Author's calculation based on the data from Economist.com (2013).

11 The Human Capital Index (HCI) was a quantified measure of how a country develops and deploys its human capital for economic development. For details, see World Economic Forum (2015).

References

BBC News (2011) 'China Overtakes Japan as World's Second-Biggest Economy,' 14 February. Available at: www.bbc.com/news/business-12427321 (Accessed on 10 February 2016).

BBC News (2015) 'China Overtakes US for Foreign Direct Investment,' 30 January. Available at: www.bbc.com/news/business-31052566 (Accessed on 10 February 2016).

Bloomberg (2014) 'China Overtakes Japan as Second-Largest Market,' 1 December. Available at: https://economictimes.indiatimes.com/news/international/business/china-overtakes-japan-as-second-largest-market/articleshow/45329780.cms (Accessed on 10 February 2016).

Borst, N. (2014) 'Reforming China's Capital Market,' *China Economic Watch*, Washington, DC: The Peterson Institute for International Economics.

Economist.com (2013) 'Labour Productivity.' Available at: www.economist.com/blogs/graphicdetail/2013/02/focus-3 (Accessed on 15 February 2016).

Garcia-Herrero, A., Le, X. and Casanova, C. (2015) 'China's Outbound Foreign Direct Investment: How Much Goes Where After Round-tripping and Offshoring?' *BBVA Working Paper*, No. 15/17, Madrid.

Guluzade, A. (2019) 'Explained, the Role of China's State-Owned Companies,' *World Economic Forum*, 7 May. Available at: www.weforum.org/agenda/2019/05/why-chinas-state-owned-companies-still-have-a-key-role-to-play/ (Accessed on 21 June 2019).

Human Development Report (2015) Available at: http://report.hdr.undp.org/ (Accessed on 14 February 2016).

National Bureau of Statistics of China (NBSC) (2014) *China Statistical Yearbook 2014.* Available at: www.stats.gov.cn/tjsj/ndsj/2014/indexeh.htm (Accessed on 4 February 2016).

Ross, J. (2013) 'China Has the World's Fastest Growth in Living Standards,' *China.org.cn.* Available at: www.china.org.cn/opinion/2013-10/24/content_30391004.htm (Accessed on 11 February 2016).

Shambaugh, D. (2013) *China Goes Global: The Partial Power*, New York: Oxford University Press.

Trading Economics (2019) 'China GDP Annual Growth Rate.' Available at: https://tradingeconomics.com/china/gdp-growth-annual (Accessed on 10 June 2019).

UNESCO Institute for Statistics (2012) *Adult and Youth Literacy, 1990–2015: Analysis of Data for 41 Selected Countries*, Montreal: UNESCO Institute for Statistics.

United Nations (2008) *Principles and Recommendations for Population and Housing Censuses: Revision 2*, New York: United Nations.

The World Bank (2015) 'China: Overview.' Available at: www.worldbank.org/en/country/china/overview (Accessed on 3 February 2016).

The World Bank (2016) 'Data: China.' Available at: http://data.worldbank.org/country/china (Accessed on 4 February 2016).

World Economic Forum (2015) *Human Capital Report 2015*, New York: World Economic Forum.ss

Zhu, L. and Leung, D. (2015) 'China's Overseas Investments, Explained in 10 Graphics,' *World Resources Institute*. Available at: www.wri.org/blog/2015/01/china%E2%80%99s-overseas-investments-explained-10-graphics (Accessed on 10 February 2016).

1 Transformation, initial success and challenges embedded

China's economic reforms that have taken place since the late 1970s have had profound and far-reaching effects on the Chinese economy, which are unprecedented in its economic history. China's four decades of economic reforms have transformed the country from a closed and centrally planned economy to a market-oriented economy integrating into the global economy, from one of the poorest countries in the world in 1978 to one of the fastest growing economies in the world, from one of the major FDI recipients to one of the major ODI investors. With its rising economic power, China has become an important and influential player challenging the US's hegemony in the global economy. The lessons and experiences of China's "success story" have been followed, to various extents, by other formerly centrally planned economies, such as Vietnam, North Korea and Cuba as well as other developing countries.

This chapter reviews the background of economic reform inaugurated since the late 1970s and the emerging issues in different stages of reforms and development. It is demonstrated that China's reform agenda can best be described as an *ad hoc suite of crisis-and-response strategy*, instead of a well thought-out reform plan. Most reforms initiatives, in particular in the early years of reforms, were ad hoc responses to the emerging problems and issues arising from the preceding phase of economic reforms and development. China's economic reform and development can broadly be divided into five phases. This chapter will first highlight the initial success of the first phase of economic reforms from 1978 to 1984, during which rural reforms brought spectacular growth in output and enhancement of living standard. The other main plank of reform in this phase was the adoption of open door policy in early 1980s, which marked China's first move to re-enter the global economy. The second phase, 1985–1991, focused on state-owned enterprises (SOEs) and price reforms. Though SOEs and price reforms were modeled upon the rural reform, that is, mainly decentralisation and marketisation, the resulting macroeconomic imbalances finally led to a political crisis in 1989, the Tiananmen Incidence. After the setback from 1989 to 1991, China embarked on another key phase of reform, marked by Deng Xiaoping's Southern tour (*nanxun*). Chinese leaders reaffirmed that market was the fundamental economic operating system. A series of extensive reforms, including financial reform, exchange rate reform and fiscal reform, were implemented to alleviate the structural and efficiency problems inherited from previous reforms. China entered the fourth phase of economic reform since its admission to the World Trade Organization (WTO) in 2001, which manifested China's further integration into the global economy and its global influence in terms of trade and financial flows. The prolong period of rapid trade expansion and growth, however, came to a halt amid the outbreak of global financial crisis (GFC) in 2008, which prompted China to initiate a 4-trillion stimulus programme to hedge against the substantial fall in external demand and stabilise the domestic economy. However, the stimulus package was implemented at the expense of generating nonperforming loans (NPLs) and massive overcapacity. The repercussions of GFC and the stimulus package drove China to move into its fifth phase of reform in 2013, with new development strategy of refocusing from extensive growth to intensive (i.e., quality) growth emphasising further market reforms, competition and efficiency. Externally, the Belt and Road Initiative (BRI) signifies China's strong intent to evolve from a passive participant in global economy to an active leader in one of major global economic cooperation programmes. The BRI extends China's arms of global influence from East Asia via Middle East to Eastern and Western Europe.[1] BRI, coupled with the China's initiative of setting up the Asian Infrastructure Investment Bank (AIIB), enables China to assume a significant role in global political economy.

Inauguration of China's economic reform: institutional changes, opening up and initial success (1978–1984)

China's journey of four decades of reforms started with institutional changes in the countryside in the late 1970s and the implementation of an open-door policy in the early 1980s. Though the reforms in the late 1970s lacked a comprehensive blueprint, the rural reform and open-door policy were by no means coincidental. The series of reforms was driven by the devastated economic conditions inherited from the pre-reform era and the political changes in the late 1970s.

The momentum behind the reforms is at least threefold. First, the Gross National Product (GNP) and GNP per capita growth rates were not very low, with respective average annual growth rates of 6.2 percent and 4.3 percent during 1952–1980 (Yeh 1996: 12). However, such growth record did not accurately reflect the living standard of households as heavy industry occupied a large share in China's GNP, which did not bring direct material wellbeing to the households. Instead, the standard of living was better gauged by per capita consumption and disposable income. Table 1.1 shows the average annual growth rate of material consumption and disposable income per capita, which were significantly lower than GNP growth. The average annual growth rates of material consumption and disposable income per capita were only 2 percent and 1.6 percent respectively over the period of 1957–1978. It indicates that benefits of economic growth could not filter down to enhance the living standard of households. From a comparative perspective, China's per capita income was $74 in 1960, which was only about half of that of Taiwan and 22 percent of that of Hong Kong. After 20 years,

Table 1.1 Average Annual Growth Rate of Material Consumption and Disposable Income Per Capita

Period	Material consumption per capita	Disposable income per capita
1957–1978	2.0	1.6
1978–1985	9.1	11.7
1985–1990	4.1	1.2

Source: Chai (1996: 248–249)

Hong Kong and Taiwan had become middle-income countries with per capita income of $5,441 and $2,341 in 1980 respectively while China's figure was just a meagre $249, which was only 10.6 percent and 4.5 percent of the per capita income of Taiwan and Hong Kong (Garnaut 1989: 41). The widening gap with neighbouring Chinese societies incentivised reform leaders to initiate and allow pragmatic and bold steps to catch up with the newly industrialising economies (NIEs). A prolonged period of a lagged-behind living standard might shake the legitimacy of the ruling party.

Second, economic growth cannot be sustained by merely increasing the amount of physical inputs such as capital, labour and land (i.e., natural resources) as they are all subject to diminishing returns. To break away from diminishing returns, long-term productivity can be enhanced by innovation, which increases output with a given amount of physical inputs. China is no exception. Inability to enhance technological innovation would mean that China's productivity would be constrained. In the 1950s, China's main sources of imported technology were the former Soviet Union and Eastern European countries. However, since its split with the Soviet Union in 1960, China had been insulated from imported technology. The Soviet Union withdrew all technical support, both hard and software, from China in 1961. In the late 1970s, China's overall level of industrial technology was 10–20 years behind world level, and 20–40 years in some specific areas (Chai 1997: 4). The technological gap prompted Beijing leaders, in particular Deng Xiaoping, to initiate open-door policy to capture foreign capital and technology.

Third, the death of Mao in 1976 and the fall of the Gang of Four offered a relaxed political atmosphere to embolden local and central cadres to take decisive steps to implement institutional changes with an aim to enhance productivity, which heightened living standard of rural households. Realising that improved living standards were vital to regain political legitimacy after two decades of disappointing growth and development, China's ruling party shifted its focus from "ideological correctness" to economic growth, with particular emphasis on improving the material wellbeing of the households (Brandt, Ma and Rawski 2013: 73). The gist of Deng Xiaoping's pragmatic approach was best captured by his "Black Cat, White Cat Theory" advocating that "it doesn't matter whether a cat is black or white, as long as it catches mice it's a good cat". He told President Carter of the US in January 1979, "The Chinese need a long period of peace to realize their full modernization". When Deng met with American businessmen, he said clearly that China needed their money and technology (Tyler 1997). Without the changed political environment, China might not be able to overcome the ideological and political hurdles to adopt such a pragmatic approach of institutional overhaul and open-door policy.

Instead of having a full-fledged reform agenda, China's reform started with an induced institutional change initiated by a spontaneous emergence of a responsibility system in poor counties of Anhui Province. The essence of the household responsibility system (HRS, *baogan daohu*) in 1978–80 was to allow farm households to sell or retain the surplus they produced after fulfilling the targets set by their collective. This institutional overhaul signified China's transformation from collective farming to household farming, which provided a much stronger effort-and-reward link than that under the commune system practised before the reform. Farmers were provided with material incentives to work and invest in their allotted land.[2] The initial reforms in the countryside accomplished impressive results. Agricultural output grew 42.23 percent in 1978–1984, and 45.79 percent of this growth was attributable to the increase in agricultural inputs, mainly the application of fertiliser. Institutional change, the implementation of HRS, contributed 46.89 percent to this growth, which demonstrated that institutional reform in rural China was as important as agricultural inputs to boost output growth during this period (Lin 1992). Measured in real terms, the annual growth rate of gross output value of agriculture (GOVA) was 6.4 percent in 1981–1985, compared with 4.7 percent in 1971–1980 and 3.05 percent in 1952–1970 (Ash 1996: 57).

China's opening up to the outside world, commonly known as the open-door policy, entails two major elements: trade expansion and utilisation of foreign direct investment (FDI). During the pre-reform period, exports were not perceived as a conducive factor for economic growth and development but only a means to earn enough foreign exchange to pay for imports. Foreign trade was limited at a minimum level. However, the "success story" of export-led growth in the NIEs, Singapore, South Korea, Taiwan and Hong Kong in the 1960s to 1970s prompted China's central leaders to reconsider the role of trade in economic growth and development. China finally attempted to capitalise its comparative advantage in producing and exporting labour-intensive products to promote economic growth. At the Fourth Meeting of the Fifth National People's Congress in late 1981, former Premier Zhao Ziyang formally announced that achieving a greater share in world trade was one of the long-term development strategies of China (Chai 1997: 139). China's exports escalated from US$9.75 billion in 1978 to US$27.36 billion in 1985 while import grew even faster from US$10.89 billion in 1978 to US$42.25 in 1985, resulting in rising trade deficit in the 1980s (National Bureau of Statistics of China 1986: 563). Instead of adopting an import substitution strategy like some NIEs and Latin American countries, China embarked on rapid expansion of imports of capital goods to accelerate its industrial growth. Imported capital goods shared 81 percent of China's total imports in 1984.[3] Though China's trade deficit reached its peak in the mid-1980s, its imported capital goods and embedded technology strengthened China's industrial base for industrial expansion in the subsequent decades.

Apart from trade expansion, the Special Economic Zones (SEZs) established in the early 1980s were another manifestation of China's open-door policy.[4] The SEZs aimed at tapping capital, technology and managerial skills, which China was lacking, from foreign investors. Favourable policies were offered in the SEZs to attract foreign investors. Such incentives included tax holidays, duty-free imported inputs, reduced land-use fees and better infrastructure (Chai 1997: 157; Rodrik 2011: 152). The setting up of SEZs was a very pragmatic and cautious approach to open up the Chinese economy. At its initial stage of reform, China certainly realised that it would not be easy to entice foreign companies worldwide, especially those in the Western countries, which were unfamiliar with Chinese business culture and environment. They were unwilling to take the risk due to severe lack of information. China therefore took a pragmatic approach to set up four SEZs with proximity to Hong Kong, Macau and Taiwan, which had a better understanding of the Chinese business environment and closer familial and cultural connections with China. Companies from these regions were more willing to invest in the SEZs. SEZs in China were not only new to foreign investors but also new to China. China adopted a cautious and experimental approach of opening up only four cities, instead of spreading the policies to all major cities. Even if the "experiment" in the SEZs was unsuccessful, its harmful effects on the Chinese economy could be contained.

From 1979 to 1984, SEZs attracted steady inflow of capital, mainly from Hong Kong, Macau and Taiwan. However, the utilised FDI increased at a much slower pace than that of the contracted FDI.[5] The ratio of utilised FDI to contracted FDI (*UC ratio*) had declined from the late 1970s to 1985 (Table 1.2). In 1985, only about one-third of the contracted FDI was actually utilised. The declining *UC ratio* demonstrated that foreign investors were reluctant to fully implement their pledged funding. Their reluctance was mainly attributable to the stringent regulations set by the Chinese government during the initial period of reforms. Some primary concerns of the foreign investors included the governance structure of joint venture (JV) and the tight control of foreign exchange.[6] Though the scale of foreign investment was limited, FDI in the early years of reform not only

Table 1.2 Contracted and Utilised FDI in China 1979–1985 (in billion US$)

Year	Contracted FDI	Utilised FDI	UC ratio
1979–1982	20.17	15.21	75.41
1983	3.43	1.51	44.02
1984	4.79	1.92	40.08
1985	9.86	3.53	35.80
1979–1985	38.25	22.17	57.96

Source: National Bureau of Statistics of China (1986: 581)

brought capital, technology and managerial skills to China but also opened a gate to collaborate with foreign investors. The business connections built between local and foreign companies constituted an important foundation for subsequent cooperation, which proved to be vital for China's economic development in the 1990s.

There was no roadmap for the first phase of economic reform. Deng adopted a pragmatic and gradual approach of "crossing the river by feeling the stones". The encouraging results of rising productivity and enhanced living standards motivated reform leaders to extend the reforms to the urban sector. While institutional reforms boosted efficiency and productivity by releasing household's initiatives in rural areas, such impact was more one-off in nature, without continual effects (Spence 2011: 36). Reformer leaders needed to explore new momentum to spread productivity and economic growth over different sectors of the economy.

SOEs reform, price reforms and setback (1985–1991)

The sweeping changes in the countryside and the unprecedented opening up in the SEZs and coastal cities not only brought rising income, productivity and living standard but also clearly demonstrated the importance of incentives, decentralisation and marketisation in reaching these arresting results. The initial success of rural reform and the open-door policy motivated central leaders to kick off enterprise reform and price reform.

The main thrust of the SOEs reform was to increase the enterprises' incentives by instituting a contract responsibility system (CRS) since 1987, similar to the nature of the HRS in agriculture. This system required SOEs to deliver a number of profit, innovation and efficiency goals. Once the assigned targets were fulfilled, the enterprises were allowed to retain the remaining profits.[7] The CRS tried to incentivise enterprises to better utilise their resources and ameliorated the problem of soft budget constraint.[8] Nevertheless, the effectiveness of using CRS to boost enterprises' incentives seemed less apparent than that of the HRS, which was attributable to two major factors. First, the process of production in industrial enterprises was much more complex than that of agriculture. A high level of division of labour was required in industrial production, which made it difficult to reward each worker according to productivity and efforts rendered. The effort-and-reward link in industrial production, particularly at workers' level, was looser than that in agriculture. The issue of separation of contribution was further complicated by the question of whether a certain SOE could fulfil the assigned targets, which depended largely on the cooperation of upstream and downstream SOEs (Zhang and Liu 2010: 6–7). It was costly and difficult to quantify efforts of individual workers and enterprises. Second, soft budget constraints remained, as the central government would not allow massive bankruptcy and layoffs for SOEs with chronic losses. Central leaders realised that massive layoffs would jeopardise public support for further reform. Based on a sample survey 300 SOEs in 1989, it was revealed that no loss-making SOEs were subject to bankruptcy. Even worse, the empirical study indicated a weak correlation between SOEs' profitability and bonus payments to workers, which implied that loss-making SOEs still paid a bonus to their workers (Chai and Tisdell 1992). The extent of soft budget constraint can be measured by the amount of fiscal subsidies to loss-making SOEs. Fiscal subsidies to SOEs declined from 50.7 billion yuan in 1985 to 32.5 billion yuan in 1986, but rose again to 37.6 billion yuan in 1987. It then increased continuously to reach its peak at 57.9 billion yuan in 1990 (Lardy 1998: 37). Given the complex nature of China's SOE system and the prevailing soft budget constraint, the result of SOE reform was much less appealing than that of rural reform. Table 1.3 shows that the percentage of loss-making state-owned industrial enterprises had increased steadily from 9.6 percent in 1985 to 25.8 percent in 1991, and the losses escalated from a small number of 3.2 billion yuan in 1985 to 36.7 billion yuan in 1991. The amount soared more than 10 times within just 6 years.

Parallel to enterprise reform, the central government initiated price reform in agriculture and industry in the mid-1980s. For agricultural products, price reform was to lift farmers' incentive to produce and better reflect the market prices of raw materials, which served as input prices for industrial production. From 1979 to 1984, the government raised the procurement prices for quota deliveries of 18 major farm products. The rise in prices ranged from 15 to 50 percent. Procurement prices for above-quota deliveries were also raised by 30 to 50 percent (Chai 1997: 103–104; Sicular 1988). The upward adjustment of procurement prices achieved the dual goals of motivating farmers to produce and reducing market distortion, but it generated an unintended outcome of raising the central government's fiscal burden, which prompted the government to abolish the compulsory purchase in 1985.

The input and output prices of industrial products were state-determined before the reform. They did not reflect relative scarcity of inputs and outputs and in turn did not mirror the true profitability of the industrial enterprises. SOEs provided with low-priced inputs and assigned with production of high-priced outputs would naturally become "profitable" and vice versa (Steinfeld 1998: 65). As profitability was one of important performance indicators under the CRS, industrial prices needed to be adjusted to align with the input (agricultural) prices

Table 1.3 Losses of State-Owned Industrial Enterprises 1985–1991

Year	Percentage of loss-making enterprises	Losses (billion yuan)
1985	9.6	3.2
1986	13.1	5.4
1987	13.0	6.1
1988	10.9	8.2
1989	16.0	18.0
1990	27.6	34.9
1991	25.8	36.7

Source: Lardy (1998: 35)

that became more market-determined after 1985. The industrial ex-factory prices rose, on average, 9.1 percent per annum from 1985 to 1991.[9]

The price reform since 1985 raised both agricultural and industrial prices, which heightened production incentives of farming households and industrial enterprises. Prices were formed more according to market forces, which reduced market distortion. Prices started to become better signals for resource allocation. Nevertheless, price reforms in the mid-1980s brought two inadvertent outcomes. First, relaxed price control imposed inflationary pressure in both rural and urban sectors. Overall retail price index skyrocketed from 108.8 in 1985 to 118.5 in 1988, which was a historic high for the 1980s and early 1990s. The urban sector was hit particularly hard by inflation, with the retail price index reaching 121.3 in 1988 (Table 1.4), which substantially raised the living costs of urban dwellers. Though a subsidy of 10 yuan per resident per month was provided by the government, it barely alleviated the hardship and discontent of urban residents (*The New York Times* 1988). Second, a dual-track price system was adopted during the initial years of price reform. Under the dual-track system, an official fixed price coexisted with an uncontrolled market price for the same product. This was a transitional arrangement as advocated to Zhao Zhiyang in 1986, which aimed at finally unifying planned and market prices for most commodities in 5 years (Rajaram 1992: 5; Chai 1997: 98–99). As shown in Table 1.5, 3 different kinds of prices existed in the market during the period 1985–1999. The market prices could be 2 to three 3 higher than the state-fixed prices (Chai 1997: 99; Rajaram 1992: 9). The existence of a dual-track price system offered immense incentives to officials vested with authority to divert outputs from plan deliveries

Table 1.4 Retail Price Indices 1978–1993 (Previous Year = 100)

	Overall retail price index	*Urban retail price index*	*Rural retail price index*
1978	100.7	102.5	100.1
1979	102.0	101.9	102.0
1980	106.0	108.1	104.4
1981	102.4	102.7	102.1
1982	101.9	102.1	101.7
1983	101.5	101.9	101.2
1984	102.8	102.5	103.0
1985	108.8	112.2	107.0
1986	106.0	107.0	105.0
1987	107.3	109.1	106.3
1988	118.5	121.3	117.1
1989	117.8	116.0	118.8
1990	102.1	100.2	103.2
1991	102.9	104.5	102.0
1992	105.4	107.7	103.9
1993	113.2	114.2	112.6

Source: National Bureau of Statistics of China (1994: 232, 236, 238)

Table 1.5 Market, State-guided and State-fixed Prices* 1978–1999

	Retail commodities			Agricultural commodities			Producer goods		
	Market	State-guided	State-fixed	Market	State-guided	State-fixed	Market	State-guided	State-fixed
1978	0	3	97	6	2	93	0	0	100
1985	34	19	47	40	23	37	n.a.	n.a.	n.a.
1987	38	28	34	54	17	29	n.a.	n.a.	n.a.
1991	69	10	21	58	20	22	46	18	36
1995	89	2	9	79	4	17	78	6	16
1999	95	1	4	83	7	9	86	4	10

Source: Lardy (2002: 25)

Note
* Market prices were free prices determined by market supply and demand. State-guided prices were prices determined by enterprises within upper and lower limits or prices set below (above) price ceiling (price floor). For details, see Chai (1997: 98); n.a. = not available.

to market sales to capture the rent generated by price differentials.[10] Some SOEs overstated their input requirement for plan deliveries and sold the excess inputs in the market to capture profits (Rajaram 1992: 5). This profiteering, more specifically rent-seeking, activities antagonised the public by raising their living costs. More importantly, the dual-track price system did not eliminate but only changed the form of price distortion and gave rise to rent-seeking behaviour.

The second phase of economic reform centring on industrial and price reforms resulted in disappointing outcomes. SOEs remained inefficient and unprofitable amid prevailing soft budget constraint. Runaway inflation, together with severe rent-seeking activities resulted from the dual-track price system, accounted for, at least partially, the June Fourth Incident in 1989.[11] The economic situation after the mid-1980s was further complicated by the rapid expansion of money supply and investment, which intensified the inflationary pressure.

Rebound and further marketisation (1992–2000)

The June Fourth Incident and subsequent military crackdown on demonstrators in Beijing brought China to the worst isolation from the West since the Cultural Revolution (Shambaugh 2013: 50). Political and economic uncertainties put a halt on capital inflow to China. Utilised FDI recorded zero growth from 1989 to 1990 (Chai 1997: 159). Domestically, rampant inflation, coupled with the impacts of the June Fourth Incident, constituted the most severe governing crisis of the ruling party since its implementation of economic reforms. An Austerity programme was implemented to rein in investment expansion and cool down the overheated economy. Sub-provincial governments were not allowed to approve new projects for 1989 and 1990. Projects in excess of 10 million yuan could still be approved by the provincial government but needed to be reported to the State

Planning Commission to ensure that the central government could keep track of major investment projects. Deposit and lending interest rates were raised to reduce loanable funds in the market (Huang 1996: 166).

To regain confidence of foreign investors and reassure the continuation of market reform, Deng embarked on a Southern tour, which proved to be the most defining event signifying China's continuation of opening up and furthering reform. The Fourteenth Party Congress in October 1992 concretised Deng's ideas by setting the goal of establishing a "socialist market economy". The "Decision on Several Issues Concerning Establishing a Socialist Market Economy" enacted in the Third Plenary Session of the Fourteenth Party Central Committee in November 1993 stipulated wide-ranging policy initiatives to deepen market reforms (Wu 2012: 22–23). Domestically, the central government put forward important reforms in SOEs, the banking sector, the tax system and the foreign exchange system.[12] The main plank of these reforms was to allow greater degree of decentralisation and marketisation. Externally, China made an ongoing endeavour to join the World Trade Organization (WTO) to further strengthen its open-door policy. However, the very nature of this endeavour was different from the initial stage of opening up, which mainly aimed at attracting FDI, – together with its embedded managerial skills – and trade expansion. China's eagerness to join the WTO was motivated by a number of strategic reasons, including exposing SOEs to foreign competition, enhancing China's technological level, avoiding annual review of China's Most Favoured Nation Status by the US and participating in formulating rules of international trade (Prime 2002). These motivations explain China's acceptance of substantial concession in order to be admitted to the WTO.

From WTO admission to post-crisis response: a return of state intervention? (2001–2013)

China entered the fourth phase of economic reform since its admission to the World Trade Organization (WTO) in 2001, which manifested China's further integration into the global economy and its global influence in terms of trade and financial flows.

China brought down the tariffs sharply and phased out subsidies in various exporting sectors, but it maintained its control on yuan (RMB) exchange rate, through which China could manipulate the effective export prices to buffer the lost protection and competitiveness after WTO admission (Rodrik 2012: 276). It explains China's reluctance in exposing yuan exchange rate determination to market mechanism. Immediately after China's WTO admission, US$:RMB exchange rate remained stable from 2002 to 2005, with RMB appreciated slightly at 1.05 percent during the same period. However, Euro:RMB exchange rate rose considerably from 1 euro to 8.01 yuan in 2002 to 1 euro to 10.19 yuan, representing a drastic devaluation of 27.35 percent of RMB against the euro within 4 years.[13] China's targeted devaluation is understandable as China's exports to Europe demonstrated remarkable growth after the late 1990s and reached US$165.63 billion yuan in 2005, which caused Europe to surpass the US as China's largest exporting market.[14]

The prolonged period of rapid trade expansion and economic growth, however, came to an abrupt adjustment amid the outbreak of global financial crisis (GFC) in 2008. China recorded 9 percent of growth in the third quarter of 2008, which was the lowest growth since 2003. Coupled with the decline in other economic indicators, China initiated a 4-trillion yuan stimulus programme in late 2008 to hedge against the substantial fall in external demand and stabilise the domestic economy. According to the plan of the central government, it would only finance 30 percent (i.e., 1.2 trillion yuan) of the stimulus program, and local governments would finance the remaining balance (i.e., 2.8 trillion yuan) (Goodstadt 2012: 12). Facing the investment targets delegated from the central government, local governments were active in setting up local government financial platforms (LGFPs) to enlarge the fund pool for local projects. As local governments are prohibited from borrowing from commercial banks or issuing bonds, they transfer their assets, such as utilities, roads and land to set up LGFPs to raise funds for their projects. LGFPs tap funds from two major channels. First, with the assets transferred from local governments, LGFPs use the assets as collaterals to borrow from commercial banks. Second, the LGFPs issue bonds and sell them to individual and institutional investors. Local officials are keen to work in response to the stimulus package handed down from the central government as working in conformity with central policy, improvement in local infrastructure and rise in income are important appraisal criteria for local officials.[15]

The immediate results of the stimulus package were impressive, giving China a quick rebound from 4.3 percent growth in the fourth quarter of 2008 to 9.5 and 11.4 percent in the first and second quarters of 2009 (Kwong 2014). The growth rates of GDP at constant prices reached 8.3 percent in 2009, followed by a more spectacular growth of 10.2 in 2010 (National Bureau of Statistics of China 2014). About 22 million jobs were created by the stimulus package in 2009 and 2010, which maintained the livelihood of the workers (China Daily Online 2010). China was widely commended for its resilience in surviving the 2008 GFC. It was one of the least affected economies by the GFC in terms of economic growth. Of equal importance, from a global perspective, China's fiscal stimulus induced demand for imports from East Asia, Europe and the United States, which prevented a more drastic post-crisis global recession (Fardoust, Lin and Luo 2012: 6–7).

While the stimulus package gave a strong boost to the economy, its notable repercussions have been far-reaching. First, loans extended to the LGFPs soared from 10.72 trillion yuan in 2010 to 17.9 trillion in 2013 (National Audit Office of the People's Republic of China 2011, 2013). The LGFPs loans were local government policy loans aiming to fulfil investment targets delegated from the central government rather than investing in projects with prudent profitability consideration. Many investment projects have been unable to generate sufficient return, more specifically cash flows, to pay off the debt, which caused rapid accumulation of nonperforming loans (NPLs) and massive overcapacity. The amount of NPLs skyrocketed from 427.9 billion yuan in 2011 to 1,091.9 billion yuan in the second quarter of 2015, representing a rise of 1.55 times within less than 4 years. Further, rapid loan expansion intensified the already pressing problem of excessive capacity, in which market demand fell short of potential output capacity. The State Council had made excess capacity its priority in 2005 to cut down redundant investment in production capacity (DeWeaver 2009). However, before Beijing's policy initiative took any effects, the 2008 stimulus package intensified the problem of excess capacity. Local governments injected capital into investment projects through LGFPs to boost economic rebound. The waning growth of domestic economy and the slow rebound of the global economy had made increasing a portion of the investment redundant. Excessive capacity spread widely in various sectors including steel, cement, glass, aluminium, and shipbuilding. The average industrial utilisation rate was 78 percent in the first half of 2013, which has been the lowest figure since 2009 (Cai 2014).

The 4-trillion yuan stimulus programme prompted the proliferation of LGFPs and rapid rise of "local policy loans", which highlights that commercial interests are still subordinate to broader political and socioeconomic consideration, especially when China faces potential economic decline. The recurrence of policy loans not only brings impediments to de facto commercialisation of the banking sector, but also indicates that state dominance in manipulating the economy is still prevalent. However, heightened risks in banking sector and worsening overcapacity urged central leaders to reassess the decades-long investment-led development strategy. The risks and efficiency losses embedded in this strategy drove China to move into its fifth phase of reform in 2013, which inaugurated an overhaul of the growth strategy.

From extensive to intensive growth: post-2013 initiatives[16]

The document "The Decision on Major Issues Concerning Comprehensively Deepening Reforms"[17] (hereafter "the Decision") endorsed at the close of the Third Plenary Session of the 18th CPC Central Committee on 15 November 2013 marked the fifth phase of China's economic reform. The overarching goal is to put forward an overhaul of the reform agenda, which focuses on three aspects: delineate the balance between market and state in reform process, upgrade the economy to avoid middle income trap and strengthen China's influence in the global economy.

Over the past decades, marketisation in various areas has been implemented, in which resource allocation is largely determined by market mechanism. However, allocation of key factor inputs, such as capital, land and energy, is still principally influenced by state forces through manipulating market prices. Distorted prices inputs are mostly channelled to state and state-connected sectors with prices lower than their market levels. The implicit subsidies of factor inputs constitute efficiency losses and industrial overcapacity. Huang and Tao (2010: 18) estimate that the factor price distortions incur efficiency loss mounting to

8.1%–12.2% of China's GDP during the period between 2000 and 2008. To curb further deterioration of the situation, the Decision clearly delineates a balance between market and state by affirming the "decisive role of the market in resource allocation" (Roberts 2013), which indicates the government's retreat from manipulating the market prices. Instead, the government will assume a strengthened role in macroeconomic management, regulation, provision of public service delivery, maintaining social stability and environmental protection (Kroeber 2013). Such a clear delineation is unprecedented, though the actual outcomes remain to be seen.

Further, the Decision highlights the significance of enhancing efficiency of the SOEs by creating a more competitive environment. First, future reforms will be targeted to establish a "mixed-ownership economy" meaning that the state-owned sector is developed alongside the private sector. Private capital is allowed in state-dominated sectors such as the banking sector. Second, prices in SOE-dominated areas such as oil, gas, power, transportation and telecommunications are to be liberalised to press the SOEs to be more competitive (Roberts 2013). Third, large SOEs will be reorganised to form financial holding companies in which the state will only be the major shareholder and the firm will assume the role of daily operation to maximise profits subject to market discipline and competition. However, such moves must not be interpreted as a drastic move to privatisation. Central leaders' intention to lift the efficiency of SOEs is apparent, but it is clear that the government's gigantic role as the major shareholder of key economic assets will remain. While the Decision signifies the coexistence of both public and non-public sectors in the economy, it also states noticeably that dominance of the public sector will remain (China Daily 2013).

The second dimension of the current phase of economic reform is the transformation of China's investment-led growth towards a more sustainable and decelerated growth through upgrading the economy. Credit and capital-driven growth have enabled China to maintain impressive growth over the past decades. However, rising credit-GDP ratios in recent years have rung the alarm that the seemingly workable growth model has gradually been losing its momentum when more credits are need to generate one unit of GDP (i.e., output). Another main pillar of China's growth model in the past was the reliance on low costs of labour and natural resources, but these comparative advantages have been undermined by neighbouring emerging economies such as Vietnam and Bangladesh. Diminishing marginal efficiency of investment and rising production costs, coupled with weakening external demand, bring China to enter a phase of post high-growth period. China needs to re-engineer its growth model to avoid falling into the "middle-income trap". In November 2014, Chinese President Xi Jinping delivered a speech at the Asia-Pacific Economic Cooperation Forum mentioning that "A new normal of China's economy has emerged with several notable features".[18] According to Xi, China's new normal entails (1) shifting from the previous high speed growth to a medium-to-high-speed growth; (2) upgrading the economy and (3) utilising technology, instead of inputs and investment, to drive economic growth and development (Robert 2014). To put forward the reform initiative in a concrete way, the State Council released an action plan "Made in China 2025" to comprehensively upgrade Chinese industry in May 2015. Nine tasks are identified to enhance China's technological innovation industry, brand building and the development of service industry. The programme also picks 10 key industrial sectors for development (Kennedy 2015).[19] China needs to take prompt and solid steps to upgrade its industry before their manufacturing competitiveness is increasingly weakened by newly emerging low-cost countries such as Vietnam, Bangladesh and India. To complement the implementation of "new normal" and the "Made in China 2025" plan, the government report released on 5 March 2016 emphasised "supply-side structural reform", which focuses on stimulating the supply of quality goods and services through tax cuts, entrepreneurship and innovation and at the same time eliminating excess capacity resulting from the previous stimulus programme and streamlining bureaucracy (Xinhuanet 2015; ShanghaiDaily.com 2016). The central leaders shifted their attention to the supply side due to the fact that the demand-side stimulus programme on the one hand has been losing its momentum and on the other hand has generated a number of unintended outcomes such as overcapacity and recurrence of NPLs as discussed previously.

The third dimension of the current phase of economic reform focuses on enhancing China's global footprint and influence. The BRI and China's initiative of setting up the AIIB demonstrates its determination to counterbalance the US's hegemony in the global political economy. The BRI involves more than 60 countries, and China has signed 1,400 infrastructure projects with a contracted amount of US$7.06 billion by July 2015 (Viehe, Gunasekaran and Downing 2015). More than 50 countries have already joined the AIIB, with initial capital of US$50 billion and finally up to US$100 billion. Though the US and Japan oppose the setting up of AIIB, the UK, Germany, Australia and South Korea are among the founding members (BBC News 2015). The presence of AIIB and influence of BRI should not be underestimated. Aside from expanding China's global influence, the BRI serves the Chinese economy in multi-faceted ways. First, the BRI captures the massive trade potential as the plan involves more than 60 countries with a population of 4.4 billion and 29 percent of global GDP (Lam 2015: 2). Second, the BRI facilitates China's "going out" policy by increasing ODI, which yields higher return than investing in US Treasury Bond.[20] Third, ODI helps alleviate China's excess capacity in heavy industry, in particular the steel industry. Last but not least, ODI facilitates China's acquisition of foreign research and development (R&D) (Ren 2013). It is evidenced by the fact that, prior to 2009, China's ODI mainly flew to developing countries and some resource-rich developed countries such as Australia and Canada, but advanced countries such as US and EU have become increasingly popular for attracting China's ODI since 2009 (Rosen and Hanemann 2012). The motivation behind this is the desire to upgrade Chinese firms' technology, acquire updated managerial skills and tap global talents to keep them globally competitive.

Conclusion

The meteoric rise of China's economy has drawn widespread attention and debate among academics and policy makers over the past decades. China's economic reforms commenced with an induced institutional change to capture potential gains to enhance living standards. China's economic reform can best be described as an "iterative process"[21] demonstrating a pattern of *ad hoc suite of crisis-and-response strategies*, instead of an overall roadmap of reform. When a new round of reforms generated some unwanted problems, a new package of reforms would be initiated to remedy the emerging problems, which was particularly true before the mid-1990s. While the world has applauded the spectacular accomplishments of China in the midst of four decades of rapid growth, China's policy makers have been increasingly aware of the impacts of development bottlenecks arising from the course of economic reforms. The lagging-behind development of the countryside, long-lasting efficiency problems of SOEs, unsolved problem of NPLs and declining competitiveness in the global market call for the urgency of revamping China's growth and development strategy. To realise a sustained growth in the long run, China needs to design an overhaul of its development strategy to address the pressing issues constraining China's long term growth. Subsequent chapters of this book will address the critical issues facing China's various economic sectors and demonstrate that, without ample effective measures to remedy current reform inadequacy, the perils of falling into the middle-income trap will become increasingly prominent in the years ahead.

Notes

1 Chinese President Xi Jinping formally announced the Silk Road Economic Belt in Kazakhstan in September 2013 and subsequently expanded the programme to include the Maritime Silk Road in February 2014, which is now commonly known as the Belt and Road Initiative (BRI). The land route starts in Western China and crosses through Central Asia via the Middle East to Europe. The maritime route links China with Europe through the South China Sea and Indian Ocean as well as connects China with the South Pacific Ocean through the South China Sea. For detailed routing of the BRI, please see Hong Kong Trade Development Council (2016).

2 A detailed discussion on the household responsibility system in rural China can be found in Chai (1997). An elaborated discussion on rural reforms, development and emerging issues will be covered in the next chapter (Chapter 2).

3 The main items of capital goods imports in the mid-1980s were machinery, transportation equipment, chemicals, textile materials, minerals, plastics and rubber.

4 The four SEZs are located in the cities of Shenzhen, Zhuhai and Shantou of Guangdong Province and the city of Xiamen of Fujian Province.

5 Contracted FDI is the fund pledged by foreign investors and approved by the government to invest, and the utilised FDI is the actual amount of foreign investment fund utilised for projects (Hornstein 2011: 92). These two figures are often different as the investors can utilise less funds than the amount stipulated in the contract.

6 See Chai (1997: 156) for more details of the early restrictions on FDI in China. A more thorough discussion on FDI is found in Chapter 5 of this book.
7 For a detailed analysis of CRS, see Chai (1997: 76–78).
8 The concept of soft budget constraint was developed by János Kornai who argues that though SOEs in planned economies were expected to maximise their profits, the loss-making SOEs were actually not allowed to fail. They were always bailed out with financial subsidies by the central government. SOEs could continue to survive even after continual losses. For details, see Kornai (1980: 306–309).
9 Calculated based on the data from National Bureau of Statistics of China (1994: 246).
10 For example, the market price for a ton of rolled steel was almost double of the price of planned delivery (Steinfeld 1998: 182).
11 Apart from inflation and rent-seeking activities, a series of sociopolitical factors contributed the occurrence of the June Fourth Incidence, which included wide-spread corruption and nepotism, rising living costs and educated youth's desire for political participation.
12 More thorough discussion of these reforms is found in subsequent chapters.
13 Calculated based on the data from the National Bureau of Statistics of China. Available at: http://data.stats.gov.cn/english/easyquery.htm?cn=C01 (Accessed on 3 May 2016)
14 China's exports to the US were US$162.89 billion in 2005. Data is derived from the National Bureau of Statistics of China. Available at: http://data.stats.gov.cn/english/easyquery.htm?cn=C01 (Accessed on 3 May 2016)
15 For a detailed discussion on the origin and operation of LGFPs and their impacts on the Chinese economy, see Kwong (2016).
16 The evolution of China's growth strategy will be discussed in greater detail in Chapter 7.
17 An abridged version of the document can be found in www.china.org.cn/china/third_plenary_session/2013-11/16/content_30620736.htm (Accessed on 9 March 2016)
18 Quoted from Robert (2014).
19 The nine tasks includes improving manufacturing innovation, integrating information technology and industry, strengthening the industrial base, fostering Chinese brands, enforcing green manufacturing, promoting breakthroughs in 10 key sectors, advancing restructuring of the manufacturing sector, promoting service-oriented manufacturing and manufacturing-related service industries and internationalising manufacturing. The 10 key sectors are new information technology, numerical control tools and robotics, aerospace equipment, ocean engineering equipment and high-tech ships, railway equipment, energy saving and new energy vehicles, power equipment, new materials, biological medicine and medical devices and agricultural machinery (China Daily 2015).
20 The yields for 3-month, 6-month, 12-month, 2-year, 5-year, 10-year and 30-year US Treasury Bond are 0.28%, 0.43%, 0.61%, 0.84%, 1.33%, 1.87% and 2.68% respectively on 18 March 2016. For details, see Bloomberg Business (2016).
21 The term "iterative process" is used by Perkins (2012: 44).

References

Ash, R. F. (1996) 'Agricultural Development in China Since 1978,' in Ash, R. F. and Kueh, Y. Y. (eds.) *The Chinese Economy Under Deng Xiaoping*, New York: Oxford University Press, pp. 55–87.

BBC News (2015) 'China-Led AIIB Development Bank Holds Signing Ceremony,' 29 June. Available at: www.bbc.com/news/world-asia-33307314 (Accessed on 20 March 2016).

Bloomberg Business (2016) 'United States Rates & Bonds.' Available at: www.bloomb erg.com/markets/rates-bonds/government-bonds/us (Accessed on 20 March 2016).

Brandt, L., Ma, D. and Rawski, T. G. (2013) 'From Divergence to Convergence: Re-evaluating the History Behind China's Economic Boom,' *Global COE Hi-Stat Discussion Paper Series*, No. 217, Tokyo: Institute of Economic Research, Hitotsubashi University.

Cai, P. (2014) 'Curbing China's Excess Capacity,' *The Australian Business Review*, 10 June. Available at: www.businessspectator.com.au/article/2014/6/10/china/ curbing-chinas-excess-capacity (Accessed on 16 November 2015).

Chai, J. C. H. (1996) 'Consumption and Living Standards in China,' in Ash, R. F. and Kueh, Y. Y. (eds.) *The Chinese Economy Under Deng Xiaoping*, New York: Oxford University Press, pp. 247–276.

Chai, J. C. H. (1997) *China: Transition to a Market Economy*, New York: Oxford University Press.

Chai, J. C. H. and Tisdell, C. (1992) 'The Two-Track System and China's Macro-Instability,' *Discussion Paper*, No. 85, Department of Economics, University of Queensland.

China Daily (2013) 'China Advances Diverse Forms of Ownership: Communique,' 12 November. Available at: www.chinadaily.com.cn/business/2013-11/12/con tent_17100460.htm (Accessed on 15 March 2016).

China Daily (2015) ' "Made in China 2025" Plan Unveiled,' *China Daily*, 19 May. Available at: www.chinadaily.com.cn/bizchina/2015-05/19/content_20760528. htm (Accessed on 21 February 2016).

China Daily Online (2010) 'China's 4 Trillion Yuan Stimulus Package Creates 22 Million Jobs,' 17 September. Available at: http://en.people.cn/90001/90776/ 90882/7143609.html (Accessed on 1 November 2015).

DeWeaver, M. A. (2009) 'China's Excess-Capacity Nightmare,' *The Korea Times*, 27 December. Available at: www.koreatimes.co.kr/www/news/opinon/2009/ 12/160_57995.html (Accessed on16 November 2015).

Fardoust, S., Lin, J. Y. and Luo, X. (2012) 'Demystifying China's Fiscal Stimulus,' *Policy Research Working Paper*, No. 6221, Washington, DC: The World Bank.

Garnaut, R. (1989) *Australia and the Northeast Asian Ascendancy: Report to the Prime Minister and the Minister for Foreign Affairs and Trade*, Canberra: Australian Government Publishing Service.

Goodstadt, L. F. (2012) 'China's LGFV Crisis 2011: The Conflict Between Local Autonomy, National Interest and Financial Reform,' *HKIMR Working Paper*, No. 03/2012, Hong Kong: Hong Kong Institute for Monetary Research.

Hong Kong Trade Development Council (2016) 'What Is Belt and Road Initiative,' *HKTDC Research*. Available at: http://beltandroad.hktdc.com/en/about-the-belt-and-road-initiative/about-the-belt-and-road-initiative.aspx (Accessed on 27 February 2016).

Hornstein, A. S. (2011) 'Where a Contract Is Signed Determines Its Value: Chinese Provincial Variation in Utilized vs. Contracted FDI Flows,' *Journal of Comparative Economics*, Vol. 39, pp. 92–107.

Huang, Y. (1996) *Inflation and Investment Controls in China: The Political Economy of Central-Local Relations During the Reform Era*, Cambridge: Cambridge University Press.

Huang, Y. and Tao, K. (2010) 'Causes and Remedies of China's External Imbalance,' *Working Paper Series*, No. 210002, Beijing: China Centre for Economic Research, Peking University.

Kennedy, S. (2015) *Made in China 2025*, Washington, DC: Centre for Strategic and International Studies. Available at: http://csis.org/publication/made-china-2025 (Accessed on 21 February 2016).

Kornai, J. (1980) *Economics of Shortage*, Amsterdam: North Holland.

Kroeber, A. R. (2013) 'Xi Jinping's Ambitious Agenda for Economic Reform in China,' *Brookings Brief.* Available at: www.brookings.edu/research/opinions/2013/11/17-xi-jinping-economic-agenda-kroeber (Accessed on 15 March 2016).

Kwong, C. C. L. (2014) 'Intended Outcome with Unintended Repercussions: China's 4-Trillion Yuan Stimulus Package,' Paper presented at the *Ninth London Business Research Conference*, Imperial College, London, 4–5 August.

Kwong, C. C. L. (2016) 'Where Is China's Banking Reform Heading for? A Dilemma Between Commercial and Policy Loans,' *Policy Paper Series*, Cycle 1, No. 1, London: Lau China Institute, King's College London.

Lam, R. (2015) 'China's "Belt and Road" Initiative: Assessing the Opportunities,' *Hong Kong Economic Monthly*, April, Hong Kong: Hang Seng Bank.

Lardy, N. R. (1998) *China's Unfinished Economic Revolution*, Washington, DC: Brookings Institute Press.

Lardy, N. R. (2002) *Integrating China into the Global Economy*, Washington, DC: Brookings Institution Press.

Lin, J. Y. (1992) 'Rural Reforms and Agricultural Growth in China,' *The American Economic Review*, Vol. 82, No. 1, pp. 34–51.

National Audit Office of the People's Republic of China (2011) *Report on the Local Government Debt Audit Work*. Available at: www.audit.gov.cn/n1992130/n1992150/n1992500/2752208.html (Accessed on 20 October 2015).

National Audit Office of the People's Republic of China (2013) *Audit Results of Nationwide Governmental Debts*. Available at: www.audit.gov.cn/n5/n25/c63642/content.html (Accessed on 21 October 2015).

National Bureau of Statistics of China (formerly State Statistical Bureau) (1986) *Zhongguo Tongji Nianjian 1985* (*Statistical Yearbook of China 1985*), Beijing: Zhongguo Tongji Chubanshe.

National Bureau of Statistics of China (formerly State Statistical Bureau) (1994) *Zhongguo Tongji Nianjian 1994* (*Statistical Yearbook of China 1994*), Beijing: Zhongguo Tongji Chubanshe.

National Bureau of Statistics of China (2014) *China Statistical Yearbook*. Available at: http://www.stats.gov.cn/tjsj/ndsj/2014/indexeh.htm (Accessed on 4 November 2019), Table 3–4.

The New York Times (1988) 'Inflation Hits Peak in China,' *The New York Times*, 29 November. Available at: www.nytimes.com/1988/11/29/business/inflation-hits-peak-in-china.html (Accessed on 10 August 2016).

Perkins, D. H. (2012) 'China's Investment and GDP Growth Boom: When and How Will It End?' in Aoki, M. and Wu, J. (eds.) *The Chinese Economy: A New Transition*, London: Palgrave Macmillan, pp. 35–59.

Prime, P. B. (2002) 'China Joins the WTO: How, Why and What Now?' *Business Economics*, Vol. XXXVII, No. 2, April, pp. 26–32.

Rajaram, A. (1992) 'Reforming Prices: The Experience of China, Hungary, and Poland,' *World Bank Discuss Paper, China and Mongolia Department Series*, No. 144.

Ren, D. (2013) 'China Overseas Direct Investment to Exceed FDI by 2017 Says Study,' *South China Morning Post*, 29 April 2006. Available at: www.scmp.com/

business/china-business/article/1225439/china-overseas-direct-investment-exceed-fdi-2017-says-study (Accessed on 20 March 2016).

Robert, D. (2013) 'The Trouble with China's Reform Plan,' *Bloomberg Business*. Available at: www.bloomberg.com/bw/articles/2013-11-18/the-trouble-with-chinas-reform-plan#p1 (Accessed on 9 March 2016).

Robert, D. (2014) 'What Is Xi's "New Normal" Chinese Economy?' *Bloomberg Business*. Available at: www.bloomberg.com/news/articles/2014-12-12/china-has-a-new-normal-too (Accessed on 16 March 2016).

Rodrik, D. (2012) *The Globalization Paradox: Democracy and the Future of the World Economy*, New York: Norton.

Rosen, D. H. and Hanemann, T. (2012) 'The Rise in Chinese Overseas Investment and What It Means for American Businesses,' *China Business Review*, July pp. 1–9.

Shambaugh, D. (2013) *China Goes Global: The Partial Power*, New York: Oxford University Press.

ShanghaiDaily.com (2016) 'China Outlines Supply-Side Structural Reform Plan,' 7 March. Available at: www.shanghaidaily.com/national/China-outlines-supplyside-structural-reform-plan/shdaily.shtml (Accessed on 20 March 2016).

Sicular, T. (1988) 'Agricultural Planning and Pricing in the Post-Mao Era,' *The China Quarterly*, No. 116, pp. 671–705.

Spence, M. (2011) *The Next Convergence: The Future of Economic Growth and Multi-speed World*, New York: Picador.

Steinfeld, E. S. (1998) *Forging Reform in China: The Fate of State-Owned Industry*, Cambridge: Cambridge University Press.

Tyler, P. E. (1997) 'Deng Xiaoping: A Political Wizard Who Put China on the Capitalist Road,' *The New York Times*. Available at: www.nytimes.com/learning/general/onthisday/bday/0822.html#top (Accessed on 24 April 2016).

Viehe, A., Gunasekaran, A. and Downing, H. (2015) 'Understanding China's Belt and Road Initiative: Opportunity and Risks,' *Foreign Policy and Security*, Centre for American Progress. Available at: www.americanprogress.org/issues/security/report/2015/09/22/121628/understanding-chinas-belt-and-road-initiative/ (Accessed on 20 March 2016).

Wu, J. (2012) 'Economics and China's Economic Rise,' in Aoki, M. and Wu, J. (eds.) *The Chinese Economy: A New Transition*, London: Palgrave Macmillan, pp. 13–31.

Xinhuanet (2015) 'Backgrounder: What Is China's Supply-Side Reform?' Available at: http://news.xinhuanet.com/english/2015-12/22/c_134941783.htm (Accessed on 20 March 2016).

Yeh, K. C. (1996) 'Macroeconomic Issues in China in 1990s,' in Ash, R. F. and Kueh, Y. Y. (eds.) *The Chinese Economy Under Deng Xiaoping*, New York: Oxford University Press,

Zhang, W. and Liu, X. (2010) 'Success and Challenges: Overview of China's Economic Growth and Reform Since 1978,' in Liu, X. and Zhang, W. (eds.) *China's Three Decades of Economic Reforms*, Oxon: Routledge, pp. 3–14.

2 The rural economy
A sector lagging behind

China embarked on its reform journey first in the countryside in the late 1970s. China's rural areas had gone through a series of far-reaching reforms, which accomplished remarkable and uncontroversial results. When reforms first took place in rural China in 1978, China was one of the most poverty-stricken countries in the world, with 60 percent of its population living below the poverty line and earning less than the World Bank standard of US$1 a day. Most of the poor were in the rural areas. With two decades of reforms since 1978, China lifted more than 200 million people out of poverty. Enhanced production incentives resulting from institutional reforms and the flourishing rural enterprises were major sources of income growth and employment creation in rural China from the mid-1980s and to mid-1990s (Kwong and Lo 2006: 3).

However, the initial benefits that peasants gained from the early rural reforms had become less glamorous when rural income had demonstrated sluggish growth and rural-urban disparity had intensified since the mid-1990s. This chapter first briefly examines the initial success of the rural economy and then analyses the sluggish growth of the countryside since the mid-1990s by looking into the problems of tapering off of rural industry, local government fiscal constraints, rural land requisition and underdevelopment of rural finance. It then scrutinises the policy initiatives made by the central government to remedy the rural problems. The final section touches upon the unsolved issues and possible solutions to the remaining problems.

Institutional changes and initial success

As discussed in Chapter 1, China's economic reforms did not commence with a full-fledged reform agenda. Instead, China's reforms started with an induced institutional change initiated by a spontaneous emergence of a responsibility system in the poor counties of Anhui Province. The essence of the household responsibility system (HRS, *baogan daohu*) in 1978–1980 was to allow farm households to sell or retain the surplus they produced after fulfilling the targets set by their collectives. This institutional overhaul signified China's transformation from collective farming to household farming, which provided a much stronger effort-and-reward link than that under the commune system practised before the reform. Under the HRS, farmers were provided with material incentives to work and invest in their allotted land. The initial reforms in the countryside accomplished impressive results. Agricultural output grew 42.23 percent in 1978–1984, and 45.79 percent of this growth was attributable to the increase in agricultural inputs, mainly the application of fertiliser. Institutional change, primarily the implementation of HRS, contributed 46.89 percent to this growth, which demonstrated that institutional reform in rural China was as important as agricultural inputs to boost output growth during this period (Lin 1992). Measured in real terms, the annual growth rate of gross output value of agriculture (GOVA) was 6.4 percent in 1981–1985, compared with 4.7 percent in 1971–1980 and 3.05 percent in 1952–1970 (Ash 1996: 57). Rural reforms were also praised for their spectacular achievement in poverty reduction. The number of rural residents living under the official poverty line shrank from 250 million in 1978 to 29 million in 2003, representing a decline of poverty incidence from 30.7 percent to 3.1 percent (Kwong 2007: 391).

However, the initial benefits that peasants gained from the early rural reforms had become less sustainable when rural income had demonstrated sluggish growth and rural-urban disparity had intensified since the mid-1990s. The annual growth rate of per capita income of rural households, measured in real terms, rose from 11.5 percent in 1986 to its historic peak of 38.5 percent in 1995 but fell continuously to a meagre 0.72 percent in 2000. Though a mild rebound of 4.08 and 5.88 percent was recorded in 2001 and 2002, the growth rate tapered off again to 3.84 percent in 2003 (Kwong and Lo 2006: 3). In relative terms, rural residents have not gained a proportional share of the economic fruits generated by the economic reforms. Table 2.1 reveals that the urban-rural gap (Yu/Yr) narrowed considerably from 2.57 in 1978 to 1.86 in 1985 due to the relatively fast growth of rural household income. The figure, however, started to rise from 2.2 in 1990 and peaked at 3.14 in 2007. The growth of rural household income, as analysed in the following sections, was constrained by the loosely defined and enforced land rights and the underdevelopment of rural finance. Without eliminating these development bottlenecks, it is difficult to foresee sustained growth and development in China's countryside.

Growth bottlenecks: land issues and rural finance

Loosely enforced property rights on land

Since the commencement of rural reforms in the late 1970s, the central government had endorsed a number of documents and laws to bestow long-term land use rights on farmers to incentivise them to invest and work on their contracted land. The No.1 Document issued in 1984 was the first important document prescribing a 15-year contract period for rural land use rights (OECD 2009: 127). The Land Management Law (LML) enacted in 1998 further stipulates that farmers are endowed with 30-year use right of the contracted land. A survey indicates that 3 years after the implementation of the LML, 47 percent of farm households had entered into the 30-year

Table 2.1 Urban-Rural Disposable Income Gap 1978–2017

Year	Yu (yuan)	Yr (yuan)	Yu/Yr
1978	343.4	133.6	2.57
1980	477.6	191.3	2.50
1985	739.1	397.6	1.86
1990	1510.2	686.3	2.20
1995	4283.0	1577.7	2.71
2000	6255.7	2282.1	2.74
2001	6824.0	2406.9	2.84
2002	7652.4	2528.9	3.03
2003	8405.5	2690.3	3.12
2004	9334.8	3026.6	3.08
2005	10382.3	3370.2	3.08
2006	11619.7	3731.0	3.11
2007	13602.5	4327.0	3.14
2008	15549.4	4998.8	3.11
2009	16900.5	5435.1	3.11
2010	18779.1	6272.4	2.99
2011	21426.9	7393.9	2.90
2012	24126.7	8389.3	2.88
2013	26467.0	9429.6	2.81
2014	28843.9	10488.9	2.75
2015	31194.8	11421.7	2.73
2016	33616.2	12363.4	2.72
2017	36396.2	13432.4	2.71

Source: *China Statistical Yearbook 2018*, Table 6.16. Available at: www.stats.gov.cn/tjsj/ndsj/2018/indexeh.htm (Accessed on 13 May 2019)

Notes
Yu = Disposable income of urban households;
Yr = Disposable income of rural households.

contract (Kwong 2011: 81). This 30-year contract was a milestone in China's development of a land contract system as it allowed a long enough contract for farmers to make their investment and, more importantly, to capture the returns on their investment. Farmers' land use rights are further enforced by the Rural Land Contracting Law (RLCL) passed in 2002, which states clearly the land use rights of the farm households and eliminates possible grounds for land readjustments and expropriations by local governments. The RLCL requires that contracts and full documents must be issued to confirm the land rights possessed by the farm households (Zhu and Li 2007: 24). To enhance the flexibility of participating in nonfarm activities by the farmers, the RLCL details farmers' right to lease (i.e., transfer) their contracted land. It enables farmers to transfer the land rights to capture potential income and retain their land rights after the transfer period.

Though the central government developed a firmer legal foundation for land use rights, the effective implementation of the RLCL was hampered by a lack of land registration system in the countryside, unlike their urban counterparts which could register their land and structures with the local offices of Ministry of Land and Resources. According to the LML and the RLCL, farmers should have been issued contracts and certificates containing the details of their contracted land and the rights they are entitled.[1] However, a survey in 2005 revealed that 63 percent of the farmers received very brief documentation for their contracted land. Among those documents, only about 10 percent of these farmers received legally compliant documentation containing the details, such as names of households, contract duration and land description of the contracted farmland (Zhu and Li 2007: 24). A follow-up survey by Prosterman et al. (2009)[2] indicates that 41.8 percent of farm households were not issued any documents regarding their land rights. This result shows that marginal progress was made towards the protection of the famers' entitlement to land rights. The loose implementation of RLCL largely explains the rampant land expropriations by local governments with partial and/or delayed compensation. The survey exposes that 34.1 percent of farm households had experienced land readjustments, and most of these readjustments were illegal.[3] On top of land readjustment, land taking poses an even bigger threat to farmers. Since the implementation of the LML in 1998, 29.2 percent of farm households reported that they had encountered one or more land takings. The LML allowed local governments to requisition land for development "in the public interest", but empirical evidence revealed that about one third of the purposes of land takings could hardly be categorised as projects for public interest (Table 2.2).[4] Since "public interest" is ambiguously defined in the LML, the local governments were entrusted with plenty legally justifiable reasons to requisition farmland (Kwong 2007: 403).

Local governments' land expropriation has become more frequent since the mid-1990s when the central government implemented the tax-assignment system (TAS, *fengshuizhi*) in 1994. Since 1978, the central share of national budgetary revenues had been rising and reached its peak at 40.5 percent in 1984. However, the share had shrunk since 1984, reaching a trough at 22 percent in 1993. To ensure an adequate and stable flow of budgetary revenues into the state finances and to regain its control in fiscal resources, the central government implemented the TAS, which centralised the major revenue sources of turnover taxes (value-added and consumption taxes) but lacked a concomitant centralisation of expenditure responsibilities. Table 2.3 indicates that the central share of

Table 2.2 Purpose of Land Seizure 2008

Purpose	Percentage
Road construction	47.4
Development zone/industrial park	12.9
Factory	9.1
Urban housing	6.4
School	5.9
Planned for non-agricultural use but currently vacant	4.0
Irrigation facility	2.7
Gas station	0.9
Others	10.7

Source: Prosterman et al. (2009: 17)

Table 2.3 Central and Local Share of Budgetary Revenue and Expenditure 1978–2015 (percent)

Year	Revenue share		Expenditure share	
	Central government	Local governments	Central government	Local governments
1978	15.5	84.5	47.4	52.6
1979	20.2	79.8	51.1	48.9
1980	24.5	75.5	54.3	45.7
1981	26.5	73.5	55.0	45.0
1982	28.6	71.4	53.0	47.0
1983	35.8	64.2	53.9	46.1
1984	40.5	59.5	52.5	47.5
1985	38.4	61.6	39.7	60.3
1986	36.7	63.3	37.9	62.1
1987	33.5	66.5	37.4	62.6
1988	32.9	67.1	33.9	66.1
1989	30.9	69.1	31.5	68.5
1990	33.8	66.2	32.6	67.4
1991	29.8	70.2	32.2	67.8
1992	28.1	71.9	31.3	68.7
1993	22.0	78.0	28.3	71.7
1994	55.7	44.3	30.3	69.7
1995	52.2	47.8	29.2	70.8
1996	49.4	50.6	27.1	72.9
1997	48.9	51.1	27.4	72.6
1998	49.5	50.5	28.9	71.1
1999	51.1	48.9	31.5	68.5
2000	52.2	47.8	34.7	65.3
2001	52.4	47.6	30.5	69.5
2002	55.0	45.0	30.7	69.3
2003	54.6	45.4	30.1	69.9
2004	54.9	45.1	27.7	72.3
2005	52.3	47.7	25.9	74.1
2006	52.8	47.2	24.7	75.3
2007	54.1	45.9	23.0	77.0
2008	53.3	46.7	21.3	78.7
2009	52.4	47.6	20.0	80.0
2010	51.1	48.9	17.8	82.8
2011	49.4	50.6	15.1	84.9
2012	47.9	52.1	14.9	85.1
2013	47.1	52.9	14.6	85.4
2014	45.9	54.1	14.9	85.1
2015	45.5	54.5	14.5	85.5

Source: *ZGTJNJ* (2000: 267–268, 2001: 257–258, 2005: 276); *ZGTJNJ 2008* CD-ROM (Table 7.3 & 7.4); *ZGTJNJ 2009* CD-ROM (Table 7.3 & 7.4); *ZGTJNJ 2016* (Table 7.1). Available at: www.stats.gov.cn/tjsj/ndsj/2016/indexeh.htm (Accessed on 17 March 2017)

total budgetary revenue escalated from 22 percent in 1993 to 55.7 percent in 1994. Since then, the central government has collected about half of the total fiscal revenues. Nevertheless, local governments have been responsible for the major share, about 70 percent, of the total expenditure since the inception of the TAS. Though the revenue shares of local governments has rose steadily from 45.9 in 2007 to 54.9 in 2015, the expenditure shares of local governments demonstrated a proportional rise for the same period. The TAS has imposed increased fiscal pressures on subnational, in particular sub provincial, finance.[5] Table 2.4 explores further the fiscal conditions of local governments. The extent of budget deficit (or surplus) is measured by the ratio of local government expenditure (LGE) to local government revenue (LGR) (column (4)), which represents a balanced budget if the ratio is equal to one. A ratio greater than one denotes a budget deficit, and a larger figure indicates a budget deficit of greater extent. A ratio less than one reflects a budget surplus, and a smaller figure registers a larger surplus. Dramatically, local governments encountered deficits for all the years from 1994 to 2015, and the magnitude of the deficits was getting more immense from 1.75 in 1994 to 1.81 in 2015.

Fiscal transfer to remedy the fiscal deficits at the local level. The pre-1994 fiscal transfer system inclined to ad hoc bilateral arrangements between the centre and provinces, with wealthier regions (coastal provinces and large cities) obtaining preferential revenue sharing arrangements. One of the important objectives of the TAS was to establish a more uniform and rules-based system. However, Wang (1997) points out that the new system failed to achieve this goal as the wealthy provinces still possesses strong bargaining power, and the amount of fiscal transfer is still primarily based on the "revenue-returned" principle, which accounted for over 40 percent of overall transfers (Dabla-Norris 2005: 12). Stringent fiscal conditions triggered local governments, especially local governments in relatively poor provinces, to explore other sources to finance their coffers. Land requisition by local governments became a commonly used means to raise local fiscal revenue.

Rural protests over land disputes have widely been reported for more than a decade. Based on survey data from four provinces, Kang (2009) revealed that the net income of the majority (53.3 percent) of households declined while only 23.8 percent of the households enjoyed higher net income after land expropriation. Of land-losing farmers, 87.7 percent regarded their compensation too low. The findings by Prosterman *et al.* (2009: 18) further illustrate that local governments/collectives derived considerable fiscal revenue from land requisition at the expense of land-losing farmers. On average, compensation per *mu*[6] was received by the collectives, which was five times the payment received by the farmer. Though available data on land requisition and compensation is sketchy and varies across different localities, the previous survey results shed some light on the discontent of the farmers and the tension between land-losing farmers and their local governments. Loosely enforced property rights on farmland generate two negative impacts on rural productivity. First, farmers are reluctant to make long-term investments in their contracted land, which in turn adversely affects

Table 2.4 Budget Balance of Local Governments 1978–2015 (billion yuan)

Year	LGR (1)	LGE (2)	LGR–LGE (3)	LGE/LGR (4)
1978	95.65	56.00	39.65	0.59
1979	91.50	62.67	28.83	0.68
1980	87.55	56.20	31.35	0.64
1981	86.47	51.28	35.19	0.59
1982	86.55	57.82	28.73	0.67
1983	87.69	64.99	22.7	0.74
1984	97.74	80.77	16.97	0.83
1985	123.52	120.90	2.62	0.98
1986	134.36	136.86	–2.5	1.02
1987	146.31	141.66	4.65	0.97
1988	158.25	164.62	–6.37	1.04
1989	184.24	193.50	–9.26	1.05
1990	194.47	207.91	–13.44	1.07
1991	221.12	229.58	–8.46	1.04
1992	250.39	257.18	–6.79	1.03
1993	339.14	333.02	6.12	0.98
1994	231.16	403.82	–172.66	1.75
1995	298.56	482.83	–184.27	1.62
1996	374.69	578.63	–203.94	1.54
1997	442.42	670.11	–227.69	1.51
1998	498.40	767.26	–268.86	1.54
1999	559.49	903.53	–344.04	1.61
2000	640.61	1036.67	–396.06	1.62
2001	780.33	1313.45	–533.12	1.68
2002	851.50	1528.14	–676.64	1.79
2003	984.99	1722.98	–737.99	1.75
2004	1189.33	2059.28	–869.95	1.73
2005	1510.07	2515.43	–1005.36	1.67
2006	1830.36	3043.13	–1212.77	1.66
2007	2357.26	3833.93	–1476.67	1.63
2008	2864.98	4924.85	–2059.87	1.72
2009	3260.26	6104.41	–2844.15	1.87
2010	4061.30	7388.44	–3327.14	1.82
2011	5254.71	9273.37	–4018.66	1.76
2012	6107.83	10718.83	–4611.0	1.75
2013	6901.12	11974.03	–5072.91	1.73
2014	7587.66	12921.55	–5333.89	1.70
2015	8300.20	15033.56	–6733.36	1.81

Source: Calculated based on the data from *ZGTJNJ* (2001: 257–258, 2005: 276); *ZGTJNJ 2008* CD-ROM (Table 7.3 & 7.4); *ZGTJNJ 2009* CD-ROM (Table 7.3 & 7.4); *ZGTJNJ 2016* (Table 7.1). Available at: www.stats.gov.cn/tjsj/ndsj/2016/indexeh.htm (Accessed on 17 March 2017)

productivity. Second, land expropriations deprive farmers of rights to lease (i.e., transfer) their land to capture the market rental. It jeopardises the income right of the farmers, which constrains their income growth.

Actually, a series of land laws and regulations had been enacted and amended since the 1980s to secure farmers' land rights,[7] but the enforcement of property rights requires an effective implementation of the relevant rules, which in turn relies on a sound legal system in the countryside. Local courts have so far been embedded in local governments, which have dominant control on the finance of the courts. The financial dependence of local courts on local governments adversely affects the impartiality of court rulings. Even when the local courts issue rulings in favour of the farmers, it is not uncommon that the local governments just neglect the courts' ruling (OECD 2009: 122). The ineffective court system in the countryside is the weakest link in protecting the land rights of the farmers. Once the land rights of the farm households are secured, farmers will have robust incentives to preserve and invest in their land to maximise productivity. As mentioned previously, secured land rights also endowed farm households with an option to lease out their land to higher value users. It not only increases the land value of the countryside but, more importantly, enhances rural household income and narrows the urban-rural income gap.

Underdeveloped rural finance

Apart from loose land security jeopardising rural households' income growth, underdeveloped rural finance creates another bottleneck in rural development. Rural households derive income from both farming and nonfarm activities that include rural industry and services. In 1985, farming generated 75.4 percent of rural household income and the figures diminished to 36.7 percent in 2015. On the contrary, nonfarm income has been gaining its share in rural income from 24.6 percent in 1985 to 63.3 percent in 2015, which indicated that rural residents have relied increasingly on nonfarm activities to maintain their income growth over the past 3 decades (Table 2.5). In addition, the proliferation of rural

Table 2.5 Farm and Nonfarm Income in Rural China 1985–2008

	Income from farming (yuan) (1)	Income from nonfarm activities* (yuan) (2)	(1) + (2)	(1)/ (1) + (2) (%)	(2)/ (1) + (2) (%)
1985	263.2	86.3	349.5	75.3	24.7
1990	456.0	201.4	657.4	69.4	30.6
1995	956.5	563.3	1519.8	62.9	37.1
2000	1090.7	1083.9	2174.6	50.2	49.8
2005	1469.6	1637.0	3106.6	47.3	52.7
2008	1945.9	2491.5	4437.4	43.9	56.1
2011	2519.9	3894.1	6414.0	39.3	60.7
2015	3431.2**	5924.2	9355.4	36.7	63.3

Source: Calculated based on the data from *ZGTJNJ* (1986: 647); *ZGTJNJ 2009* CD-ROM (Table 9.20); *ZGTJNJ 2012* (Table 10.20). Available at: www.stats.gov.cn/tjsj/ndsj/2012/indexeh.htm (Accessed on 19 March 2017)

Notes
* Transfer income is not included in nonfarm income.
** The disclosure of household income from farming has been changed since 2012. The figures of 2015 are estimated by the author based on the data from 1985 to 2015.

industry in the 1980s and 1990s assumed an important function of absorbing surplus labour released from agriculture. Rural enterprises employed 30 million workers in 1980, and the number skyrocketed to 111.69 million in 1990, demonstrating a growth of 2.72 times during the 1980s (*ZGTJNJ* 2005:121). However, employment creation by rural enterprises was impeded by the implementation of banking reform in 1994, which aimed at commercialising the four state-owned specialised banks (SOCBs)[8] by separating commercial lending from policy lending, unintentionally resulted in noticeable capital constraints facing the small- and medium-sized private enterprises, particularly those in rural areas. Since the SOCBs were required to operate on commercial principles, 44,000 county branches of SOCBs ceased to operate during 1998–2001 to cut operation costs.[9] Loans extended to township-village enterprises (TVEs) and private enterprises (PEs) increased in absolute term from 1985 to 2009, but their share in total lending by financial institutions demonstrated a decreasing trend (Table 2.6), which

Table 2.6 Share of Loans to Rural Enterprises 1985–2009 (billion yuan)

	Total lending by financial institutions	Loans to agriculture	Loans to TVEs	Loans to PEs and self-employed individuals
1985	643.09	41.66 (6.48)*	32.13 (5.0)^	n.a.
1990	1683.78	103.81 (6.17)	83.13 (4.94)	n.a.
1995	5398.90**	192.16 (3.56)	110.04 (2.04)	n.a.
2000	9937.1	488.9 (4.92)	606.1 (6.09)	65.5 (0.66)
2001	11231.47	571.15 (5.08)	641.3 (5.71)	91.8 (0.82)
2002	13129.39	688.46 (5.24)	681.23 (5.19)	105.88 (0.81)
2003	15889.62	841.14 (5.29)	766.16 (4.82)	146.16 (0.92)
2004	17819.78	984.31 (5.52)	806.92 (4.53)	208.16 (1.17)
2005	19469.04	1152.99 (5.92)	790.18 (4.06)	218.08 (1.12)
2006	22543.72	1320.82 (5.86)	622.2 (2.76)	266.76 (1.18)
2007	26169.1	1542.9 (5.90)	711.3 (2.72)	350.8 (1.34)
2008	30339.5	1762.9 (5.81)	745.4 (2.46)	422.1 (1.39)
2009	39968.5	2162.3 (5.41)	902.9 (2.26)	711.7 (1.78)

Sources: Calculated based on the data from *ZGTJNJ* (1991: 643, 1996: 614, 2001: 638, 2004: 762); *ZGTJNJ* CD-ROM (2007: Table 20.2, 2009: Table 19.2), *ZGTJNJ* 2002 (Table 19–3). Available at: www.stats.gov.cn/english/statisticaldata/yearlydata/YB2002e/ml/indexE.htm (Accessed on 28 March 2017.); *ZGTJNJ 2006* (Table 20.3). Available at: www.stats.gov.cn/tjsj/ndsj/2006/indexeh.htm (Accessed on 28 March 2017.); *ZGTJNJ* 2007 (Table 20.2). Available at: www.stats.gov.cn/tjsj/ndsj/2007/indexeh.htm (Accessed on 28 March 2017.); *ZGTJNJ 2009* (Table 19.2). Available at: www.stats.gov.cn/tjsj/ndsj/2009/indexeh.htm (Accessed on 28 March 2017.); *ZGTJNJ 2011* (Table 19.2). Available at: www.stats.gov.cn/tjsj/ndsj/2011/indexeh.htm (Accessed on 28 March 2017)

Notes
* Figures in parentheses are the respective share in total lending.
** Figures before 1995 were total lending from the four SOCBs while figures since 2000 covered all financial institutions.
^ Figures from 1985 to 1995 were combined loan amounts to TVEs, PEs and self-employed individuals.
n.a. Not available.

reached a historic low of 2.26 percent in 2009. Compared with the output share of rural enterprises in GDP, which remained at about 25 percent since 2000 (Naughton 2007: 286; OECD 2009: 64), the negligible share of total lending acquired by rural enterprises exhibited the difficulties of accessing credit in the countryside. The enterprises have to utilise their accumulated profits to finance their production and investment. However, rural enterprises face keen competition among flourishing TVEs and the state-owned enterprises (SOEs) that have much easier access to bank credit. Rural enterprises are less likely to acquire ample capital to invest in product design and quality improvement. The expansion of rural enterprises is thus inhibited and it impairs the ability of rural enterprises to absorb rural labour. The growth rate of employment in rural enterprises has been decreasing since 1995, and negative growth was recorded for two consecutive years in 1997 and 1998. Though the figure rebounded to 4.5 percent in 2005, it declined once again in recent years (Table 2.7). The average annual growth rate of employment in rural enterprises was 9.97 percent during 1990–1995, while, in

Table 2.7 Growth of Employment in Rural Enterprises 1990–2010

	Workers employed in rural enterprises * *(million)*	*Growth rate (%)*
1990	111.69	19.2
1991	113.41	1.5
1992	124.87	10.1
1993	145.42	16.5
1994	148.84	2.4
1995	163.87	10.1
1996	173.67	6.0
1997	171.72	(1.1)
1998	171.29	(0.25)
1999	175.00	2.2
2000	168.93	(3.5)
2001	169.02	0.05
2002	171.73	1.6
2003	175.87	2.4
2004	179.56	2.1
2005	187.61	4.5
2006	194.59	3.7
2007	199.49	2.5
2008	203.98	2.2
2009	209.92	2.9
2010	217.80	3.8

Source: Calculated based on the data from *ZGTJNJ* (1991: 295, 2005: 121); *ZGTJNJ* CD-ROM (2009: Table 4.2); *ZGTJNJ* (2010: Table 4.2). Available at: www.stats.gov.cn/tjsj/ndsj/2010/indexeh.htm (Accessed on 20 March 2017); *ZGTJNJ* (2011: Table 4.2). Available at: www.stats.gov.cn/tjsj/ndsj/2011/indexeh.htm (Accessed on 20 March 2017)

Note
* Figures include workers employed in TVEs, PEs and self-employed individuals. Figures in parentheses indicate negative growth rates.

stark contrast, such figures shrank to 1.91 percent for the period 1996–2010. As depicted earlier, the income from nonfarm activities has become a major source of rural household income, dwarfing employment creation by rural enterprises that certainly have direct bearing on household income.

Since the retreat of SOCBs in the countryside, rural credit cooperatives (RCCs) have become the most important financial institutions in rural areas to meet the credit demanded by the rural enterprises. The merge of rural credit cooperatives over the past decade, however, further decreased the number of county financial institutions. As of the end of 2007, the number of county financial outlets dropped by 9,811 or 7.3% since 2004, declining to a total of 124,000 outlets. Towns and villages are the most adversely affected areas. At the end of 2005, only 3.28% of the administrative villages had financial institutions. Despite an increase in deposit in RCCs, a rising amount of funds has been channelled out of rural areas through depositing funds into the People's Bank of China or purchasing bonds for which the returns are more stable and less risky. Even with the repeated emphases by central leaders on the importance of rural finance in rural development, the amount of loans extended to agriculture and rural enterprises is still disproportionately small as revealed in Table 2.6. The empirical study by Tang, Huan and Lansing (2010) demonstrates evidence that the credit markets in rural China are unable to cater to the credit demand of the households. The study shows that those who are likely to need the credit the most (with more land and off-farm opportunities) are most likely to face credit constraints. It further illustrates that households' distance from financial institutions significantly reduces their probability of obtaining credit. Banking reform since 1994 has focused on the institutional overhaul of the banking sector in urban areas. After three decades of reform, the rural financial reforms still lag behind, thus creating the risk of slowing down further expansion of rural enterprises and rural development as a whole.

Concerted efforts have been made to ensure adequate financial services rendered to the countryside. The China Postal Savings Bank (CPSB) was established in 2007 to take over the rural financial services previously provided by the post offices. The new bank provides a network of 37,000 branches providing banking services, including small loans to individuals, in rural areas (Kwong 2009: 17). However, since the postal saving system was not allowed to extend loans to rural households and enterprises before June 2006, it is not certain whether the newly established CPSB has adequate expertise in credit and risk evaluation. In addition, the China Banking Regulatory Commission (CBRC), China's banking regulator, designed a plan to set up 1,294 new financial institutions in rural areas over a 3-year period (2009–2011) to cater for the escalating demand for financial services in the rural sector. Nevertheless, the response of local and foreign banks has been lukewarm as average size of each loan application in rural areas remains small, which lowers the cost-effectiveness of processing each loan application. Further, the lack of collateral for farmers increases the default risks of the loans. Lower profitability and higher risks deter the banks from taking bold steps to tap into the rural business, particularly in poor regions. Setting up an extensive credit-reporting system is a necessary step to allow lenders to better manage their risks in rural lending by reducing information asymmetry, which enables financial institutions to increase their lending to the underserved areas. A further relaxation of interest rates charged by rural financial institutions can provide an adequate risk premium for the lenders, which induces more loans to risky borrowers. Notwithstanding, higher interest rates may deter farm households from borrowing from financial institutions. Therefore, the problem of inadequate financial services in rural China cannot be solved solely by market means. Government initiatives, such as government-subsidised microfinance, tax exemption and concessionary land rent for financial institutions, must be instituted to promote lending to rural households and enterprises.

China's new socialist countryside: good, but not enough

The lagged-behind development of rural areas had drawn the attention of central leaders, who recognised that ongoing discontent among rural dwellers could be destabilising factors for national development. The number of peasant protests reached a historic high of 87,000 in 2005, which registered a growth of 6.6 percent from 2004. Increasing numbers of protests turned violent (So 2009). To avoid intensifying the problem, China proposed to build a "new socialist countryside" (NSC) in the eleventh Five-Year Plan (2006–2010) in order to advance rural development and livelihood. The new initiative was drafted in December 2005 and formally announced in February 2006. Though the primary goal of the policy was to raise the development and livelihood of the countryside, it embedded a broader aim of modernising the nation by enhancing rural residents' wealth and consumption (Watts 2006). The central leaders realised that China's modernisation would be impeded if half of the population lived with only one third of the income and consumption of the remaining population. A number of concrete policies have been implemented since 2006.[10]

First, central funds have gradually been increased to support agriculture and infrastructure investment in the countryside. Table 2.8 indicates that total investment in agriculture, forestry, animal husbandry and fishing (Ka) rose substantially from 2,749.9 million yuan in 2006 to 21,042.7 million yuan in 2015, an average annual growth rate of 27.84 percent that was higher than the average annual growth rate of total investment in fixed assets of the whole country (Kc') by 5.14 percentage points during the period 2006 to 2015.[11] The rising ratio of Ka/Kc further illustrates the central government's concrete efforts in transferring more investment to fixed assets in rural areas. The ratio demonstrated a continuous rise from 2.5 percent in 2006 to 3.74 percent in 2015. However, it is worth noting that agriculture, forestry, animal husbandry and fishing shared 9.2 percent of China's GDP in 2015,[12] the ratio Ka/Kc of 3.74 percent indicates that fixed assets investment in agriculture is still proportionally lagging behind its share in GDP.

Second, a practical step to alleviate local fiscal burden is the fundamental reform on education financing at local levels, which was implemented in 2006.

Table 2.8 Total Investment in Fixed Assets in Agriculture, Forestry, Animal Husbandry and Fishing 2003–2015 (100 million yuan)

Year	Kc	Kc'	Ka	Ka'	Ka/Kc (%)
2003	55566.6	n.a.	1652.3	n.a.	2.97
2004	70477.4	26.83	1890.7	14.43	2.68
2005	88773.6	25.96	2323.7	22.90	2.62
2006	109998.2	23.91	2749.9	18.34	2.50
2007	137323.90	24.84	3403.5	23.77	2.48
2008	172828.4	25.85	5064.5	48.80	2.93
2009	224598.8	29.95	6894.9	36.14	3.07
2010	278121.9	23.83	7923.1	14.91	2.85
2011	311485.1	12.00	8757.8	10.54	2.81
2012	374694.7	20.29	10996.4	25.56	2.93
2013	446294.1	19.11	13478.8	22.57	3.02
2014	512020.7	14.73	16573.8	22.96	3.24
2015	561999.8	9.76	21042.7	26.96	3.74

Source: Author's calculation based on *ZGTJNJ* 2016, Available at: www.stats.gov.cn/tjsj/ndsj/2016/indexeh.htm (Accessed on 17 February 2017)

Notes
Kc = Total investment in fixed assets in the whole country
Kc'= Annual growth rate of Kc
Ka = Total investment in fixed assets in agriculture, forestry, animal husbandry and fishing
Ka'= Annual growth rate of Ka

Before the tax-for-fees reform implemented in 2000, education in rural areas was financed by town/township governments and village committees that relied mainly on the tax and fees collected from farm households. The burden of education financing at local levels was almost solely shouldered by farmers. After the tax-for-fees reform, education fundraising and surcharge were prohibited and the burden of education funds on farmers shifted to local governments. Under the NSC, school fees in rural areas in Western provinces were waived in 2006, and such a policy was extended to all provinces in 2007. To compensate for the abolition of school fees, the central government earmarked 218 billion yuan to be spent on rural education during the period 2006–2011 to lighten the fiscal pressure on county and town/township governments. Compulsory education in rural areas has gradually been financed primarily by central and provincial vaults. It provides a cure, at least partially, for the lasting fiscal imbalance at town/township and village levels and makes education more accessible to rural dwellers.

Third, with the aim of easing the financial burden of the farmers at a faster pace, central leaders decided in the annual rural work conference, held in December 2005, to abolish the agricultural tax in 2006, instead of phasing out the tax by 2008 as originally scheduled. The earlier elimination of agricultural tax certainly benefits the farmers, but the blessing of the reform is achieved at the expense of the added financial burden on local governments, especially for those in agriculturally based provinces. The central government planned to compensate the sub-provincial governments by fiscal transfer of 103 billion yuan annually to aid local finances. However, the central government's fiscal transfer was insufficient to make up for the fiscal losses to local governments. It was estimated that a quarter of fiscal losses caused by the abolition of agriculture tax was shouldered by local governments. That said, the elimination of agricultural tax increased farmers' net income by 4.8 percent (The Economist 2006), which enhanced their purchasing power and living standard.

The policy initiatives under the NSC programme signified central leaders' awareness of the severity of rural problems. Though a number of rural problems remains unsolved, the NSC initiative indicates the Chinese government's intention of forging a more balanced growth between urban and rural areas with an aim to develop a more harmonious country. Central leaders were willing to trade off economic growth for more even distribution of income to avoid escalating social unrest. One of the major contributing factors for income inequality at a national level arises from inequality between the countryside and cities. Similarly, recent decline in inequality is mainly attributable to the narrowing income gap between rural and urban areas, which were partially realised by the NSC programme. The urban-rural income ratio was 3.14 in 2007 and since then has been tapering off for 6 consecutive years, reaching 2.71 in 2017 (Table 2.1).

Though the income gap has been narrowed, rural households still lack access to urban living standards and social services due to the household registration system, the *hukou* system. The *hukou* system has its origin in the late 1950s when many rural residents fled to the cities to seek relief from starvation taking place in 1959–1961. The implementation ended the free flow of migrants from rural to urban areas. Rural residents without urban registration were expelled from the cities, and rural residents were not allowed to leave their place of residence without official approval (Frazier 2013). Since then the pro-urban development bias continues; the rural-urban gap has not only been reflected in terms of income but also in terms of infrastructure, welfare and medical and educational provisions. To address the issue, the Chinese government announced in March 2014 a bold new plan to resolve the rural-urban welfare gaps by a large-scale urbanisation plan aiming at turning rural people into urban residents. The plan is targeted to raise the population ratio in urban areas from 53.7 percent in 2014 to 60 percent in 2020, which at the same time will mean that the proportion of households with urban household registration will rise from 35.7 percent in 2013 to 45 percent in 2020. This decisive attempt will bring an additional 100 million people into new cities who will enjoy benefits equal to those of existing urban residents (Zhu 2014). However, the effectiveness of the plan to alleviate rural-urban disparity is subject to scrutiny. First, the number of rural migrant workers reached 268.94 million by the end of 2013 (Zhu 2014). Even if the plan can fully move 100 million people into new cities and grant them urbanite status, there is still a sizable 168.94 million migrant works who cannot benefit from the plan. Second, more significantly, this plan mainly focuses on settling the migrant workers who have already moved and worked in the cities while neglecting 45.4 percent of population, amounting to 621 million people, residing in the countryside.[13] The rural residents' livelihood is unlikely to be improved much by this urbanisation plan. Third, with its excess capacity in construction materials such as cement, steel, flat glass and aluminium, China will not encounter many difficulties in providing hardware infrastructure, such as transport network and housing estates. However, it may run into problems in delivering adequate software infrastructure, including education and medical and social services, to serve the population in new cities. If China had already possessed the capacity to provide these services, it would not have been so reluctant to relax the household registration system in the past decades.

A more effective and workable solution to the rural problems is to enhance the income and welfare of rural residents in their locality, instead of moving a huge rural population to new cities. It is less costly to enhance rural income by further institutional reforms in the countryside than a massive urbanisation programme. An institutional reform of clear delineation and enforcement of land rights is a precondition for establishing a market for rural land. When rural land is tradable, it means that rural dwellers can exercise their right to transfer land to capture exclusive income. Tradable rural land brings marked benefits to the rural economy and the economy as a whole. First, protecting land rights increases peasants' incentive to invest and develop their land, which heighten the productivity of land and thus farmers' income. Second, a rural land market will increase the land value as land will be transferred from low value users (e.g., farmers) to high value users (e.g., commercial crops growers, property developers). Farmers' wealth will be increased through land transfer and the wealth effect will increase their propensity to spend. Third, well-protected land rights reduce land disputes and protests in the countryside. It alleviates the pressure on central leaders and enhances the ruling party's legitimacy. Put together, protected and transferable land rights are conducive to productivity as well as increase in income and wealth. It is one of the most effective means of narrowing the long-lasting urban-rural disparity, which fosters social harmony and stability. The Ministry of Agriculture put forward a plan in 2015 to issue land-use certificates in rural areas and aimed to complete the work by 2020 (Xinhua 2013). The confirmation and registration of land use right was widely regarded as a prelude to the land reform endorsed by the Third Plenum of the 18th CPC Central Committee in 2013, which allowed farmers to transfer, mortgage and collateralise their land-use rights (Yuen 2014: 61). However, the impacts of the reform may not be very remarkable for two major reasons. First, the land reform kicked off with so-called rural construction land for commercial use (*jingyingxing jianshe yongdi*), which was a very small portion, about 2.4 percent, of the total area of cultivated land in 2014[14] and was equal to 8.5 percent of non-agricultural land use in China. In addition, some land plots are sparsely distributed and some located in areas of low commercial value. It is uncertain how many benefits farmers can actually derive from trading their land in an open market. It may bring limited momentum to boost farmers' incomes. Second, the success of the reform rests on the smooth completion of land-use registration and certification. More importantly, whether the farmers can really capture the benefits of the land reform lies vitally in farmers' understanding of their legal rights and the protection of the legal rights by local courts, which is still the weakest link in rural China.

Apart from land reform, expansion of rural finance is vital to sustain an increase in rural income. Land and labour productivity in agriculture has stayed at very low level when compared with upper-middle and high income countries. Gross agricultural output per unit of land in China was only about 55 percent of that of the high income countries over the period 2006–2011. Gross agricultural output per unit of labour was only a meagre of 9 percent of the high income counterparts (OECD 2015: 42). The very low levels of land and labour productivity are closely related to the amount and quality of physical and human capital that work with a given amount of land and labour. The availability of better physical inputs, such as quality seeds and fertilisers and human capital, such as technical knowhow, are crucial in enhancing land and labour productivity. The provision of physical and human capital is largely depended on the availability of ample bank credit. Given the fact that loans to rural households are around 5 percent of total outstanding loans in the country (Lai 2012), and the total investment in fixed assets in agriculture has been below 4 percent of the total investment in fixed assets in China, it appears that underdeveloped rural finance in China continues to constrain the productivity growth in the countryside. As discussed in the previous section, market forces may not effectively boost the development of rural finance as risks and profitability in extending loans to rural areas are not in proportion. NPL ratio in agriculture, forestry, animal husbandry and fishing was 3.54 percent in 2015, which was the second highest ratio among all economic sectors (*ZGTJNJ* 2016: 198). Profitability growth of rural credit cooperatives (RCCs)[15] was 24.9 percent, which was in stark contrast with the figure of 57.7 percent for all financial institutions for the period 2011–2015.[16] High risks and lower profitability growth explain the reluctance of financial institutions to re-enter the rural market. From a market failure perspective, government participation, such as subsidised microfinance, is justifiable to render adequate financial services to rural residents and enterprises to aid their development. Without ample financial resources to lift the quality and quantity of physical and human capital, land and labour productivity will further be constrained and the urban-rural gap will likely remain in the coming years.

Conclusion

This chapter reveals the initial reforms of China's rural areas, which released robust incentives for rural households to produce and invest. The results were impressive in terms of both rural income and living standards. The abundant supply of surplus labour in the countryside, together with local governments' support in sourcing bank loans, facilitated the proliferation of TVEs. TVEs performed the dual function of absorbing surplus labour and generating non-farm income for rural households. The spectacular growth and development in the countryside encountered bottlenecks when the central government implemented fiscal and banking reform in 1994. The fiscal reform, more specifically the TAS, hit the fiscal condition of local governments hard, which motivated local governments to appropriate land for commercial development to ease their financial burden. Land acquisitions have hampered the livelihood of rural residents and impeded peasants' incentive to invest in their allotted land. On another front, banking reform in 1994 further aggravated the lagged-behind growth of rural areas. The efficiency-enhancing banking reform, which aimed at commercialising the SOCBs, unintentionally led to shrinking financial services in the countryside. SOCBs were required to operate according to market discipline, which prompted banks to withdraw their business from the countryside, which demonstrated low profitability and high risks. Financial repression limited the growth of nonfarm activities and productivity in agriculture, which in turn has constrained rural income growth since the mid-1990s. The lagged-behind income growth intensified the yawning urban-rural gap. Rising protests and discontent among rural dwellers pushed central leaders to initiate the SNC programme in 2006 to boost rural development. The results were encouraging, with urban-rural income ratio narrowed from 3.14 in 2007 to 2.71 in 2017. That said, the SNC initiatives were far from providing a solution to the root cause of rural China's lagged-behind development. To sustain income growth and improve the livelihood of rural residents, the Chinese government must effectively address the issues of land rights protection and financial deepening. Land rights must be well defined and enforced. The land use value can be heightened if the market for transferring use right of land can be expanded and legally protected. Households can freely transfer out their land to earn a rental income or transfer in land plots to expand their farm and nonfarm activities. Both transferors and transferees can capture mutual gains from voluntary market transactions. Aside from the land issue, financial deepening is vital for raising land and labour productivity. No economy can sustain its long term growth without investing in physical capital, human capital and technical knowhow. China is no exception.

The significance of accelerating rural growth, apart from narrowing the urban-rural gap, is at least threefold. First, there are still 55 million people living in poverty,[17] and the majority of them reside in the countryside (Zhang 2017). Lifting rural income will mean a further step towards the eradication of poverty in 2020 as targeted by the central government. Second, given the fact that rural residents account for almost half of the population, raising rural income can heighten domestic consumption, which enables China to be less reliant on export- and investment-driven growth. Last but not least, the legitimacy of China's ruling party rests largely on the state's ability to promote growth and improve living standards. A successful income-enhancing institutional change in the countryside will assuage the discontent among rural dwellers and bestow the ruling party with stronger legitimacy.

Notes

1 A contract is signed between the collectives and the farm households while a certificate contains the details of the contract, which is issued by a higher level government (see Prosterman et al. 2009: 21).

2 The survey covered 1,773 households in 1657 villages and 945 counties in 17 provinces. For details, see Prosterman et al. (2009).
3 According to the RLCL, only a natural disaster constitutes a valid reason for readjustment of contracted land. However, the survey results indicated that only about 1 percent of the land readjustment was due to natural disasters. See Prosterman et al. (2009: 9, 14).
4 Here, the items "development zone/industrial park", "factory", "urban housing" and "gas station" are not categorised as projects mainly for the "public interest" of local communities.
5 For a detailed discussion of the impacts of TAS on local finances, see Lee and Kwong (2003), and Kwong (2007).
6 1 *mu* = 0.165 acre = 798.6 square yards = 667.8 square metres.
7 A comprehensive collection of land laws and regulations since the 1980s can be found in OECD (2009: Annex 3.A2). Available online: http://dx.doi.org/10.1787/548456516500 (Accessed on 19 March 2017)
8 The four SOCBs are Agricultural Bank of China (ABC), Industrial and Commercial Bank of China (ICBC), China Construction Bank (CCB), and Bank of China (BOC).
9 For the impact of 1994 banking reform on rural enterprises, see Kwong and Lee (2005).
10 The discussion of NSC policies are derived mainly from Kwong (2007). For concrete policies announced by the Chinese government on NSC, see "Facts and Figures: China's Drive to Build New Socialist Countryside.". Available at: www.gov.cn/english/2006-03/05/content_218920.htm (Accessed on 19 February 2017)
11 Kc' and Ka' was 22.7 percent and 27.84 for the period 2006–2015 respectively. Growth rates are calculated based on the figures in Table 2.3.
12 Data from *ZGTJNJ 2016*. Available at: www.stats.gov.cn/tjsj/ndsj/2016/indexeh.htm (Accessed on 19 February 2017)
13 Calculated based on data from Chinability.com. Available at: www.chinability.com/Population.htm (Accessed on 19 October 2016)
14 The "rural construction land for commercial use" was about 50 million *mu* (33,333 km²) while the total area of cultivated land was 1.35 million km² in 2014. Data derived from Yuen (2014) and *ZGTJNJ* 2016. Available at: www.stats.gov.cn/tjsj/ndsj/2015/indexeh.htm (Accessed on 6 March 2017)
15 Since the retreat of commercial banks from the countryside in the late 1990s, RCCs have become the main financial institutions extending loans in rural China.
16 Calculated based on the figures on CBRC (2016: 195).
17 China's poverty line is an annual income of 2,300 yuan as of 2017. See Zhang (2017).

References

Ash, R. F. (1996) 'Agricultural Development in China Since 1978,' in Ash, R. F. and Kueh, Y. Y. (eds.) *The Chinese Economy Under Deng Xiaoping*, New York: Oxford University Press, pp. 55–87.

China Banking Regulatory Commission (CBRC) (2016) *China Banking Regulatory Commission 2015 Annual Report*, Beijing: Zhongguo Jingrong Chubanshe.

Dabla-Norris, E. (2005) 'Issues in Intergovernmental Fiscal Relations in China,' *IMF Working Paper*, No. WP/05/30.

The Economist (2006) 'Planning the New Socialist Countryside,' 9 March. Available at: www.economist.com/node/5609082 (Accessed on 20 February 2017).

Frazier, M. W. (2013) 'Narrowing the Gap: Rural-Urban Inequality in China,' *World Politics Review*, September. Available at: www.worldpoliticsreview.com/arti cles/13241/narrowing-the-gap-rural-urban-inequality-in-china (Accessed on 19 October 2016).

Kang, L. (2009) 'Shidi nongmin bei zhengyong tudi de yiyuan jiqi yingxiang yinsu (Land-Losing Farmers' Attitude Towards Land Requisition and Its Determining Factors),' *Zhongguo Nongcun Jingji* (*Chinese Rural Economy*), No. 8, pp. 53–62.

Kwong, C. C. L. (2007) 'Where Is China's Rural Economy Heading for: A Brighter Future or Problems Unsolved?' in Cheng, Y. S. (ed.) *Challenges and Policy Pro-grammes of China's New Leadership*. Hong Kong: City University of Hong Kong Press, pp. 389–412.

Kwong, C. C. L. (2009) 'From Commercialization to WTO Accession: What Lies Ahead for China's Banking Reform,' *The Chinese Economy*, Vol. 42, No. 5, pp. 8–20.

Kwong, C. C. L. (2011) 'Sustaining China's Rural Development Under Global Eco-nomic Instability: Key Policy Issues,' *Asia Journal of Global Studies*, Vol. 4, No. 2, pp. 78–91.

Kwong, C. C. L. and Lee, P. K. (2005) Bad Loans Versus Sluggish Rural Industrial Growth: A Policy Dilemma of China's Banking Reform,' *Journal of the Asia Pacific Economy*, Vol. 10, No. 1, pp. 1–25.

Kwong, C. C. L. and Lo, H. W. C. (2006) 'Guest Editors' Introduction,' *The Chinese Economy*, Vol. 39, No. 4, July–August, pp. 3–9.

Lai, J. (2012) 'Rural Finance in China: Opportunities and Challenges,' Paper pre-sented at the *CICA Annual Meeting*, Hong Kong, 16 November.

Lee, P. K. and Kwong, C. C. L. (2003) 'From Developmental to Predatory Govern-ment: An Institutional Perspective of Local Cadres' Strategic Economic Behav-iour,' in Cheng, J. Y. S. (ed.) *China's Challenges in the Twenty-First Century*, Hong Kong: City University of Hong Kong Press, pp. 383–407.

Lin, J. Y. (1992) 'Rural Reforms and Agricultural Growth in China,' *The American Economic Review*, Vol. 82, No. 1, pp. 34–51.

National Bureau of Statistics of China (various issues) *China Statistical Yearbook* (*Zhongguo Tongji Nianjian, ZGTJNJ*), Beijing: China Statistics Press.

Naughton, B. (2007) *The Chinese Economy: Transitions and Growth*, Cambridge: MIT Press.

Organisation for Economic Co-operation and Development (OECD) (2009) *OECD Rural Policy Review: China*, Paris: OECD Publishing.

Organisation for Economic Co-operation and Development (OECD) (2015) *OECD Economic Survey: China*, Paris: OECD Publishing.

Prosterman, R., Zhu, K., Ye, J., Riedinger, J., Li, P. and Yadav, V. (2009) 'Secure Land Rights as a Foundation for Broad-Based Rural Development in China: Results and Recommendations from a Seventeen-Province Survey,' *NBR Special Report*, No. 18, The National Bureau of Asian Research.

So, A. Y. (2009) 'Peasant Conflict and the Local Predatory State in the Chinese Countryside,' *The Journal of Peasant Studies*, Vol. 34, Nos. 3–4, pp. 560–581.

Tang, S., Guan, Z. and Lansing, E. (2010) 'Formal and Informal Credit Markets and Rural Credit Demand in China,' Paper presented at the *Agricultural & Applied Economics Association 2010 AAEA,CAES, & WAEA Joint Annual Meeting*, Den-ver, Colorado, 25–27 July.

Wang, S. (1997) 'China's 1994 Fiscal Reform: An Initial Assessment,' *Asian Survey*, Vol. 37, No. 9, pp. 801–817.

Watts, J. (2006) 'China Vows to Create a "New Socialist Countryside" for Millions of Farmers,' *The Guardian*, 22 February. Available at: www.theguardian.com/world/2006/feb/22/china.jonathanwatts (Accessed on 20 November 2016).

Xinhua (2013) 'China to Complete Land-Use Right Registration in 5 Years,' *Xinhuanet*, 25 December. Available at: http://news.xinhuanet.com/english/china/2013-- 12/25/c_132996241.htm (Accessed on 6 March 2017).

Yuen, S. (2014) 'China's New Land Reform? Assessment and Prospects,' *China Perspectives*, No. 1, pp. 61–65.

Zhang, R. (2017) 'China's Local Governments Set Poverty Reduction Goals,' *CCTV. com*. Available at: http://english.cctv.com/2017/01/17/ARTIEFkSz4dwyjU569 jQ0cwO170117.shtml (Accessed on 25 April 2017).

Zhu, K. and Li, P. (2007) 'Rural Land Rights Under the PRC Property Law,' *China Law and Practice*, November Issue, pp. 23–26.

Zhu, N. (2014) 'China Unveils Landmark Urbanization Plan,' *Xinhuanet*, 16 March. Available at: http://news.xinhuanet.com/english/china/2014-- 03/16/c_133190495.htm (Accessed on 19 October 2016).

3 State-owned enterprises
Big and strong?

An increasing number of China's enterprises has been ranked on the *Fortune* Global 500 list in the world in terms of total revenue. China had only 10 enterprises on the list in 2000 and 46 in 2010. China registered a spectacular jump to 98 on the list in 2015, which was only second to the US, which had 128 enterprises on the list. The rapid rise of Chinese companies on the list is impressive. However, when taking a closer look, China's rise in *Fortune* Global 500 begins to look less remarkable. The top 12 Chinese companies are all state-owned. They include state-owned commercial banks (SOCBs) and oil companies under the control of the central government through the State-Owned Assets Supervision and Administration Commission of the State Council (SASAC), which is endowed with the authority of key staff appointments and major investment decisions. More importantly, these giant state-owned enterprises (SOEs) are granted quasi oligopoly/monopoly status and have easy access to bank loans. These dual benefits foster the swift expansion of the SOEs. Among the 98 Chinese companies on the *Fortune* Global 500 list, only 22 were private enterprises (Cendrowski 2016). This chapter will first provide a snapshot of China's SOE reforms implemented since early 1980s. It will then focus on the major challenges facing SOE reforms. This will be followed by analysing how a substantial state sector has constrained the growth of private enterprises and its bearing on efficiency. The concluding section highlights that though central leaders are clearly aware of the inefficiency embedded in the SOEs, it is likely that SOEs will continue their policy roles in the economy.

SOE reforms: a snapshot

Under China's centrally planned economy before the late 1970s, SOEs were directly controlled and monitored by central and/or local governments, which set input, output and pricing decisions. SOEs were entrusted with little autonomy in making investment and production decisions. Apart from fulfilling production targets assigned by the government, SOEs had to shoulder social responsibilities including provision of lifetime employment and social services such as clinics, schools, and a retirement pension for its employees and their families. In order to ensure ample inputs available for fulfilling production targets, cadres in charge of SOEs tended to ask for more than necessary inputs from industrial ministries, which were prone to accommodate SOEs' requests as under-fulfilment of one industrial sector might create bottlenecks in other production sectors. As fulfilling production targets, instead of profitability, were of paramount importance for SOEs, cadres in SOEs had very limited incentives to minimise the use of resources in production, which gave rise to the problem of soft budget constraint.[1] As a result, pre-reform SOEs were highly inefficient, in particular in terms of productive efficiency.[2]

Reform policies in the 1980s focused on decentralisation by offering SOEs more decision-making autonomy and incentives through profit sharing. SOEs' reforms in the 1980s to early 1990s represented a search for an optimal incentive system for SOEs to enhance their efficiency. The main plank of the reforms was to institute a contract responsibility system (CRS) that allowed SOEs to retain a bigger portion of profits and enhance the income rights of the SOE managers and workers after fulfilling their assigned tasks and production targets. SOEs were expected to shoulder profit and loss in order to harden enterprises' soft budget constraint. However, the CRS in SOEs was not as successful as that implemented in the countryside. As discussed in Chapter 1, SOE reforms were hindered by two major factors. First, production process in industrial enterprises was much more complex than that of agriculture. It involved a high level of division of labour, which made it difficult to reward each worker and manager according to productivity and efforts rendered. The effort-and-reward link in industrial production, particularly at managers'/workers' level, was much looser than that in agriculture. The issue of separation of contribution was further complicated by the question of whether a certain SOE could fulfil the assigned targets, which depended largely on the cooperation of upstream and downstream SOEs (Zhang and Liu 2010: 6–7). Second, soft budget constraints remained, as the central government would not allow massive bankruptcy and layoffs for SOEs with chronic losses. Central leaders realised that massive layoffs would jeopardise public support for further reform. Based on a sample survey 300 SOEs in 1989, it was revealed that no loss-making SOEs were subject to bankruptcy. Even worse, the empirical study indicated a weak correlation between SOEs' profitability and bonus payments to workers, which implied that loss-making SOEs still paid bonus to their workers (Chai and Tisdell 1992). Soft budget constraints were best reflected by the amount of government subsidies to SOEs. Fiscal subsidies to SOEs declined from 50.7 billion yuan in 1985 to 32.5 billion yuan in 1986 but rose again to 37.6 billion yuan in 1987. It then increased continuously to reach its peak at 57.9 billion yuan in 1990 (Lardy 1998: 37). Table 1.3 in Chapter 1 indicates that the percentage of loss-making state-owned industrial enterprises had increased steadily from 9.6 percent in 1985 to 25.8 percent in 1991, and the losses escalated from a small amount of 3.2 billion yuan in 1985 to 36.7 billion yuan in 1991. The amount soared more than 10 times within just 6 years. The complex nature of China's SOE system and the prevailing soft budget constraint made the result of SOE reform much less appealing than that of rural reform.

The huge losses incurred by SOEs in the early 1990s prompted the central government to take a decisive step to remedy the situation. The SOE reforms under Zhu Rongji represented an emphasis on efficiency and embarked on an unprecedented large-scale privatisation programme of loss-making or less strategically important businesses.[3] More notably, the government encouraged rapid expansion of the non-state sector by endowing private enterprises with equal political status with the state sector. This ideological breakthrough was motivated by the central government's intention to expand the private sector to absorb layoffs from the SOEs. As expected, the move of privatisation was far from full-fledged. Central government allowed the privatisation of some small- and medium-sized SOEs but retained dominant control of large SOEs in strategic sectors such as communication, energy, finance and national defence, thereby ensuring its control over the whole economy and national security. This stage of SOE reforms was best captured by the official slogan of "grasping the big and letting go of the small (SOEs)" and the state sector "advancing (in some areas) while retreating (from other areas)" (Zhang and Freestone 2013). Further, the Chinese government allowed more bankruptcy of insolvent SOEs. As the huge losses accumulated in SOEs in the early 1990s, local governments, the owners of the smaller SOEs, had strong incentive to restructure them into joint-stock companies (JSCs) or private enterprises through management buyouts (MBOs). Some of the JSCs were listed in stock exchanges and the companies' shares have been traded in the stock market. The JSCs are, in principle, owned jointly by the government and the private shareholders, but the major shares are still under direct and indirect control of the local governments and government departments. To better manage state assets in the companies, the SASAC was established in 2003 to monitor the major SOEs and a local SASAC was set up afterwards to manage the state assets owned by local governments and departments (Zhang and Yuan 2016: 6–7).

The progress of privatisation was slowed down after the early 2000s for at least two reasons. First, massive privatisation in the 1990s generated about 30 million laid off workers, whose living standards were adversely affected (The Economist 2008). With an aim of building a "harmonious society" under Hu-Wen leadership,[4] the government chose to gear down the pace of privatisation in exchange for greater social stability. Second, more importantly, since the mid-1990s, central government allowed smaller SOEs to be sold, either through MBOs or sales to outsiders (usually through auctions). MOBs refer the management of the enterprise which utilises its own (internal) and external fund, mainly through lending facilities to buy the shares of the enterprise and finally privatise the firm. This process of privatisation, also known as *gaizhi*,[5] converted about 25 percent of China's 87,000 industrial SOEs into private enterprises (Lu and Dranove 2007: 4). However, MBOs in China offered opportunities for enterprise managers to artificially press down the profit before privatisation in order to lower purchase price. The managers who bought the enterprise gained windfalls while the government shouldered losses of state assets. Lu and Dranove (2007) use survey data of 683 firms in 11 cities, 309 of which had completed *gaizhi* by the end of 2002, to show that firms privatised by insiders experienced a U-shaped pattern of profitability relative to other firms. SOEs sold to insiders experienced a significant reduction in profitability and productivity in the period just before privatisation. However, profitability returned to earlier levels after privatisation was completed. Other than managers, local government officials were also prone to give low evaluation of less promising SOEs so as to sell the local SOEs more easily to outsiders (i.e., joint venture or foreign investors). Local officials were eager to do so as the pace of restructuring ailing SOEs was one of the major criteria for their performance appraisal. Though there was no accurate gauge and consensus of the size of asset stripping, it is estimated that the asset loss of SOEs was around 100 to 300 million per day in the 1990s, with an estimate of 500 million on the high side.[6] The central government responded to the rising severity of asset stripping by substantially winding down the practice of MBOs. Asset stripping constituted one of the major motivations for the State Council to establish the SASAC in 2003 to strengthen its supervision of SOEs and avoid siphoning state assets through MBOs and other channels.

SOE reform reached a turning point when Xi Jinping highlighted the importance of speeding up SOE reform at the third plenary session of the central committee of the Communist Party of China (CPC) in November 2013. Unlike previous reforms intending to liberalise SOEs through decentralisation and liberalisation, Xi emphasised that SOEs must deepen their reforms in order to "become important forces to implement the decisions of the party" (Zhao 2016). The Party has used its political apparatus to tighten the control on SOEs. All SOEs are required to have a Party organisation headed by a Party secretary and all important decisions of the enterprises must first be scrutinised and approved by the Party committee before the plans are implemented. This ensures that the CPC has sufficient monitoring of enterprise operation and management and that the SOEs' development plans align with state targets and priorities. Further, the CPC warrants its control by overlapping (i.e., concurrent) appointments, which require that the Party secretary and chairman of the board must be the same person. This practice of overlapping appointments has made the Party become the political core of the enterprise. It is especially true for the largest key SOEs. The appointment of the top leaders of the 53 largest SOEs is not made by SASAC but by the Party's Organization Department. Their positions are ranked at vice-ministerial level. These SOE leaders take up senior government or Party positions after they have served the SOEs with good performance, which incentivises the SOE leaders to work in line with state policy targets. Xi's firm political grip on SOEs fundamentally reverses Deng Xiaoping's policy of separating the government and enterprises (Brødsgaard 2018). Efficiency enhancement is once again subordinated to political missions.

Contrary to tightening control, the government has introduced the concept of mixed ownership of SOEs, which promotes cross-holdings among state capital, collective capital and private capital. Investment by private capital in SOEs through equity purchase, convertible bond subscription and equity swap has received greenlight from the government. In additional, the government, in principle, allows more private capital to invest in new SOE projects in some strategic areas such as oil and gas, power, railway, telecommunication and resources (Chan 2015: 1–2). However, under government's tight control, it is unlikely that private investment would have any real impact on SOEs' corporate governance and efficiency enhancement. As pointed out by Hsu (2017), China's mixed ownership reform is targeted for tapping funding from the non-state sector rather than relaxing state control in SOEs. It is unconvinced that the Party would relinquish its control over SOEs to private investors due to the central government's strong intention to rein in the autonomy of SOEs.

Another main plank of Xi's SOE reforms is to encourage merger and requisition to generate synergy and reduce excessive capacity. One of the most eye-catching cases was the merger of Wuhan Iron and Steel and Baosteel in November 2016, which created China's largest steelmaker. Other mergers include COSCO and China Shipping in December 2015 – resulting in the fourth largest container shipping company in the world – and China Minmetals Corp's acquisition of China Metallurgical Group in December 2015 (Hsu 2017). The mergers and acquisitions reduce the number of big SOEs, but no systematic evidence indicates the presence of expected synergy and efficiency enhancement. Instead, one thing is clear: this round of mergers and acquisitions has created more and stronger monopolies that may further shrink efficiency. Merging huge state firms without downsizing redundant manpower and production capacity will only keep SOEs' long-lasting problems of soft budget and operation inefficiency intact. Nonetheless, generating synergy and reducing excessive capacity may not be the primary targets of the central government. Against the background of Belt and Road Initiative (BRI), mergers between big SOEs exist to strategically develop giant SOEs to become natural monopolies,[7] which boost SOEs' international competitiveness. For instance, the merger of China Power Investment Corporation (CPIC) and State Nuclear Power Technology Corporation (SNPTC) to form State Power Investment Corporation in 2015, in which CPIC's vast capital resources complemented SNPTC's advanced technology. Another example of forming a state monopoly is the merger of CSR Corporation and CNR Corporation to create the China Railway Rolling Stock Corporation, which became one of the world's largest companies in the railway sector, which is a key sector of BRI. The pace of merging large SOEs is clearly accelerating. Only 5 mergers of central SOEs were completed between 2012 and 2014. However, between 2015 and November 2016, 11 central SOE mergers took place in various industrial sectors including shipping, commerce, construction, steel, services and energy (Leutert and Godement 2016).

SOE reform after the Third Plenum in 2013 can best be captured by the phrase that "state ownership is a central pillar of the economy" (Shambaugh 2016: 42). The Plenum also pointed out the decisive role of markets in SOE reform, but, as illustrated previously, it is not difficult to observe that this is more in principle than in practice. The reform under Xi is a retreat from decentralisation and marketisation, but from the central leaders' perspective it serves the best interest of the government to control the most important part of state assets and ensure that SOEs are effective levers to reach state targets. Moreover, mergers of SOEs reflect the central government's intention to create giant state monopolies to increase their presence in the international market under the BRI and "going out" strategy.

SOEs: bigger but not stronger

By 2016, there were about 19,022 SOEs[8] at central and local levels that engaged in a wide range of industries including energy, commodities, telecommunication, finance, hotel and retail business. SOEs' development and efficiency have long been trapped by rigid political monitoring, high debt ratios, redundancy and making social responsibility a higher priority than profitability. Since the financial crisis in 2008, despite China's rebound in its growth in 2010, average SOE profitability has been declining. Returns on investment for SOEs are at around 5 percent, compared to over 9 percent for private firms (Tiezzi 2015). Among the country's nearly 2,800 A-share listed companies in 2016, the biggest loss-making firm was Sinopec Oilfield Service Corp, which registered a loss of about 16 billion yuan. The figures were very close to the record high losses incurred by Chalco in 2014.[9] Actually, most of biggest losers in the industrial sector were SOEs over the past decade.[10] Financial indicators of SOEs in various sectors have been deteriorating over the past years. The return on equity (ROE) of nearly 300 non-financial SOEs listed in mainland stock exchanges declined from 15.6 percent in 2007 to 7.0 percent in 2017. The ROE dropped by almost half over a decade (Cho and Kawase 2018).

Zhang and Yuan (2016) examine empirically the financial performance of all publicly listed firms in China from 2003–2013. It appears that both direct and indirect government ownership have a negative impact on the performance, in terms of ROA[11] and Tobin's Q ratio,[12] of publicly listed firms in China. Firms with direct government ownership and immediate control demonstrate the worst performance. Firms indirectly owned by the government, through SOEs or through local and central SASACs, perform slightly better than their counterparts under direct government ownership and control. In stark contrast, firms owned and controlled by private individuals perform best, followed by firms controlled by companies. These results suggest once again that SOEs record a far weaker returns on assets than private firms.

Table 3.1 shows the major indicators of SOEs and private enterprises (PEs). There are two observations worth noting. First, the number of SOEs has been decreasing from 20,680 in 2007 to 19,022 in 2016 while the number of PEs has been rising from 177,080 to 214,309 for the same period. However, these figures could not be interpreted as a rapid expansion of PEs. SOEs possessed 44.8 percent of national total assets while the respective figure for PEs was only 15.1 percent in 2007. After years of promoting the development of the private sector, the percentage share of national assets for SOEs declined to 38.5 percent, registering a drop of only 6.3 percentage points over the past decade. Correspondingly, the percentage share for PEs rose to 22.1 percent in 2016, representing a rise of 7 percentage points over the same period. These figures reveal

Table 3.1 Major Indicators of State-owned Enterprises[13] and Private Enterprises

	2007		2012		2016	
	SOEs	PEs	SOEs	PEs	SOEs	PEs
Number of Enterprises	20,680	177,080	17,851	189,289	19,022	214,309
National Total Assets (billion yuan)	35,304		76,842		108,587	
Total Assets of Enterprises (billion yuan)	15,819	5,330	31,209	15,255	41,770	23,954
Assets/Enterprise (million yuan)	765.0	30.0	1748.3	80.6	2195.9	111.8
Total Profit (billion yuan)	1,080	505	1,518	2,019	1,232	2,549
Profit Rate (%)	6.8	9.5	4.9	13.2	2.9	10.6

Source: *China Statistical Yearbook* (2008, 2013, 2017)

that SOEs still control a dominate share of national assets. More remarkably, the average size of an SOE and a PE in terms of assets was 765 million yuan and 30 million yuan respectively in 2007. The average size of a SOE was 25.5 times of a PE. Though PEs have exhibited a rise in asset value, an SOE's asset value was still 19.6 times that of a PE in 2016. The firm size constraints are directly related to the fact that SOEs are more accessible to formal finance. SOEs got access to about 55 percent of the total corporate loans in 2016 but only produced 22 percent of GDP (Chow and Anderson 2017: 2).

Second, a more severe problem for SOEs revealed in Table 3.1 is their deteriorating financial performance since the 2008 global financial crisis. Credit expansion and investment-driven growth after the financial crisis successfully boosted growth by increasing factor inputs rather than raising factor productivity. Total profits of SOEs rose from 1,080 billion yuan in 2007 to 2,549 billion yuan in 2016, representing a growth of 136 percent. During the same period, total assets of SOEs soared from 15,819 billion yuan to 41,770 billion yuan, registering a growth of 164 percent. The growth rate of SOE assets outpaced that of the profits, which resulted in a decline of profit rate from 6.8 percent in 2007 to 4.9 percent in 2012 and tapered off further to 2.9 percent in 2016. In stark contrast, profit rates of PEs have been consistently higher than that of SOEs by 2.7 to 8.3 percentage points over the past decades. SOEs' rapid accumulation of assets was mainly caused by high financial leverage, measured by liability-to-asset ratio, of SOEs, especially for heavy industrial sectors dominated by state firms. Table 3.2 depicts liability-to-asset ratios of SOEs and non-SOEs. The ratio for SOEs was 8.5 percentage points higher than that of non-SOEs. More noticeably, the most-leveraged sectors, mainly SOEs, had an average ratio of 66.6 percent while the average ratio for the least-leveraged sectors was 41.7 percent; the former is higher than the latter by 24.9 percentage points. The high leverage generates overcapacity of SOEs, which accounts for their dwindling profitability.

Table 3.2 Financial Leverage: Liability-to-asset Ratio (%) for
SOEs and Non-SOEs (June 2017)

All industrial enterprises	55.9
SOEs	61.2
Non-SOEs	52.7
Most-leveraged sectors	
Coal mining	68.7
Ferrous metal processing	66.3
Fabricated metals manufacturing	64.9
Least-leveraged sectors	
Printing	42.9
Wood and wood products	41.6
Medical devices and pharmaceuticals	40.7

Source: Chow and Anderson (2017: 3)

Private enterprises: a rising sector?

Though PEs have been encountering hurdles to expand business and facing keen competition from private and state counterparts, the private sector as a whole has gathered momentum to flourish over the past two decades. With about one-fifth of national assets and one-third of corporate loans, it produced 60 percent of China's Gross Domestic Product (GDP) and contributed more than 50 percent of tax revenue.[14] More noteworthy is that PEs have accomplished an important mission of absorbing the layoffs from downsized SOEs and generating new jobs for the labour force, which constitute a cornerstone of social stability. It is of vital importance to maintain the legitimacy of the ruling party. Table 3.3 indicates that the number of workers employed by PEs in urban areas skyrocketed from 45.81 million in 2007 to 75.57 million in 2012 and soared to 120.83 in 2016. In contrast, employment in SOE has shrunk from 64.24 to 61.7 million workers in 2007 and 2016 respectively. Taking a broader perspective, the state sector only created 14.9 percent of urban employment and the non-state sector brought about 85.1 percent of urban employment in 2016.[15] Though PEs in rural areas generated less employment than in urban areas, workers employed by PEs recorded a rise of 121.3 percent from 2007 to 2016, and its share in total rural employment rose from 6 percent to 16.3 percent. The percentage share rises to 28.1 percent in 2016 when self-employed individuals are added to the number of workers employed by PEs.

The private sector plays an important role in the entire economic system, contributing more than 50% of tax revenue, more than 60% of gross domestic product, more than 70% of technological innovation, more than 80% of urban labor employment, and more than 90% of the number of new employment opportunities and newly founded enterprises.

Table 3.3 Employment in State and Non-state Sector 2007–2016 (in millions, selected years)

	2007	*2012*	*2016*
Total national employment	753.21	767.04	776.03
Total urban employment	309.53	371.02	414.28
SOEs	64.24	68.39	61.70
PEs	45.81	75.57	120.83
Self-employed individual	33.10	56.43	86.27
Total rural employment	443.68	396.02	361.75
PEs	26.72	37.39	59.14
Self-employed individual	21.87	29.86	42.35

Source: *China Statistical Yearbook 2017*. Available at: www.stats.gov.cn/tjsj/ndsj/2017/indexeh.htm (Accessed on 22 October 2018)

Despite central leaders' reemphasis of the importance of the private sector and repeated pledges to render more support to PEs, concrete measures are still rare. To illustrate, SOEs still get access to almost half of the total corporate loans while the small and medium-sized private enterprises received only 32.3 percent of total corporate loans in the first half of 2018. In terms of new corporate loans issued in the first two quarters of 2018, PEs received only 20.9 percent, which is the lowest figure since 2012 (Wang 2018).

Trade war with the US that emerged in the mid-2018 further twisted China's path of SOE reform towards more centralisation. On the surface, the US makes use of the trade war to insert pressure on China to open up its market. What's behind the US trade action is the intent to create hurdles to China's industrial upgrade programme "Made in China 2025", which is an initiative made by the Chinese government to drive manufacturing innovation, strengthen the industrial base and promote breakthroughs in key industrial sectors, with the ultimate goal of enhancing international competitiveness and improving the image and quality of Chinese brands. The central government has targeted 9 tasks and 10 key sectors to develop.[16] This plan is one of the most prominent elements in China's thirteenth Five-year Programme. When China rolled out this high-profile industrial upgrade programme in 2015, it did not draw much attention from the advanced Western countries. However, when the Chinese acquired a number of German manufacturing firms in 2016, including Midea's acquisition of robot maker Kuka, ChemChina's acquisition of machinery maker KraussMaffei, Shanghai Electric Group's acquisition of hi-tech equipment manufacturer Manz and Shang Gong Group's acquisition of knitting machine maker H. Stoll (Tse 2016), it triggered a nerve for the West, in particular the US.[17] The US fears China's challenge against the US's economic and technology hegemony if China can easily acquire the necessary technology to fulfil "Made in China 2025". The concern of the US is not without grounds, as China has demonstrated a strong ability to apply and replicate imported technology for manufacturing in a cost effective way. In response, the US government announced in mid-2018 that it would restrict firms with at least 25 percent Chinese ownership from investing in US companies with "industrially significant technology" including those related to "Made in China 2025".[18]

Central leaders have been fully aware that China is on the disadvantageous side when both China and the US impose retaliation tariffs, as China has long been maintaining a trade surplus with the US. Instead of lengthening its bargaining with the Trump administration, China will probably move to two directions to minimise its reliance on the US. First, China will likely diversify its export markets. Second, it will shrink the dependence on importing high-tech parts and semi-finished products such as semi-conductors and robotic parts from the US and advanced European countries. Further, China will not rely on investing in foreign firms to acquire hi-tech for manufacturing as more hurdles are expected to be imposed on China. The central government's target of "self-reliance" on technological innovation was best captured by Xi's comments when he toured at the Gree Electric Appliances in Zhuhai, one of the country's biggest manufacturers, on 22 October 2018:[19]

> To go from a big country to a strong one, we must give paramount importance to the development of the real economy. . . . Manufacturing is a key to the real economy, and the core strength of manufacturing is innovation, or the control of core technologies. . . . We must . . . seek innovation by relying on ourselves, and I hope all enterprises will work in this direction.

The private enterprises are vibrant forces for innovation especially in the IT sector where PEs dominate, with prominent successful firms such as Alibaba, Tencent, Huawei, Sina and Baidu. However, the Chinese government, instead of relying on private firms, inclines to maintain its dominance in the SOEs to make sure that the state enterprises are heading to fulfil the government's targets. Further, hi-tech research and development is capital-intensive and risky. It involves substantial investment with very uncertain outcomes. To reach quick results, government dominance and huge capital injection are unavoidable.

The central government's firm control of SOEs is also attributable to the long standing principle of maintaining stable employment in SOEs though the state sector shared only about 14.9 percent of urban employment in 2016 as indicated previously. It was originally planned to cut 1.8 million workers in the SOEs in 2009 with a further cut of 5–6 million workers in 2019. However, a total of 2,663 labour protests were recorded during 2014–2016. The undercurrent of social instability prompted China's Premier Li Keqiang to highlight in 2016 that it was important to cut excessive workers in SOEs but that firm leaders must arrange new posts for the layoffs. Even more explicitly, the SASAC head Xiao Yaqing emphasised that SOE restructuring should not be achieved at the expense of the wellbeing of the workers and social stability (Economy 2018: 109).

Continued support (including easily accessible loans and maintenance of monopoly/oligopoly status) of SOEs not only creates unfair competition for PEs but also diverts resources from more productive PEs to less productive SOEs.

Numerous performance indicators illustrated previously convey a clear message that same amount of financial resources in private sectors would likely generate more output, employment and profits. Nonetheless, the current stage of SOE reform seems to place more emphasis on reaching government targets than raising efficiency. The more immediate targets are to upgrade manufacturing technology and expand China's presence on the global stage. To reach these goals, the central government will continue its firm control of the 100-odd large central SOEs under the direct monitoring of SASAC and amalgamate its central SOEs to establish monopolies that could be more competitive abroad. The private sector will continue to develop, but supportive policy from the government will be limited relative to their state counterparts.

Conclusion

The Chinese government has initiated a series of reforms since the 1980s with an aim to enhance the efficiency of SOEs. The results are spectacular, with a rising number of SOEs that are now ranked on the *Fortune* Global 500 list. China's SOEs reform started with a contract responsibility system in the 1980s, which was an attempt to search for an optimal incentive system to motivate SOE managers to take into account profit and loss when they carried out production plans. However, the outcome was less impressive than that of rural reform. One of the primary reasons was that soft budget constraints largely remained in SOEs. Managers were rewarded for making profits and meeting state targets but did not shoulder the responsibility of incurring losses and overspending. Zhu Rongji's attempt in the 1990s to curb the mounting losses of SOEs by privatising some of the SOEs brought about unintended outcomes of asset stripping and sizable unemployment. The pace of privatisation and marketisation were considerably slowed down by Zhu's successors, Hu Jintao and Wen Jiabao, who put "social harmony" over efficiency. Since Xi Jinping assumed his leadership in 2013, a trend of recentralisation and amalgamation of SOEs has been underway. Though low profitability and inefficiency embedded in SOEs have long been a concern of central leaders, Xi's reluctance to diminish the role of SOEs in the economy implies limited market reform under his leadership.

China will not put a halt to the expansion of the private sector as it effectively generates the much needed GDP growth and employment, but it is unrealistic to hope that China will turn into a de facto market-driven economy. A major overhaul of the SOEs similar to the scale done by Zhu Rongji in the 1990s seems out of the question. Instead, China will run its economic system with firm control of the state sector with elements of a market economy. The blend between state control and marketisation finally relies on the priority of state targets and efficiency considerations at the point of policy making. When policy goals and efficiency consideration appear to be fundamentally contradictory, central leaders under Xi's leadership incline to make efficiency considerations subordinate to policy targets.

Notes

1 The concept of soft budget constraint was developed by János Kornai who argues that though SOEs in planned economies were expected to maximise their profits, the loss-making SOEs were actually not allowed to fail. They were always bailed out with financial subsidies by the central government. SOEs could continue to survive even after continual losses. For details, see Kornai (1980: 306–309).

2 A firm is said to achieve productive efficiency if it minimises its average costs in production. However, SOEs were not responsible for their profit and loss. They have no incentive to minimise their production costs.

3 Zhu Rongji was appointed Vice-premier of the State Council in 1991 and served concurrently as Governor of the central bank. Zhu became Premier in March 1998 and retired and was succeeded by Wen Jiabao by 2003. For a more detailed discussed of Zhu's SOE reforms, see Zheng and Chen (2007).

4 Hu Jintao and Wen Jiabao officially succeeded Jiang Zemin, Li Peng and Zhu Rongji in 2003.

5 The Chinese term *gazhi* means change in institution or restructuring.

6 For the various estimates and forms of asset loss of SOEs in the 1990s, see Smyth (2000).

7 A natural monopoly is a giant firm that can lower its long run average total cost through economies of scale, which can drive away some competitors in the global market.

8 SOEs include state-owned and state-holding enterprises. State-owned enterprises, originally known as state-run enterprises with ownership by the whole society, are non-corporate economic entities registered according to the *Regulation of the People's Republic of China on the Management of Registration of Legal Enterprises*, where all assets are owned by the state. State-holding enterprises are a sub-classification of enterprises with mixed ownership, referring to enterprises where the percentage of state assets (or shares by the state) is larger than any other single shareholder of the same enterprise, which indicates that the state maintains a controlling share of the enterprise. See explanatory note from *China Statistical Yearbook 2007*. Available at: www.stats.gov.cn/tjsj/ndsj/2007/indexeh.htm (accessed on 20 October 2018); *China Statistical Yearbook 2013*. Available at: www.stats.gov.cn/tjsj/ndsj/2013/indexeh.htm (accessed on 20 October 2018); *China Statistical Yearbook 2017*. Available at: www.stats.gov.cn/tjsj/ndsj/2017/indexeh.htm (Accessed on 20 October 2018)

9 The major shareholder of Chalco is Aluminum Corporation of China, also known as Chinalco, which is an SOE. Chalco registered a loss of 16.2 billion yuan in 2014, which was a record high for a subsidiary of an SOE.

10 Some of the biggest losers included Wuhan Iron & Steel Co in 2015, COSCO in 2011–2012 and China Eastern Airlines in 2008 (South China Morning Post 2017).

11 Return on assets (ROA) is an indicator of a firm's profitability, which is measured by net income divided by total assets. It also indicates how efficiently the management uses the firm's assets. See "Return on Assets – ROA". Available at: www.investopedia.com/terms/r/returnonassets.asp (Accessed on 13 October 2018)

12 Tobin's Q ratio is developed by Nobel Laureate James Tobin to indicate a firm's development potential in the market, which is measured by the total market (stock) value of the firm divided by the total asset value (i.e., replacement costs). If the ratio is greater than 1, it shows some unmeasured or unrecorded assets of the company. It is worth it for the firm to invest more in capital. A ratio less than 1 implies that the firm cannot earn enough to compensate for the investment of total assets. See "Q Ratio (Tobin's Q Ratio)". Available at: www.investopedia.com/terms/q/qratio.asp (Accessed on 13 October 2018)

13 See note 7.
14 See "Those Who Don't Support Development of Private Enterprises Must Be Corrected: Liu He", *Caixin*. Available at: www.caixinglobal.com/2018-10-20/those-who-do-not-support-the-development-of-private-enterprises-must-be-resolutely-corrected-liu-he-101337150.html (Accessed on 22 October 2018)
15 The non-state sector includes private enterprises; collective enterprises; joint ownership enterprises; limited liability corporations; shareholding corporations; enterprises with funds from Hong Kong, Macao and Taiwan; foreign funded enterprises and self-employed individuals.
16 For the details of the 9 tasks and 10 key sectors, please see note 19 in Chapter 1.
17 At almost the same time, some other Chinese firms have already acquired some German companies including ChemChina's acquisition of machinery-maker KraussMaffei, Shanghai Electric Group's acquisition of hi-tech equipment manufacturer Manz and Shang Gong Group's acquisition of knitting machine maker H. Stoll (Tse 2016).
18 It includes the technology in robotics, aerospace and aviation equipment, clean energy cars and medical equipment. See "Donald Trump to Hit US$50 Billion of Chinese Imports with 25 Per cent Tariffs and Restrict Investment in US Hi-tech Industries". Available at: www.sino-us.com/35/09555096502.html (accessed on 24 October 2018) and Aleem (2018).
19 Quoted in He (2018).

References

Aleem, Z. (2018) 'Trump Is About to Escalate His Trade War with China.' Available at: https://www-vox-com.cdn.ampproject.org/v/s/www.vox.com/platform/amp/world/2018/6/26/17500848/trump-china-trade-war-invest-export?_gsa=1&usqp=mq331AQCCAE%3D&amp_js_v=0.1 (Accessed on 24 October 2018).

Brødsgaard, K. E. (2018) 'Can China Keep Controlling Its SOEs?' *The Diplomat*. Available at: https://thediplomat.com/2018/03/can-china-keep-controlling-its-soes/ (Accessed on 13 October).

Cendrowski, S. (2016) 'China's Global 500 Companies Are Bigger than Ever – And Mostly State-Owned,' *Fortune*. Available at: http://fortune.com/2015/07/22/china-global-500-government-owned/ (Accessed on 8 May 2017).

Chai, J. C. H. and Tisdell, C. (1992) 'The Two-Track System and China's Macro-Instability,' *Discussion Paper*, No. 85, Department of Economics, University of Queensland.

Chan, B. (2015) 'Balancing Autonomy with Control: China's Latest SOE Reform Plan,' *Linklaters*. Available at: http://content.linklaters.com/pdfs/mkt/shanghai/A30433792%20v0.3%20Chinas%20Latest%20SOE%20Reform%20Plan.pdf (Accessed on 14 October 2018).

China Statistical Yearbook 2008. Available at: www.stats.gov.cn/tjsj/ndsj/2008/indexeh.htm (Accessed on 21 October 2018).

China Statistical Yearbook 2013. Available at: www.stats.gov.cn/tjsj/ndsj/2013/indexeh.htm (Accessed on 21 October 2018).

China Statistical Yearbook 2017. Available at: www.stats.gov.cn/tjsj/ndsj/2017/indexeh.htm (Accessed on 21 October 2018).

Cho, Y. and Kawase, K. (2018) 'How China's State-Backed Companies Fell Behind,' *Nikkei Asian Review*. Available at: https://asia.nikkei.com/Spotlight/Cover-Story/How-China-s-state-backed-companies-fell-behind (Accessed on 13 October 2018).

Chow, M. and Anderson, H. (2017) 'Tackling China's Debt Mountain Needs More than SOE Reform,' *Market Bulletin*, J. P. Morgan.

The Economist (2008) 'The Second Long March,' 11 December. Available at: www.economist.com/node/12758848 (Accessed on 10 June 2017).

Economy, E. C. (2018) *The Third Revolution: Xi Jinping and the New Chinese State*, New York: Oxford University Press.

He, H. (2018) 'Xi Jinping Urges China to Become More Self-Reliant During Tour of Southern Manufacturing Hub,' *South China Morning Post*, 23 October. Available at: www.scmp.com/economy/china-economy/article/2169779/xi-jinping-urges-china-become-more-self-reliant-tour-southern?aid=197778625&sc_src=email_2377018&sc_llid=28074&sc_lid=156214316&sc_uid=onlcRnJcdo&utm_source=emarsys&utm_medium=email&utm_campaign=GME-O-TradeWar&utm_content=hkrow-181023 (Accessed on 24 October 2018).

Hsu, S. (2017) 'China Goes in Circles: Another Attempt to Reform State-Owned Enterprises Doesn't Do Enough,' *Forbes*. Available at: www.forbes.com/sites/sarahsu/2017/06/13/china-goes-in-circles-another-attempt-to-reform-state-owned-enterprises-doesnt-do-enough/#4916f8a64912 (Accessed on 11 October 2018).

Kornai, J. (1980) *Economics of Shortage*, Amsterdam: North-Holland.

Lardy, N. R. (1998) *China's Unfinished Revolution*, Washington, DC: Brooking Institution Press.

Leutert, W. and Godement, F. (2016) 'Big Is Beautiful? State-Owned Enterprise Mergers Under Xi Jinping,' *European Council on Foreign Relations*. Available at: www.ecfr.eu/publications/summary/china_state_owned_enterprise_mergers_under_xi_jinping7196 (Accessed on 30 October 2018).

Lu, S. F. and Dranove, D. (2007) 'Profiting from Gaizhi: Management Buyout During China's Privatization.' Available at: https://ssrn.com/abstract=1348277 or http://dx.doi.org/10.2139/ssrn.1348277 (Accessed on 11 June 2017).

Shambaugh, D. (2016) *China's Future*, Cambridge: Polity Press.

Smyth, R. (2000) 'Asset Stripping in Chinese State-Owned Enterprises,' *Journal of Contemporary Asia*, Vol. 30, No. 1, pp. 3–16.

South China Morning Post (2017) 'Massive Loss by China's Sinopec Unit Raises Tough Questions on State Owned Enterprise Reform,' 20 February. Available at: www.scmp.com/news/china/economy/article/2072196/massive-loss-chinas-sinopec-unit-raises-tough-questions-state (Accessed on 22 May 2017).

Tiezzi, S. (2015) 'Xi's New Year's Resolution: Reform China's State-Owned Enterprises,' *The Diplomat*, 14 January. Available at: http://thediplomat.com/2015/01/xis-new-years-resolution-reform-chinas-state-owned-enterprises/ (Accessed on 24 May 2017).

Tse, E. (2016) 'Midea's Move for German Robot Maker Kuka May Be a Turning Point for Chinese Manufacturing,' *South China Morning Post*, 21 August. Available at: www.scmp.com/comment/insight-opinion/article/2006054/mideas-move-german-robot-maker-kuka-may-be-turning-point (Accessed on 24 October 2018).

Wang, O. (2018) 'Brother Can You Spare a Dime: China's Small Firms Can't Get Loans Even with the Government's Push,' *South China Morning Post*, 29 August. Available at: www.scmp.com/business/china-business/article/2161759/brother-can-you-spare-dime-chinas-small-firms-cant-get-loans (Accessed on 22 October 2018).

Zhang, D. and Freestone, O. (2013) 'China's Unfinished State-Owned Enterprise Reforms,' *Economic Roundup*, Issue 2, The Treasury, Australian Government.

Zhang, S. and Yuan, S. (2016) *The Performance of State-Owned Enterprises in China: An Empirical Analysis of Ownership Control Through SASACs*, Singapore: Chartered Institute of Management Accounts and Centre for Governance, Institutions and Organisations, NUS Business School.

Zhang, W. and Liu, X. (2010) 'Success and Challenges: Overview of China's Economic Growth and Reform Since 1978,' in Liu, X. and Zhang, W. (eds.) *China's Three Decades of Economic Reforms*, Oxon: Routledge, pp. 3–14.

Zhao, G. B. (2016) 'Could SOE Reform in China Usher in the Next Economic Revolution?' *South China Morning Post*, 16 November. Available at: www.scmp.com/comment/insight-opinion/article/2046165/could-soe-reform-china-usher-next-economic-revolution (Accessed on 13 October 2018).

Zheng, Y. and Chen, M. (2007) 'China's Recent State-Owned Enterprise Reform and Its Social Consequences,' *Briefing Series*, Issue 23, China Policy Institute, The University of Nottingham.

4 The banking sector

Struggle between commercial and policy loans

China is now the largest manufacturing country in the world. For any economy, a rapid expansion of the real sector has to be backed by an effective money sector which channels loanable funds to finance the projects in the real sector. China is no exception. China has made multidimensional efforts to enhance the efficiency of the banking sector over the past decades. The highlight of the banking reform was the commercialisation of state banks in 1994, which aimed at enhancing efficiency of the banking sector by transforming state banks into state-owned commercial banks (SOCBs) that operate according to market disciplines. The achievement has been unprecedented, in particular in improving the balance sheets and corporate governance of the SOCBs. However, evidence shows that SOCBs are still dominated by state policy direction over the past two decades and a de facto commercial banking system is still far from complete, which has direct bearing on the efficiency of the banking sector. This chapter will first review briefly the pre-1994 banking reforms, followed by an analysis of the commercialisation of state banks taken place since 1994. It will then demonstrate how the 4-trillion yuan stimulus package implemented after the 2008 global financial crisis (GFC) caused a retreat from the decade-long reform of commercialising the SOCBs. It argues that though a state-dominated banking sector with policy targets hampers efficiency of allocating loanable funds, the Chinese government will not initiate fully-fledged market reform in banking sector, which may abate the government's ability of leveraging the banking sector to reach policy targets. This chapter concludes that a complete withdrawal of government influence on banking decisions is unlikely, though some market reforms, such as interest rate liberalisation, have gradually been implemented since the assumption of Xi-Li leadership in late 2013. However, as financial stability and fulfilment of state policy targets still top central leaders' agendas, the state's decisive role in the banking sector will remain prevalent.

Pre-1994 banking reform: an overview

In the 1950s, China had a simple and highly centralised banking system consisting of the Bank of China (BOC) and the Construction Bank of China (CBC), which were subordinate to the People's Bank of China (PBOC) and the Ministry of Finance (MOF) respectively. The BOC functioned as a foreign exchange division of PBOC while the CBC disbursed funds to finance state-owned enterprises (SOEs) and capital-investment projects blueprinted in the government's economic plan (Eckstein 1977: 176–181).

During the Cultural Revolution (1966–1976), a mono-banking system was established, under which all financial institutions merged into the PBOC or the MOF (Okazaki 2007: 6). The PBOC became a mono-bank performing the dual functions as a central bank (regulating money supply and determining interest rate) and as a commercial bank (financing SOEs and state projects). However, the "commercial" functions of the PBOC by no means correspond to those performed by commercial banks operated in market economies. The PBOC before the reform can best be perceived as the state's fiscal agent to allocate funds to fulfil the planned targets (Lardy 1998: 61).

From 1979 to 1984, 4 state-owned specialised banks (SBs) were re-instituted and separated from the PBOC. The Agricultural Bank of China (ABC) was re-established in 1979 to handle deposits and lending in rural areas. The BOC was re-instituted under the State Council (SC) in 1979 to manage the country's foreign exchange. The People's Construction Bank of China (PCBC) (renamed as China Construction Bank in 1996) was made subordinate to the SC in 1979 to undertake financing construction and fixed assets investment while the Industrial and Commercial Bank (ICBC), established in 1984, specialised in funding business activities (Okazaki 2007: 8; Lardy 1998: 61–64). On top of re-instituting the SBs, the central government transformed the PBOC into a formal central bank in 1984 by transferring its deposit and lending activities to ICBC. The re-establishment of the SBs and the setting of a formal central bank laid the important foundation of separating central bank and commercial bank functions. Aside from re-establishing the SBs, new commercial banks and nonbank financial institutions (NBFIs) were allowed to open to cater for different financial needs in urban and rural areas. Nine national and regional banks, such as the Bank of Communications (BOCOM) and the Guangdong Development Bank, were set up in the 1990s. NBFIs also flourished in the decade. Up to 1994, about 60,000 rural credit cooperatives (RCCs), 1,500 urban credit cooperatives (UCCs) and 590 trust and investment companies (TICs) were set up (Chai 1997: 123). SBs' specialised roles had started to blur since the 1980s with each SBs facing increasing competition from other SBs and the new financial institutions.

The re-instituting of SBs and the diversification of financial institutions in the 1980s represented only a hierarchical and structural transformation. Limited competition was introduced and the SBs still dominated the banking sector – with 71.2 percent of assets in the banking sector managed by the SBs in 1986 (Lardy 1998: 224–225) – and continued to perform the fiscal functions assigned by the central government. Prior to the mid-1990s, the financial role as fiscal agents assumed by the SBs remained basically intact. The primary problem associated with policy lending is that loans were extended to state entities on the basis of social and political consideration instead of profitability and business criteria. To avoid massive layoffs by ailing SOEs from the pre-reform period to the mid-1990s, the SBs shouldered the key responsibility of extending "soft loans" to SOEs to maintain the operation of many loss-making SOEs. In 1997, almost 40 percent of SOEs incurred operating losses, rising from 19 percent in 1978. The total losses accumulated from 4.2 billion yuan in 1978 to 74.4 billion yuan in 1997, representing a spectacular jump of 17.7 times (Wolf 2003: 128). This strategy reduced the number of losers under reform and helped to maintain social and political stability. Nonetheless, policy lending at the same time piled up non-performing loans (NPLs) of the SBs (Naughton 2007: 460–461). The ratio of NPLs of the SBs reached 20.4 percent in 1994 and was estimated to increase by 2% annually (Lardy 1998: 121–122). The "soft loans" resulted in a spectacular rise in money supply and inflation rates. Money supply (M2) increased from 31.3 percent in 1992 to 34.5 percent in 1993, while the inflation demonstrated a hyper growth from 6.4 percent in 1992 to 24.1 percent in 1994.[1] The runaway inflation alarmed the central leaders regarding the possible macroeconomic instability resulting from quasi uncontrolled bank loans by the SBs. Externally, since the transformation of the GATT (General Agreement on Tariffs and Trade) to WTO (World Trade Organization) in 1995, China started to request its membership in WTO. As part of the commitments to WTO accession, China was required not only to reduce its tariff and non-tariff barriers for imports but also open up its telecommunication, banking, financial and insurance sectors to foreign investors (Okazaki 2007: 18). Foreseeing the intensifying competition from foreign banks, China was motivated to initiate reforms in various dimensions to meet the international banking standards and to cope with encroaching competition.

1994 banking reform: a halfway commercialisation

Facing both domestic and external pressures on its banking sector, the central government embarked on an overhaul of the banking system in 1994 with an aim to raise the efficiency and competitiveness of the banking sector. The reform focuses on two major areas. First, it develops the PBOC into an independent full-scale central bank to regulate the banking sector and maintain macroeconomic stability. The Law of the People's Republic of China on the People's Bank of China (PBCL) was enacted in 1995 to establish a legal foundation for the superior status of the PBOC. The PBCL stipulates that the PBOC, under the leadership of the State Council, devises and implements monetary policy and monitors the operations of the financial sector (Article 2). Article 7 of the PBCL entrusts the PBOC with a high level of independence by specifying that the PBOC is free from the intervention of local governments, government departments, organisations and individuals when it performs its central bank functions. The central government's decision explicitly urged the establishment of a "sound macroeconomic control system". It is clearly stated that "the central bank, the People's Bank of China, under the leadership of the State Council, should implement monetary policy independently". The independent status is further elucidated in that "the power of the central bank and local authorities over economic administration should be rationally delineated" and "the branches of the People's Bank of China are certified as agencies of its head office" (Mehran et al. 1996: 2; PBCL 1995). However, it is worth noting that the independence of PBOC in policy making and implementation should not be overemphasised. Under China's socialist market economy, the PBOC is subordinate to the State Council. The governor of the PBOC is nominated by the State Council Premier and endorsed by the National People's Congress. The governor is then appointed by the president of the state. Further, the drafting and implementation of the budget of the PBOC are monitored by the financial department under the State Council (Article 38 of PBCL 1995). The independence of the PBOC is merely in relation to local governments and government departments but not the State Council (Leung 1998).

Second, in dealing with the mounting NPLs, the banking sector overhaul took a decisive step to commercialise the four SBs by separating commercial lending from policy lending (Lo 2001; World Bank 1996). It was endorsed in the Third Plenum of the 14th Central Committee that the 4 SBs would gradually be transformed into SOCBs. Policy-based loans were designated for the 3 policy lending banks established in 1994.[2] By doing so, the SOCBs could be freed from the burden of "soft loans" and concentrate their businesses in commercial lending based on market disciplines. However, the transfer of policy lending from the SOCBs to the 3 policy lending banks was more complicated than expected. Two points deserve mention. First, the newly established policy banks were reluctant to accept the policy responsibilities, particularly lending to SOEs, previously assumed by the SBs. The SOCBs continued to be a major government-directed funding source for SOEs. Almost half of the short-term loans of SOCBs were extended to SOEs in 1997 (*ZJTJNJ* 1998). Second, since the policy banks did not receive deposits from the public, their operation was financed by the state fund by issuing financial bonds to existing financial institutions, primarily the SOCBs. The state banks were under constant pressure and directives from the PBOC to absorb the financial bonds issued by the policy banks.[3] As a result, commercialisation of state banks did not substantially improve the balance sheets of SOCBs in the 1990s.

Commercialising the SBs in 1994 aimed at separating policy and commercial lending, through which the efficiency of the state banks could be enhanced. However, in practice, the reform failed to institute a credit culture based on market disciplines. Lending decisions were still mainly influenced by state directives instead of profitability considerations. The reform was also constrained by a lack of Chinese bankers well-vested with knowledge of running commercial banks (Chen and Shih 2004). The rising fragility of China's banking sector was evident by the escalating NPLs in the 1990s. Some estimates indicated that the ratio of NPLs of the Big Four stayed at an alarmingly high level of 40 percent by the end of 1998 (Woo 2003). The Big Four were technically insolvent in the late 1990s. The situation was further complicated by the occurrence of the Asian financial crisis in 1997–1998. Though China was least affected by the crisis due to its relatively closed financial system, central leaders did observe the financial chaos in other Asian countries such as Thailand, Indonesia and Korea (Stent 2017: 82–83). To speed up the pace of relieving the NPLs from the SOCBs, the Ministry of Finance (MOF) injected US$34 billion into the Big Four in

1998. The recapitalisation was supposed to alleviate the financial burden of the SOCBs arising from the past policy lending. Such recapitalisation by the central coffer was planned to be "first and final" (Anderson 2007: 172). However, the subsequent establishment of 4 asset management companies (AMCs) in 1999 to absorb 1.4 trillion yuan of NPLs from the Big Four – and the further recapitalisation amounting to US\$75 billion – of the SOCBs in 2003–2006 defeated the initial design of an "once-and-for-all" relief plan for China's debt-ridden state banking system. The official financial support rendered to the state banking sector reached an amount of US\$402 billion (Anderson 2007: 173), which was about 16 percent of China's GDP in 2006.[4]

Substantial recapitalisation of SOCBs swiftly recovered the health of state banks' balance sheet. The capital adequacy ratio (CAR) of the SOCBs was lifted to a level higher than the international standard of 8 percent[5] and reduced the NPL ratio to an official figure of 7.83 percent in 2007 (Q3).[6] However, this quick fix did not bring much enhancement of state banks' performance. To illustrate, from 2005 to 2006, the smaller city commercial banks, such as the Zhuzhou City Commercial Bank and the Bank of Dalian, achieved a much faster growth of profitability than the SOCBs though the city commercial banks received no capital injection from the government (KPMG 2007). These figures are consistent with the study by Yao et al. (2007), which uses panel data of 22 Chinese banks from 1995 to 2001 to assess their performance. The results indicate that non-state banks are 8–10 percent more efficient than their state counterparts. The relative inefficiency of state banks was attributable to the government protection while the non-state banks were facing a hard budget constraint. Lin and Zhang (2009) reaffirm the findings by Yao et al. (2007). Based on the data from 60 Chinese banks during the period 1997–2004, Lin and Zhang reveal that the SOCBs were less efficient and profitable, in terms of ROA (return on asset) and COI (costs to operating income), than the joint stock commercial banks (JSCBs), city commercial banks (CCBs) and foreign banks. The underperformance of the SOCBs raises the issue of the moral hazard and cost-effectiveness of bailing out the state banks. It implies that the bailout has not fundamentally changed the state banks' corporate governance and lending practice. SOCBs were supposed to operate in response to market signals, such as risk factor and profitability, but their operation was still considerably influenced by the government. Though China has fulfilled most of the 25 Core Principles adopted by the BIS (Bank for International Settlements) committee on banking regulation and supervision, some principles are not truly fulfilled. To illustrate, Principle 1 requires the regulatory agency to have full autonomy, power and resources to exercise its supervisory and monitoring role. However, the China Banking Regulatory Commission (CBRC)[7] is hierarchically under the State Council, which can veto the decision made by CBRC, and the appointment of key officials in CBRC was still under the control of the Communist Party. The state banks are also required to recruit independent directors to oversee the decision-making process and operation of the SOCBs, but most of the independent directors are either government officials or ex-bank staff, who can rarely perform an independent supervisory role (Kudrna 2007).

2008 global financial crisis: reemergence of policy loans

Though the banking reform in the mid-1990s could not completely change the credit culture and fully commercialise the SOCBs, the operations of SOCBs and their non-state counterparts have been more responsive to market signals and discipline. The reform reached some remarkable milestones of declining NPLs, enhancing corporate governance and complying with international best practices.[8] Nonetheless, the 2008 global financial crisis (GFC) put China once again in the dilemma between policy and commercial loans, which has reshaped China's banking reform over the past decades. China is widely commended for its rapid rebound from the 2008 GFC and the contribution to global economic recovery by boosting consumption and investment domestically and overseas after the crisis. However, these noteworthy accomplishments were achieved by paying substantial costs, in particular in the financial sector. In order to maintain a stable growth after the GFC, the central government initiated a 4-trillion yuan stimulus package which drove the proliferation of local government financial platforms (LGFPs) and rapid credit expansion through shadow banking. Substantial amount of credit was channelled to project low returns and even create sizable excess capacity. Deteriorating credit quality with rising overdue loans and NPLs heightens the risks in China's banking sector.

The emergence of LGFPs can be traced back to the mid-1990s during which the tax assignment system (TAS, *fengshuizhi*) was implemented in 1994. To ensure an adequate and stable flow of budgetary revenues into the state finances, the central government implemented the TAS, which centralised the major revenue sources of turnover taxes (value-added and consumption taxes) but lacks a concomitant centralisation of expenditure responsibilities. The central share of total budgetary revenue escalated from 22 percent in 1993 to 55.7 percent in 1994. Since then, the central government has collected about half of the total fiscal revenues. Nevertheless, local governments have been responsible for the major share, about 70 percent, of the total expenditure since the inception of the TAS. The TAS has imposed increased fiscal pressures on subnational, in particular sub provincial, finance.[9] The fiscal strain of local governments was hardened by the fact that they are prohibited from borrowing from commercial banks or issuing bonds. To find more leeway to release their fiscal burden, local governments transfer their assets, such as utilities, roads and land, to set up limited-liability companies, which become local government financial platforms (LGFPs) to raise funds for their projects. LGFPs tap funds from two major channels. First, with the assets transferred from local governments, LGFPs use the assets as collateral to borrow from commercial banks. Second, the LGFPs issue bonds and sell them to individual and institutional investors. In recent years, it is a more common practice that the LGFPs issue bonds to commercial banks and trust and investment companies, which repackage the bonds into structured financial products and then market to the individual and institutional investors.

According to the Company Law, LGFPs are municipal SOEs (Tong and Yao 2010: 39). Some local governments even guarantee loans for the LGFPs, though such practice is actually prohibited by law.[10] With strong tie and backup by local governments, the LGFPs are able to acquire loans without much difficulty. The LGFP loans can best be interpreted as "local policy loans" since these loans are extended mainly for policy instead of profitability consideration. The upsurge of LGFP loans was largely due to the announcement of the 4 trillion yuan stimulus package by the State Council in late 2008 to buffer the anticipated economic downturn amid global financial crisis. According to the plan of the central government, it only financed 30 percent (i.e., 1.2 trillion yuan) of the stimulus program and local governments would finance the remaining balance (i.e., 2.8 trillion yuan) (Goodstadt 2012: 12). Facing the investment targets delegated from the central government, local governments were active in setting up more LGFPs to enlarge the fund pool for local projects. Local officials are keen to work in response to the stimulus package handed down from the central government as working in conformity with central policy, improvement in local infrastructure and rise in income are important appraisal criteria for local officials. Studies show that economic performance of a locality is closely related to the promotion of local officials (Lin 2008; Burns and Zhou 2010). Though performance criteria has been broadened in recent years by incorporating other performance indicators such as provision of 15 years of education for young people and the extent of guarantee for minimum livelihood for farmers, successful fulfilment of these "other performance indicators" once again hinges on steady and satisfactory economic growth. This explains why local officials are ardent to accomplish the targets, in particular those economic ones, delegated from higher level governments, as it serves their best interest.

According to the China Banking Regulatory Committee (CBRC), 8,221 LGFPs had been operating at provincial, regional, county and municipal government levels by mid-2009 (Walter and Howie 2011: 121). Since LGFP loans take many forms, including bank loans, bonds and packaged financial products, it is difficult – and always debatable – to gauge accurately the exact loan amount. The lack of a consistent definition of LGFP loans in China makes accurate estimate of the loan size even more difficult. That said, Table 4.1 shows some of the more representative and widely quoted estimates of LGFP loans from 2008 to 2016. The National Audit Office announced in June 2011 that local government debt totalled 10.72 trillion yuan ($1.66 trillion) at the end of 2010 (National Audit Office of the People's Republic of China 2011). Though the estimates in Table 4.1 are an not exact measure of LGFP loans, it is clear that the growth of LGFP loans is spectacular, rising from about 1 trillion yuan in 2008 to 10.72 trillion yuan in 2010, and skyrocketing to 17.9 trillion yuan in mid-2013, which amounted to 31.5 percent of China's GDP in 2013.[11] The growth of LGFP loans from 2010 to mid-2013 demonstrated a growth of 67 percent. Though the amount of LGFP loans demonstrated a decline in 2014, it rebounded to 17.1 trillion yuan in 2016.

The immediate results of the stimulus package were impressive, making China a quick rebound from 4.3 percent growth in the fourth quarter of 2008 to 9.5 and 11.4 percent in the first and second quarters of 2009 (Kwong 2014). The

Table 4.1 Size of LGFP Loans (trillion yuan)

Year	Estimated amount of LGFP loans
2008	1[a]
2009	5[b], 5.66[c], 7.1[d]
2010	10.72[e]
2011	9.1[f]
2012	12.0[g]
2013	17.9[h]
2014	15.4[i]
2015	16.0[j]
2016	17.1[k]

Notes

a and b were released by Ba Shusong, Deputy Director (2003–2007) of the Institute of Finance of the Development Research Centre. The figures are quoted from Wang (2009)

c and are derived from the estimates from Lardy (2012: 27) and d from Brainard and Zhuang (2010: 4).

e is derived from the National Audit Office of the People's Republic of China (2011).

f is estimated LGFP loans as of 30 Sept 2011 by the Shanghai Securities News (quoted from China Daily (2012)). Since the figure only covers the first 9 months of 2011, it is estimated that the year-end figure is around 10 trillion yuan (Wang and Yang 2013: 91).

g estimated figure by Changjiang Securities (Wei 2013); see also Wang and Yang (2013: 91).

h is a mid-year estimate of 2013 by the National Audit Office of the People's Republic of China (2013).

i, j and k are estimated by Chen, He and Liu (2017: 52).

growth rates of GDP at constant prices reached 8.3 percent in 2009, followed by a more spectacular growth of 10.2 in 2010 (*ZGTJNJ* 2014). About 22 million jobs were created by the stimulus package in 2009 and 2010, which maintained the livelihood of the workers (China Daily Online 2010). From a global perspective, China's fiscal stimulus induced demand for imports from East Asia, Europe and the United States, which prevented a more drastic post-crisis global recession (Fardoust, Lin and Luo 2012: 6–7). While the stimulus package gave a strong boost to the economy, its notable repercussions have been far-reaching. The recurrence of policy loans brings impediments to de facto commercialisation of the banking sector, heightened risks in banks' operation and worsening overcapacity.

Table 4.2 shows that both NPL ratios and balance had declined for 3 years after the rolling out of the stimulus programme. It seems that the huge fiscal push did not worsen much of commercial banks' assets quality. However, the relatively low NPL ratios and balance from 2009 to 2011 was mainly attributable to the fact that 24 percent (2.6 trillion yuan) of the 10.72 trillion yuan LGFP debt accumulated up to 2010 was due on 2011 and afterwards. Another 30 percent of LGFP debts was due in 2016 (Lu and Sun 2013: 11). Therefore, any impact on assets quality would only be reflected after 2011. It is also worth noting that the relatively low NPL ratios were kept since the commercial banks continued to extend loans at a rapid pace with annual growth rates between

Table 4.2 Major Supervisory Indicators of China's Commercial Bank 2009–2017

	NPL ratio (%)	NPL balance (billion yuan)	NPL balance growth rates (%)	Provision coverage ratio (%)	Capital adequacy ratio (CAR) (%)
2009	1.58	497.3		155.0	9.2
2010	1.14	429.3	-13.7	218.3	12.2
2011	1.0	427.9	-0.33	278.1	12.7
2012	0.95	492.9	15.2	295.51	13.25
2013	1.0	592.1	20.1	282.7	9.95
2014	1.25	842.6	42.3	232.06	13.18
2015	1.67	1274.4	51.2	181.18	13.45
2016	1.74	1512.2	18.7	176.4	13.28
2017	1.74	1705.7	12.8	181.42	13.65

Source: China Banking and Insurance Regulatory Commission (n.d.)

about 14 and 32 percent during 2008–2012 (Li 2013: 2). The NPL balance is a better indicator of credit quality as it measures the absolute amount of NPLs, which demonstrated a double-digit growth since 2012, with a historic high of 51.2 percent in 2015. Though banks tried to enlarge the credit base to lower NPL ratio, the escalation of NPLs was so tremendous that it eventually raised the NPL ratio, which registered a 0.74 percentage point rise from 1.0 to 1.74 from 2011 to 2017. The stimulus package undoubtedly deteriorated the banks' balance sheets, but it is worth mentioning that the rising NPL ratio and balance do not necessarily imply that a financial crisis in China will likely happen, as some outside observers predict. First, as indicated in Table 4.2, the provision ratio for bad debts is required by CBRC to be kept at or above 150 percent. The ratio increased noticeably from 155 percent in 2009 and peaked at 295.51 percent in 2012, which provided a very safe buffer against piling up of NPLs. It also met the recommendations by the Basel Committee on Banking Supervision that provisions should be kept higher in years of economic boom and used to cover loan losses in years of economic downturn (Stent 2017: 129). Though the ratio has declined since 2013, it still maintains a ratio above the required standard of 150 percent. Second, a full default without paying back any interest and principal is unlikely. Therefore, the provisions are far more than enough to deal with the bad debts. Third, debtors' collateral can be sold to cover part of the loan losses, which will not use up the entire provision (Prasad 2017: 193–194).

Despite the remoteness of a financial crisis, the emergence of "local policy loans" has had remarkable impacts on heightening risks in the banking sector and shrinking loan efficiency. The 4-trillion yuan motivated commercial banks to extend credits through off-balance-sheet (OBS) financing such as issuance of wealth management products (WMPs) and trust products to circumvent PBOC's regulations. Since OBS financing activities are not recorded in banks' balance sheets, these credit extension activities are generally referred as shadow banking. The term "shadow bank", coined by economist Paul McCulley in 2007, refers mainly to nonbank financial intermediaries that engaged in maturity transformation. Such transformation entails the activities of raising short-term funds in the money markets and use the accumulated funds to buy assets in the capital market with longer-term maturities. The scope of shadow banking is later broadened by the Financial Stability Board, which refers to lending activities undertaken by nonbank financial institutions that operate outside the regular banking sector.[12] Commercial banks in China have heavily engaged in shadow banking activities to circumvent PBOC's prudential regulations; commercial banks extend more credits through OBS financing. A common form of OBS financing is that banks securitise local projects, bonds and stocks and repackage them into WMPs offering rates of return much higher than bank deposit rates. Among the 4 most popular categories of shadow banking activities associated with commercial banks, namely WMPs, entrusted loans, bank-trust cooperation and bank-security firm cooperation, WMPs are the most important vehicles to channel funds from investors (lenders) to borrowers who otherwise could not acquire funds from the regular banking sector.[13] The total assets of WMPs was not significant till 2010, but its size skyrocketed to 7.1 trillion yuan in 2012 (Lu et al. 2015: 42) and further up to 8.2 trillion yuan as of the end of March 2013 (Bloomberg News 2013). By mid-2015, WMPs managed by commercial banks exceeded 18 trillion yuan, increasing at a compound annual growth rate of 30 to 40 percent since 2005 (Jiang 2015). The popularity of WMPs among investors has been attributable to its superbly high rate of return, which reached 10 percent in 2011, compared to the 3 percent of annual deposit interest rate (Chovanec 2011). Though the returns on WMPs have been tapering off in the past years, it still reached an average annualised 5.2 percent in the first half of 2014 (Bloomberg News 2014).

Shadow banking provides abundant funding for LGFPs while banks can raise their profit by extending loans through shadow banking activities. However, the risks embedded in shadow banking have been intensifying for several reasons. First, most WMPs securitised a wide range of financial products including bonds, stocks and many other types of debt products. They are sold with severe asymmetric information with limited regulation and disclosure of what they contain. Unlike the commercial banks' deposit-taking business, WMPs are not subject to prudential bank regulation, and they cannot borrow from the central bank in case of a liquidity problem. The investors bear their own risks as their investment funds are not covered by deposit insurance. Second, according to the estimates by the National Audit Bureau, 79 percent of funding for the LGFPs was financed by bank loans (Lu and Sun 2013: 9). Any default of the LGFPs will adversely affect the balance sheets of the banks. To avoid cash-strapped LGFPs going bankrupt, banks are willing to offer new short-term loans to pay for the interest of existing loans. Constrained by the CAR and the cash reserve ratio (CRR) set by the CBRC and PBOC respectively, banks evade the regulatory requirements by issuing WMPs (Wang and Yang 2013: 92). However, most of the WMPs, almost 97 percent, have maturity below 1 year, and about 45 percent of the WMPs have a maturity ranging from 1–3 months (Lu et al. 2015: 42). Such a short maturity severely mismatches the long-term policy loans extended under the stimulus programme to finance infrastructure projects. Severe maturity mismatch pushes banks to issue WMPs on a rolling basis to ensure adequate cash flow to honour payments of WMPs, though this practice only delays and does not solve the problem of maturity mismatch. The embedded risks of WMPs are easily overlooked by investors, particularly for individual investors, as the cases of default related to trust products have not been very frequent so far. One of the main reasons for the small number of default cases surfacing in the market is the central government's intention to underwrite possible default cases before they leak in the market. A typical example was the takeover of two property trusts by China Huarong, a state-owned asset management company, in 2012 when the two property trusts were on the verge of collapse (Ren 2013). Another representative case took place in early 2014 when a WMP, issued by China Credit Trust (CCT) in 2012 on behalf of Zhenfu Energy Group and sold by Industrial and Commercial Bank of China (ICBC) was unable to honour its payment when the WMP was due on 31 Jan 2014. CCT, whose major share is owned by state-affiliated firms, ICBC and the provincial government of Shanxi, where Zhenfu Energy Group is based, collectively bailed out the 3 billion yuan of WMP (Pei 2014). This move aims at pacifying the discontent among investors and avoiding negative ripple effects to the stability of the financial sector. This anecdotal evidence may not indicate widespread defaults of OBS financing products, but increasing defaults are highly possible when we examine the credit-to-GDP ratio in China. During 2009 and 2010, total social financing (TSF)[14] amounted to 26.7 trillion yuan, representing a 71% increase over a 2-year period. The credit-to-GDP ratio jumped by 46 percentage points from 120 percent at the end of 2008 to 166 percent by March 2011 and soared to 200 percent in mid-2014.[15] The ratio experienced another enormous jump to 230 percent in 2016.[16] The ratio measures the amount of credit needed to realise a given level of GDP, which has been rising since the 2008 fiscal stimulus. The rising ratio not only reveals the declining efficiency of the credit but also implies that less income is generated by each unit of credit, which undermines borrowers' repayability. In October 2014, the Ministry of Finance allowed several municipalities to issue Munibonds to leverage their financial sources to repay the LGFP loans. This reform was likely a response to the mounting rollover pressure of local commercial banks. A rapid growth of Munibonds was observed under the so-called local government bond-swap program (i.e., issuing Munibonds to repay existing due debt) and the majority of Munibonds (87 percent) were held by commercial banks in 2016 (Chen, He and Liu 2017: 12). However, the issuance of Munibonds to replace rollover loans only changes sources and types of loans and does not fundamentally alter the fact that "local policy loans" have re-emerged and expanded since the 2008 GFC. The rollover loans may not have immediate impact on the risk and efficiency of the banking sector provided that deposit growth is faster than loan growth. However, recent loan and deposit data deserve more attention. The loan-to-deposit ratio swelled from 65.8 percent in June 2015 to 71.2 percent at the end of March 2018. New deposits reached their peak in 2015 and have failed to keep pace with lending growth since then. Loan-to-deposit ratio for new loans amounted to 100.1 percent in 2017 and rose further to 104 percent in 2018. These figures imply that banks encounter pressure on extending rollover loans to borrowers who are unable to repay their loans. To ease liquidity constraints in the market, the PBOC has injected a total of 1.5 trillion US dollar loans to commercial banks. The PBOC allows commercial banks to use the newly acquired loans from the central bank to cover expired short-term loans by rolling in medium- and long-term loans, which have shared 85 percent of new loans in the banking sector since January 2017 (Balding 2018). Loans extended by the central bank to the commercial banks, with an aim to ease liquidity, actually heighten the problem of moral hazard in the banking sector. The commercial banks are encouraged to use medium- and long-term loans to cover unpaid short-term loans, with the central bank as last resort to provide liquidity in the market. Commercial banks will become less prudent to offer loans, and borrowers are less motivated to repay the loans if banks can be kept afloat by rollover loans.

Post-2013 banking reform: heading for further marketisation?

Since the inauguration of Xi-Li leadership in 2013, banking reform has made limited progress when compared to that in the 1990s. That said, there have been two important reforms implemented since 2013. First, the most significant step taken towards a more market-based banking system was the abolition of the deposit interest rate ceiling in 2015 after eliminating the lending interest rate floor in 2013 (Lo 2015). Interest rate liberalisation marks a milestone of allowing market signals to allocate loanable funds and banks to better price loans to reflect the risk involved. Deposit rates offered to savers will be pitched at competitive levels in the market. It ends the decades long "financial depression" that officially pressed deposit rate to provide cheap loans to subsidise SOEs and state projects. Second, with the introduction of deposit insurance in April 2015, the Chinese government attempts to alter the public's conventional belief that it will bail out banks with liquidity problems. It also conveys a clear message to bank operators that they will be responsible for their losses if they run their banks improperly. China is trying to bring the concept of risk into the banking sector (Gough 2015).

In principle, the new reform measures will make banks orient their operations towards market disciplines. Banks will make loan decisions based on creditworthiness of the borrower and interest rates charged should more appropriately reflect the risks and market situation. However, China still have a challenging path to travel before reaching a real market-based banking sector for several reasons. First, though the lending interest rate floor and deposit interest rate ceiling were abolished, the benchmark interest rate is still set by the PBOC. Local governments and SOEs can borrow from banks at a benchmark rate (Lo 2015), which is in general lower than the market rate, especially when the market demand for loanable funds is substantial. Amid the close link between SOEs and state banks, "soft loans" are still easily accessible to SOEs and local government projects at a "subsidised" interest rate. This practice is to make sure that ample funds are available for SOEs and state projects at low borrowing cost. Second, the central bank states clearly that it will intervene if competition for deposits is so keen that it may jeopardise the stability of the banking sector and that the state remains the dominant owner of the banking system (Bloomberg News 2015). It indicates that the paramount concern of the Chinese government is the stability of the banking sector, and full liberalisation is still remote as the government will not surrender its close monitoring in the sector. Third, deposit insurance has been in place since 2015 to alleviate the moral hazard in the banking sector, which reduces the likelihood of the government to bail out problematic banks. However, the bailout of WMP in recent years discussed earlier indicates that central government will not allow mounting risks in OBS financing activities to shake the stability of the financial sector. As a major owner and monitor of the banking sector, the Chinese government has robust incentive to bail out problematic banks before they transform into a systemic crisis.

Conclusion

The banking reform since the mid-1990s has accomplished noticeable results in cleaning up state banks' balance sheets, enhancing corporate governance, implementing international best practice and motivating banks to be more responsive to market signals. However, risks have emerged since the 2008 GFC. Rapid credit expansion and proliferation of shadow banking resulted in rising NPL ratio and balance as well as occasional defaults of WMP. It seems that China has not been facing a "real" financial crisis as its NPLs are still under control. The problem of NPLs can be contained mainly because banks continue to enlarge their deposit to maintain a high NPL provision coverage, which was still about 181.42 percent in 2017, which is a reasonably safe level. Some analysts worry that the deposit base can be shaky in the coming years as deposit growth is very much dependent on economic growth, which has shown signs of slowdown since 2010. This concern is valid, but a huge portion of domestic deposits comes from non-financial enterprises – mainly SOEs – and the government,[17] which is a "stabiliser" in the banking system.

Though it is unlikely that the banking system will encounter severe systemic risks, recent developments in the banking sector have much bearing on the issue of efficiency. The credit-to-GDP ratio soared from 120 percent in 2008 to a record high of 300 percent in 2016. The ratio indicates that the amount of credit needed to realise a given level of GDP has been rising since the 2008 fiscal stimulus programme. It implies that more and more credit is needed to generate one unit of GDP. Productive efficiency is unavoidably falling. Equally bad, some credit has been diverted to unproductive projects, which give rise to overcapacity and hamper allocative efficiency. In addition, the close link between SOEs and state banks make loans more available to SOEs and state projects and at the same time crowd out the financial resources to private enterprises, which are more productive and efficient than their state counterparts. The misallocation of loanable funds causes deteriorating productive and allocative efficiency, which is a real concern for China's long-term growth. The Chinese government is fully aware of the efficiency problem embedded in the banking sector, but central leaders are hesitant to enlarge the scope of market reforms as it will lessen government's ability to use the banking sector as an economic lever for accomplishing policy targets.

Notes

1 Calculated based on the data from *ZGTJNJ* (2003: 313, 704).
2 The 3 policy lending banks are the Agricultural Development Bank of China, Export-Import Bank of China and the State Development Bank of China.
3 For example, the State Development Bank sold 77.5 billion yuan of financial bonds to beef up its capital; 42.9 billion yuan was sold to the SOCBs (Lardy 1998).
4 Calculated based on the figures from www.stats.gov.cn/tjsj/ndsj/2006/indexeh. htm and www.china.org.cn/english/BAT/194852.htm (Accessed on 7 January 2008)
5 At end-2005, the CARs of BOC, CCB and ICBC was 10.42%, 13.75%, and 10.26% respectively (see Hansakul 2006: 4).
6 www.cbrc.gov.cn/english/home/jsp/docView.jsp?docID=2007051774830DB D1F20010BFFD7F4A6791F6F00 (Accessed on 7 January 2008)
7 CBRC was set up in 2003 to formulate supervisory rule governing the banking institutions in China. For details of the supervisory roles of CBRC, see www.cbrc. gov.cn/showyjhjjindex.do (Accessed on 9 November 2018)
8 For a detailed discussion on the banking reform in the mid-1990s, see Kwong (2009, 2010). For an empirical study of how corporate governance reforms affect the performance of SOCBs, see Lo and Ng (2009).
9 For a detailed discussion of the impacts of TAS on local finances, see Lee and Kwong (2003) and Kwong (2007).
10 The Law of the People's Republic of China on Commercial Banks was promulgated in 1995 to establish an independent status of the SOCBs. Article 4 of the CBL emphasises that the banks should be run based on the business principles of efficiency, portfolio risks and liquidity. The provision of Article 41 reinforces the independence of the SOCBs by stipulating that no agency or individual is allowed to force the commercial banks to extend loans to designated projects.
11 China's GDP was 56.9 trillion yuan in 2013. See National Bureau of Statistics of China (2014).
12 The Financial Stability Board (FSB) is an international body, set up after the 2009 G-20 London summit in April 2009, which monitors and makes recommendations about the global financial system. For a more detailed discussion on the definition and scope of shadow banking, please see Kodres (2013).
13 For a thorough discussion on various shadow banking activities, see Lu et al. (2015).
14 TSF is a more comprehensive measure of total credit supplied by including total credit extended not only by domestic financial institutions but also by domestic households and non-financial institutions. For details, see Chicago Tribunal (2012).
15 See Asian Banking and Finance (2011) and The Economist (2014).
16 See Wallace (2017). Even before the global financial crisis, expanding credit had already brought increasing risks to China's banking sector. For an empirical analysis, see Baradwaj, Flaherty and Shao (2014).

17 Deposits by non-financial enterprises and the government shared 51.6 percent of domestic deposits in 2016. Calculated based on the data from *ZGTJNJ 2017*. Available at: www.stats.gov.cn/tjsj/ndsj/2017/html/EN1812.jpg (Accessed on 2 December 2018)

References

Anderson, J. (2007) 'China's New Banking System,' in Hoffmann, W. J. and Enright, M. J. (eds.) *China into the Future: Making Sense of the World's Most Dynamic Economy*, Singapore: Wiley, pp. 163–212.

Asian Banking and Finance (2011) 'Debt Threats: China's Alarming Credit-to-GDP Ratio Jumps from 120% to 166% in March 2011,' 21 June. Available at: http://asianbankingandfinance.net/lending-credit/news/debt-threats-china%E2%80%99s-alarming-credit-gdp-ratio-jumps-120-166-in-march-2011 (Accessed on 15 November 2015).

Balding, C. (2018) 'China's Banks Are Still in Trouble.' Available at: www.bloomberg.com/opinion/articles/2018-06-14/china-s-banks-are-still-in-trouble (Accessed on 28 November 2018).

Baradwaj, B. G., Flaherty, S. M. V. and Shao, Y. (2014) 'The Impact of Lending Growth on the Riskiness of Chinese Banks,' *The Chinese Economy*, Vol. 47, Nos. 5–6, pp. 29–49.

Bloomberg News (2013) 'Wealth Products Threaten China Banks on Ponzi-Scheme Risk,' 16 July. [Online] Available at: www.bloomberg.com/news/articles/2013-07-15/wealth-products-threaten-china-banks-on-ponzi-scheme-risk (Accessed on 14 November 2015).

Bloomberg News (2014) 'China Plans Wealth-Product Rules to Cut Shadow Banking Risks,' 5 December. [Online] Available at: www.bloomberg.com/news/articles/2014-12-05/china-plans-wealth-product-rules-to-limit-shadow-banking-risks (Accessed on 19 October 2015).

Bloomberg News (2015) 'Unshackling $21 Trillion: China's Risky Bid to Reform Banking,' *Bloomberg News*, 26 October. [Online] Available at: www.bloomberg.com/news/articles/2015-10-26/unshackling-21-trillion-china-s-risky-bid-to-reform-banking (Accessed on 20 November 2015).

Brainard, L. and Zhuang, B. (2010) 'Is China's Local Government Debt a Serious Problem?' *China Macro Policy*, April, London: Trusted Sources.

Burns, J. and Zhou, Z. (2010) 'Performance Management in the Government of the People's Republic of China: Accountability and Control in the Implementation of Public Policy,' *OECD Journal on Budgeting*, Vol. 2010, No. 2, pp. 1–28.

Chai, J. C. H. (1997) *China: Transition to a Market Economy*, New York and Oxford: Clarendon Press.

Chen, C. H. and Shih, H. T. (2004) *Banking and Insurance in the New China: Competition and the Challenge of Accession to the WTO*, Cheltenham: Edward Elgar.

Chen, Z., He, Z. and Liu, C. (2017) 'The Financing of Local Government in China: Stimulus Loans Wane and Shadow Banking Waxes.' Available at: http://w3.bm.ust.hk/fina/2017symposium/paper/Zhiguo%20He_StimulusloanMCB_201711. (Accessed on 11 November 2018).

Chicago Tribunal (2012) 'What Is China's Total Social Financing Indicator?' *Chicago Tribune*, 13 November. Available at: http://articles.chicagotribune.com/

2012-11-13/news/sns-rt-china-tsf-factboxl3e8m24an-20121112_1_central-bank-yuan-loans-interest-rates (Accessed on 15 November 2015).

China Banking and Insurance Regulatory Commission (n.d.) Available at: http://www.cbirc.gov.cn/cn/index.html (Accessed on 7 November 2019).

China Daily (2012) 'China to Boost Local Gov't Debt Clean-up,' 2 March. Available at: http://english.people.com.cn/90778/7745294.html (Accessed on 24 September 2013).

China Daily Online (2010) 'China's 4 Trillion Yuan Stimulus Package Creates 22 Million Jobs,' 17 September. Available at: http://en.people.cn/90001/90776/90882/7143609.html (Accessed on 1 November 2015).

Chovanec, P. (2011) 'Caixin on China's Risky Wealth Funds.' [Online] Available at: https://chovanec.wordpress.com/2011/07/25/caixin-on-chinas-risky-wealth-funds/ (Accessed on 19 October 2015).

Eckstein, A. (1977) *China's Economic Revolution*, Cambridge: Cambridge University Press.

The Economist (2014) 'China's Debt-to-GDP Level 200% and Counting,' 16 July. Available at: www.economist.com/free-exchange/2014/07/16/200-and-counting (Accessed on 17 July 2019).

Fardoust, S., Lin, J. Y. and Luo, X. (2012) 'Demystifying China's Fiscal Stimulus,' *Policy Research Working Paper*, No. 6221, Washington, DC: The World Bank.

Goodstadt, L. F. (2012) 'China's LGFV Crisis 2011: The Conflict Between Local Autonomy, National Interest and Financial Reform,' *HKIMR Working Paper*, No. 03/2012, Hong Kong: Hong Kong Institute for Monetary Research.

Gough, N. (2015) 'China Rethinks Safety Net for Its Banking System,' *The New York Times*, 30 April. [Online] Available at: www.nytimes.com/2015/05/01/business/dealbook/china-rethinks-safety-net-for-its-banking-system.html?_r=0 (Accessed on 20 November 2015).

Hansakul, S. (2006) 'China's Banking Sector: Ripe for the Next Stage,' *Current Issues-China Special*, Frankfurt: Deutsche Bank Research.

Jiang, X. (2015) 'Wealth Management Business to Reach $19b in 10 Years,' *China Daily*, 11 September. [Online] Available at: www.chinadaily.com.cn/business/2015-09/11/content_21843627.htm (Accessed on 19 October 2015).

Kodres, L. E. (2013) 'What Is Shadow Banking?' *Finance & Development*, Vol. 50, No. 2, June, pp. 42–43.

KPMG (2007) 'Mainland Banking Survey 2007,' *KPMG Report*.

Kudrna, Z. (2007) 'Banking Reform in China: Driven by International Standards and Chinese Specifics,' *MPRA Paper*, No. 7320, Moscow.

Kwong, C. C. L. (2007) 'Where Is China's Rural Economy Heading for: A Brighter Future or Problems Unsolved?' in Cheng, J. Y. S. (ed.) *Challenges and Policy Programmes of China's New Leadership*, Hong Kong: City University of Hong Kong Press.

Kwong, C. C. L. (2009) 'From Commercialization to WTO Accession: What Lies Ahead for China's Banking Reform?' *The Chinese Economy*, Vol. 42, No. 5, pp. 8–20.

Kwong, C. C. L. (2010) 'Mission Completed or Problems Unsolved? A Policy Review of China's Banking Reform,' in Liu, X. and Zhang, W. (eds.) *China's Three Decades of Economic Reforms*, Oxon: Routledge, pp. 17–27.

Kwong, C. C. L. (2014) 'China's 4-Trillion Yuan Stimulus Package: Its Repercussion on the Banking System,' Paper presented at the *Ninth Annual Conference of The Asian Studies Association of Hong Kong "Culture and Society in Asia: Thematic Issues and Methodologies"*, The University of Hong Kong, 14–15 March.

Lardy, N. R. (1998) *China's Unfinished Economic Revolution*, Washington, DC: Brookings Institute Press.

Lardy, N. R. (2012) *Sustaining China's Economic Growth*, Washington, DC: Peterson Institute for International Economics.

The Law of the People's Republic of China on Commercial Banks 1995 (*CBL Zhonghua Remin Gongheguo Shangye Yinhang Fa*), Beijing: Zhongguo Fazhi Chubanshe.

The Law of the People's Republic of China on the People's Bank of China 1995 (*PBCL Zhonghua Remin Gongheguo Zhongguo Remin Yinhang Fa*), Beijing: Zhongguo Fazhi Chubanshe.

Lee, P. K. and Kwong, C. C. L. (2003) 'From Developmental to Predatory Government: An Institutional Perspective of Local Cadres' Strategic Economic Behavior,' in Cheng, J. Y. S. (ed.) *China's Challenges in the Twenty-First Century*, Hong Kong: City University of Hong Kong Press.

Leung, T. T. Y. (1998) 'Central Bank Independence: Application in the PRC,' *Hong Kong Lawyer*. Available at: www.hk-lawyer.com/InnerPages_features/0/589/1998/1 (Accessed on 3 March 2011).

Li, C. (2013) 'Shadow Banking in China: Expanding Scale, Evolving Structure,' *Asia Focus*, April, Federal Reserve Bank of San Francisco.

Lin, T. (2008) 'Explaining Intra-Provincial Inequality in Education in China: The Roles of Institutions and Provincial Leaders,' Unpublished PhD thesis, University of Hong Kong.

Lin, X. and Zhang, Y. (2009) 'Bank Ownership Reform and Bank Performance in China,' *Journal of Banking and Finance*, Vol. 33, pp. 20–29.

Lo, W. C. (2001) 'A Retrospect on China's Banking Reform,' *The Chinese Economy*, Vol. 34, No. 1, pp. 15–28.

Lo, C. (2015) 'Here's What Interest Rate Liberalisation Means for China,' *South China Morning Post*. Available at: www.scmp.com/business/banking-finance/article/1877144/heres-what-interest-rate-liberalisation-means-china (Accessed on 1 December 2018).

Lo, W. C. and Ng, M. C. M. (2009) 'Banking Reform and Corporate Governance,' *The Chinese Economy*, Vol. 42, No. 5, pp. 21–39.

Lu, Y., Guo, H., Kao, E. H. and Fung, H. G. (2015) 'Shadow Banking and Firm Financing in China,' *International Review of Economics and Finance*, Vol. 36, pp. 40–53.

Lu, Y. and Sun, T. (2013) 'Local Government Financing Platforms in China: A Fortune or Misfortune?' *IMF Working Paper*, No. WP/13/243.

Mehran, H., Quintyn, M., Nordman, T. and Laurens, B. (1996) *Monetary and Exchange System Reforms in China: An Experience in Gradualism*, Washington, DC: International Monetary Fund.

National Audit Office of the People's Republic of China (2011) *Report on the Local Government Debt Audit Work*. Available at: www.audit.gov.cn/n1992130/n1992150/n1992500/2752208.html (Accessed on 20 October 2015).

National Audit Office of the People's Republic of China (2013) *Audit Results of Nationwide Governmental Debts*. Available at: www.audit.gov.cn/n5/n25/c63642/content.html (Accessed on 21 October 2015).

National Bureau of Statistics of China (formerly State Statistical Bureau) (various issues) *Zhongguo Tongji Nianjian* (*ZGTJNJ* hereafter, *China Statistical Yearbook 2003*), Beijing: Zhongguo Tongji Chubanshe.

National Bureau of Statistics of China (2014) *China Statistical Yearbook* 2014, Table 3–1. Available at: http://www.stats.gov.cn/tjsj/ndsj/2014/indexeh.htm (Accessed on 7 November 2019).

Naughton, B. (2007) *The Chinese Economy: Transition and Growth*, Cambridge: MIT Press.

Okazaki, K. (2007) 'Banking System Reform in China: The Challenge of Moving Toward a Market-Oriented Economy,' *Occasional Paper*, The RAND Corporation.

Pei, M. (2014) 'Shadow Banking: China's Wobbly House of Cards,' *Fortune*, 29 January. Available at: http://fortune.com/2014/01/29/shadow-banking-chinas-wobbly-house-of-cards/ (Accessed on 15 November 2015).

Prasad, E. S. (2017) *Gaining Currency: The Rise of Renminbi*, New York: Oxford University Press.

Ren, D. (2013) 'Guarantor Repays Principal on Failed Huaxia Product,' *South China Morning Post*, 23 January, p. B1.

Stent, J. (2017) *China's Banking Transformation: The Untold Story*, New York: Oxford University Press.

Tong, S. Y. and Yao, J. (2010) 'China's Rising Local Government Debts Spark Concerns,' *East Asian Policy*, Vol. 2, No. 4, October/December, pp. 38–49.

Wallace, T. (2017) 'China's Debt Boom Could Lead to Financial Crisis, IMF Warns,' *Telegraph*, 15 August. Available at: www.telegraph.co.uk/business/2017/08/15/chinas-debt-boom-could-lead-financial-crisis-imf-warns/ (Accessed on 17 July 2019).

Walter, C. E. and Howie, F. J. T. (2011) *Red Capitalism: The Fragile Financial Foundation of China's Extraordinary Rise*, Singapore: John Wiley & Sons (Asia).

Wang, B. (2009) 'Systematic Risks' Warning,' *China Daily*, 9 November, p. 7.

Wang, P. and Yang, Z. (2013) 'China to Rectify Local Governmental Debt,' *Caijing*, No. 1, pp. 88–95.

Wei, T. (2013) 'Rating Agency Looks at Local Government,' *China Daily*, 22 January, p. 1.

Wolf, C., Yeh, K. C., Zycher, B., Eberstadt, N. and Lee, S. (2003) *Fault Lines in China's Economic Terrain*, Santa Monica: RAND.

Woo, W. T. (2003) 'The Macroeconomic Consequences of China's Partially-Reformed Economy: The Key to Eradicating the Deflation Bias Lies in Establishing an Efficient Financial Intermediation Mechanism,' *China Perspectives*, No. 50, November–December, pp. 1–9. Available at: www.cefc.com.hk/uk/pc/articles/art_ligne.php?num_art_ligne=5001 (Accessed on 25 March 2008).

World Bank (1996) *The Chinese Economy: Fighting Inflation, Deepening Reforms*, Washington, DC: The World Bank.

Yao, S., Jiang, C., Feng, G. and Willenbockel, D. (2007) 'On the Efficiency of Chinese Banks and WTO Challenges,' *Applied Economics*, Vol. 39, pp. 629–643.

5 China and the world

A new form of integration

China's opening up to the outside world since the early 1980s has fundamentally transformed China from a closed economy into an active and influential player in the global economy. China has been the largest exporter in the world since 2009 and with its export value reached a historic high of US$2.097 trillion in 2017.[1] China also surpassed the US as the largest trading nation in the world in 2013; its trade volume amounted to US$4.12 trillion.[2] In 2015, China's US$145.7 billion of outbound direct investment (ODI) for the first time exceeded inbound foreign direct investment (FDI) with a total of US$135.6 billion. This milestone figure marked China as a net exporter of capital. China also surpassed Japan to become the second largest ODI country in 2015 (KPMG 2016). China's dramatic global expansion not only brings fundamental overhaul to its economy but also remarkably impacts the structure of the global economy.

This chapter argues that China's open door policy started with a trial-and-error detour from its past and gradually evolved into a determining actor in the global political economy. China's unprecedented global presence is welcomed by the world for its gigantic demand for overseas goods and services, which becomes an important stabiliser of global growth in particular, after the global financial crisis (GFC) in 2008. Nonetheless, the blessings brought by China are somewhat counterweighted by the worry and threat felt by the advanced powers such as the US, Japan and some EU members such as Germany. These powers have initiated numerous protective – and even confrontational – measures to undermine the pace and extent of China's rise and international presence. Whether China can further enhance its global footprint depends primarily on China's capabilities in expanding mutually beneficial cooperation with partner countries and bolstering its soft power in the global arena.

From closed door to open door: foreign direct investment and trade participation

The centrally planned economy, together with the Great Leap Forward and Cultural Revolution, implemented during the pre-reform period, proved to be counterproductive. The living standard, economic growth and technological level were far behind the world standards in the 1970s. In contrast to China's "closed door policy" adopted in the 1950s-1970s, the neighbouring Newly Industrialised Economies (NIEs, South Korea, Taiwan, Singapore and Hong Kong) embraced a more outward-oriented approach of trade participation and attracting FDI, which resulted in remarkable economic growth, enhancement of living standards and technological innovation. Strong drive to modernise China and catch up with the world economy prompted a group of more liberal and pragmatic leaders, led by Deng Xiaoping, to initiate an open door policy that departed from the previous policy of self-sufficiency and isolation. The first stage of China's open door policy is marked by the establishment of 4 Special Economic Zones in 1979, Shenzhen, Zhuhai, Xiamen and Shantou, bestowed with special rights to attract FDI. Hainan was later granted the same special rights to attract FDI, followed by the opening up of 14 Open Coastal Cities in 1984. With initial success, preferential policies were extended to the Yangtze River Delta and Pearl River Delta, Xiamen-Zhangzhou-Quanzhou Triangle in south Fujian, Shangdong Peninsula, Liaodong Peninsula, Hebei and Guangxi into an open coastal belt. In 1990, the Pudong New Zone in Shanghai was set up to form an extensive open economic belt, with Shanghai's Pudong as the "dragon head".[3] China's cautious approach is understandable and rational. Even if the experimental opening up of 4 SEZs was unsuccessful, it was only confined to a number of small areas, which would not trigger huge damage and impact the whole economy. If it turned out to be successful, the experience of SEZs could be extended to other regions and provinces. During the initial years of opening up, the amount of realised FDI was limited, with a total amount of US\$ 4.1 billion in 1979–84. The June Fourth Incident in 1989 posed a challenge to the Chinese government as Western countries had imposed various sanctions on China, but the impact on FDI was minimal. Though the growth of FDI shrank dramatically from 38.1 percent in 1988 to 6.3 percent in 1989, it swiftly rebounded to 25.2 percent in 1991, followed by 2 consecutive years of spectacular growth in 1992 and 1993. Such resurgence was attributable to two main factors. First, the political situation in China after the Incidence had gradually regained its stability and did not show signs of further deterioration. In particular, Deng Xiaoping's Southern Tour in 1992 reassured that China would continue more progressive and bolder reforms in opening up to the outside world. Foreign investors interpreted Deng's important speech positively and FDI has kept on pouring into China since 1992 (Table 5.1). Second, Western countries imposed a range of economic and military sanctions aimed at isolating and pressurising China, but Asian countries opted to detach from those sanctions in order to maintain harmonious diplomatic relations with China. Japan, the third biggest foreign investor in China,[4] was the only Asian country that explicitly condemned China's use of force against students and civilians. South Korea only stated that the Incidence was "regrettable". Thailand and Malaysia took an even more neutral stand, saying that the event was China's "internal affair" and other ASEAN countries remained almost silent (Shambaugh 2013: 95–96). Given the fact that Asian countries/regions, including Hong Kong (and Macau), Taiwan and Japan, have been China's major sources of FDI,[5] military and economic sanctions from the West did not constitute much negative impact on China's FDI.

Table 5.1 FDI Realised 1979–2017 (US$ billion)

Year	FDI realised	Growth (%)
1979–84	4.10	
1985	1.96	30.7*
1986	2.24	14.3
1987	2.31	3.1
1988	3.19	38.1
1989	3.39	6.3
1990	3.49	2.9
1991	4.37	25.2
1992	11.01	151.9
1993	27.52	150.0
1994	33.77	22.7
1995	37.52	11.1
1996	41.73	11.2
1997	45.26	8.5
1998	45.46	0.4
1999	40.32	(11.3)
2000	40.72	1.0
2001	46.88	15.1
2002	52.74	12.5
2003	53.51	1.5
2004	60.63	13.3
2005	60.33	(0.5)
2006	63.02	4.5
2007	74.77	18.6
2008	92.40	23.6
2009	90.03	(2.6)
2010	105.74	17.4
2011	116.01	9.7
2012	111.72	(3.7)
2013	117.59	5.3
2014	119.56	1.7
2015	126.27	5.6
2016	126.0	(0.2)
2017	131.04	4.0

Source: China Statistical Yearbook 2018 (Table 11.13). Available at: www.stats.gov.cn/tjsj/ndsj/2018/indexeh.htm (Accessed on 26 January 2019)

Note
* Growth rate in 1985 is calculated based on the data from Chai (1997: 159).

China's FDI has entered a phase of steady growth since 1992 amid some ups and downs. More obvious decline was recorded after the 1997 Asian Financial Crisis and the 2008 GFC, but were both followed by rapid rebound. Several points are noteworthy for China's gigantic inflow of foreign capital over the past 4 decades. First, China prefers FDI to foreign loans in tapping foreign capital. The Latin American debt crisis in 1982 alarmed the Chinese government that huge external debts would make its domestic economy vulnerable to external shocks. FDI could also avoid regular repayment and minimise interest costs, which reduced financial risks and costs of utilising foreign funds. Second, empirical studies in the 1980s and 1990s revealed that FDI not only filled China's capital gap in the 1980s but also generated a number of economic benefits including income growth, employment creation and export growth (Chai 1983; World Bank 1988; Hiemenz 1990; Kueh 1992; Chi 1994). Foreign enterprises are the main driver of China's export-oriented strategy. After 2 decades of foreign capital inflow, foreign-funded enterprises contributed 44 percent of China's total exports in 1998, and the figures maintained a similar level at 43.2 percent in 2017.[6] Third, of equal importance to the quantitative economic benefits, FDI brought about qualitative benefits of technology transfer and managerial knowhow, notably in the first 2 decades of opening up. Foreign investors brought in machinery, equipment and production knowhow as well as managerial skills. Chinese managers were trained with skills of enterprise management such as cost control, inventory control and quality assurance (Pomfret 1991: 135–136). Empirically, Buckley, Clegg and Wang (2002) uses cross-section data of Chinese manufacturing industries in 1995 to examine the relationship between FDI and technology transfer. The results indicate that non-Chinese foreign firms generate technological and international market access spill over benefits for Chinese firms, which contributed to technological enhancement and new product development of Chinese industrial enterprises. The qualitative value-added of FDI is vital to the upgrading of Chinese industry. Last but not least, though foreign investors' complaint against unfavourable business and investment environment has never faded away, the ongoing influx of foreign capital into China proves that it is mutually beneficial for China and foreign investors under various forms of FDI. The benefits to the foreign investors must outweigh the costs of the claimed unfavourable investment environment. FDI in the 1980s and 1990s was mainly incentivised by China's low labour and land costs, which helped reduce production costs and raise profitability while the FDI since 2000 has been mainly driven by China's burgeoning domestic market with rising wealth. From the China side, FDI has been an integral part of the Chinese economy in terms of income growth, employment creation, trade growth and technology transfer. The complementarity between foreign investors and their Chinese counterparts sustained the inflow of foreign capital into China over the past decades. Increasing presence and unfailing incentive to enter new investment sectors by foreign investors indicate that China's opening up to tap FDI has been incredibly successful.

Another main plank of China's open door policy is trade liberalisation and participation. During the pre-reform period, China adopted the policy of autarky, which emphasised economic independence and self-sufficiency. Trade was kept at minimum and the limited amount of exports was to earn adequate foreign exchange to purchase necessary imports. The State Planning Commission (SPC) determined more than 90 percent of imports, and the export plans were devised in physical quantities to finance the imports permitted by the SPC. Imports were mainly equipment, raw materials and factor inputs needed to fulfil the production targets set by planning authorities (Lardy 2002: 29–30). As trade was not used to promote growth, central planners were not concerned much about the market signals of international prices and exchange rates to guide the composition of imports and exports. Export prices and exchange rates were set by central authorities. The import and export plans deliberated by the SPC would then be carried out by 12 foreign trade corporations (FTCs), which were under the control of Ministry of Foreign Trade. FTCs monopolised the trading right and separated the producers and end-users between China and the international markets. China's exporting industries did not have any information about the consumers (i.e., end-users) preference and price signals in the international market. China's products were thus not exported according to comparative advantage, which caused substantial efficiency loss. With its endowment of abundant labour supply, China in principle should export more labour-intensive products. However, China exported a large amount of capital-intensive products such as crude oil and petroleum products in the 1970s and the first half of 1980s. Almost all petroleum products were exported during this period though China had faced severe shortage of these products domestically (Lardy 2002: 31–32). On the contrary, the NIEs in Southeast and East Asia adopting an export-oriented growth strategy based on comparative advantage in the 1970s and 1980s had achieved spectacular growth records. This contrast growth experience prompted the pragmatic leaders to give up the strategy of autarky and isolation. Several decisive steps were taken to speed up trade participation. First, trading rights were decentralised and FTCs no longer possessed the monopoly in trading. The number of FTCs was dramatically increased from 12 in 1978 to over 7,000 in mid-1994 (Chai 1997: 140). Trading rights were later decentralised further to local authorities, enterprises and joint venture trading companies. A total of 35,000 domestic companies was allowed to engage in trade in 2001 (Lardy 2002: 41). Second, together with the decentralisation of trading rights, goods under foreign trade plans were sharply reduced. During the pre-reform period, about 3000 export commodities and almost 90 percent of imports were under a foreign trade plan, but there were only 38 export commodities and 11 import commodities under the plan after reform. Third, related to the previous two points, to foster trade liberalisation, trading units were allowed to set prices according to the world market situation in order to maintain price competition. Further, Renminbi (RMB) has been devalued since 1978 to reflect a more realistic exchange rate. The RMB:US exchange rate experienced a dramatic drop from 1.56 in 1978 to 5.76 (Chai 1997: 145), representing a 2.69 times devaluation. RMB were overvalued before the reform with an aim to reduce the costs of imports. The post-reform devaluation not only better reflects the real value of RMB but also largely enhances the competitiveness of China's exports. The bundle of trade liberalisation measures implemented since the late 1970s prompted a rapid rise in both imports and exports. China's trade participation ratio (the share of imports plus exports in GDP), which is a measure of openness, rose from 9.7 percent in 1978 to an all-time high of 64.2 percent in 2006 (Table 5.2). In addition, except the period of import spree in the 1980s,

Table 5.2 China's Imports, Exports and Trade Balance 1952–2017 (100 million yuan)

Year	Exports (EX)	Imports (IM)	IM+EX	EX−IM (NX)	GDP	IM+EX/ GDP	NX/ GDP
1952	27.1	37.5	64.6	−10.4	679.0	9.5	−1.53
1957	54.5	50.0	104.5	4.5	1068.0	9.8	0.42
1962	47.1	33.8	80.9	13.3	1149.3	7.0	1.16
1965	63.1	55.3	118.4	7.8	1716.1	6.9	0.45
1970	56.8	56.1	112.9	0.7	2252.7	5.0	0.03
1975	143.0	147.4	290.4	−4.4	2997.3	9.7	−0.15
1978	167.6	187.4	355.0	−19.8	3678.7	9.7	−0.54
1980	271.2	298.8	570.0	−27.6	4587.6	12.4	−0.60
1985	808.9	1257.8	2066.7	−448.9	9098.9	22.7	−4.93
1986	1082.1	1498.3	2580.4	−416.2	10376.2	24.9	−4.01
1987	1470.0	1614.2	3084.2	−144.2	12174.6	25.3	−1.18
1988	1766.7	2055.1	3821.8	−288.4	15180.4	25.2	−1.90
1989	1956.0	2199.9	4155.9	−243.9	17179.7	24.2	−1.42
1990	2985.8	2574.3	5560.1	411.5	18872.9	29.5	2.18
1991	3827.1	3398.7	7225.8	428.4	22005.6	32.8	1.95
1992	4676.3	4443.3	9119.6	233.0	27194.5	33.5	0.86
1993	5284.8	5986.2	11271.0	−701.4	35673.2	31.6	−1.97
1994	10421.8	9960.1	20381.9	461.8	48637.5	41.9	0.95
1995	12451.8	11048.1	23499.9	1403.7	61339.9	38.3	2.29
1996	12567.4	11557.4	24133.9	1019.0	71813.6	33.6	1.42
1997	15160.7	11806.6	26967.2	3354.1	79715.0	33.8	4.21
1998	15223.5	11626.1	26849.7	3597.4	85195.0	31.5	4.22
1999	16159.8	13736.5	29896.2	2423.3	90564.4	33.0	2.68
2000	20634.4	18638.8	39273.3	1995.6	100280.1	39.2	1.99
2001	22024.4	20159.2	42183.6	1865.3	110863.1	38.1	1.68
2002	26947.9	24430.3	51378.2	2517.6	121717.4	42.2	2.07
2003	36287.9	34195.6	70483.5	2029.3	137422.0	51.3	1.48
2004	49103.3	46435.8	95539.1	2667.6	161840.2	59.0	1.65
2005	62648.1	54273.7	116921.8	8374.4	187318.9	62.4	4.47
2006	77597.9	63376.9	140974.7	14221.0	219438.5	64.2	6.48
2007	93627.1	73296.9	166924.1	20330.2	270232.3	61.8	7.52
2008	100394.9	79526.5	179921.5	20868.4	319515.5	56.3	6.53
2009	82029.7	68618.4	150648.1	13411.3	349081.4	43.2	3.84
2010	107022.8	94699.5	201722.3	12323.3	413030.3	48.8	2.98
2011	123240.6	113161.4	236402.0	10079.2	489300.6	48.3	2.06
2012	129359.3	114801.0	244160.2	14558.3	540367.4	45.2	2.69
2013	137131.4	121037.5	258168.9	16094.0	595244.4	43.4	2.70
2014	143883.8	120358.0	264241.8	23525.7	643974.0	41.0	3.65
2015	141166.8	104336.1	245502.9	36830.7	689052.1	35.6	5.35
2016	138419.3	104967.2	243386.5	33452.1	743585.5	32.7	4.50
2017	153311.2	124789.8	278101.0	28521.4	827121.7	33.6	3.45

Source: China Statistical Yearbook 1999 (Table 17.3; Table 3.1). Available at: www.stats.gov.cn/english/statisticaldata/yearlydata/YB1999e/q03e.htm; China Statistical Yearbook 2018 (Table 11.2; Table 3.1). Available at: www.stats.gov.cn/tjsj/ndsj/2018/indexeh.htm (Accessed on 28 January 2019)

China has experienced trade surplus in most of the subsequent years, which contributes positively to China's economic growth.

China's opening up in the 1980s generated enormous economic benefits in terms of income growth, employment creation, and accumulation of foreign reserves. However, even more important is China's exposure to the global market, which brings in immense valuable information for China's later development. Moreover, the positive results prompt China to embrace the notion that integration into the world economy would not jeopardise but rather speed up its long-term development. It is undebatable that adoption of open door policy is attributable to the push factors resulting from the poor conditions of the domestic economy and the rise of more pragmatic and liberal leaders at the upper echelon. However, opening up could not be feasible without a changed international environment, in particular China's diplomatic relationship with the US. Since Henry Kissinger's historic visit to Beijing in 1971, China-US relations had undergone subtle changes from hostility to normalisation and later to cooperation. The US had strong incentive to ally with China to shield Soviet influence in the Far East. Further, after signing the Joint Declaration with the UK on the return of sovereignty of Hong Kong to China, China endeavoured to improve relationships with Taiwan by advocating "reunification with Taiwan" rather than "liberation of Taiwan" (Huan 1986: 3–4). Amid improved relations, the US and Taiwan became the second and third largest foreign investors in China and major trade partners in the mid-1990s. Change in diplomatic relations served as a facilitator for China's opening up.

From opening up to "going out"

The opening up since the late 1970s had furnished China with new growth momentum fostered by substantial inflow of FDI and its associated technology and managerial know-how. In addition, extensive participation in foreign trade utilised China's comparative advantage to expand its overseas market, which not only boosted China's economic growth and foreign reserves, but also enabled China to access important information regarding foreign markets. With accumulated foreign reserves, building up of stronger enterprises (mainly SOEs) and gathered experience in dealing with foreign business partners, China started to scrutinise its global presence by reversing its policy direction: from opening up to "going out". Without doing away the open door policy, key central leaders in the 1990s held the view that "going out" could enlarge China's economic benefits by increasing ODI and overseas acquisition.

Like other policy change in China, it is difficult to state precisely the commencement of the "going out" policy. However, its origin could be traced back to some internal speeches by Jiang Zemin,[7] former President of the PRC, delivered in mid-1992 prior to the Fourteenth Party Congress in Autumn 1992. A more explicit statement made by Jiang on the "going out" policy was made on 26 July 1996 after his visit to Africa. In his speech, he encouraged Chinese enterprises to "go out". Another statement by Jiang delivered in the Fifteenth Party

Congress in 1997 followed this speech, which clearly propounded the notion of "bring [investment] in and go out". After that Jiang repeatedly raised the new policy initiative in different speeches and occasions. The "going out" policy was formally discussed at a Politburo on 20 January 2000 (Shambaugh 2013: 175).[8] The "going out" strategy was mainly motivated by the swift accumulation of foreign exchange. After two decades of open door policy since the early 1980s, Chinese exports have expanded remarkably to create huge trade surplus, in particular with the US. The United States' trade deficit skyrocketed from US$96 billion in 1995 to $380 billion in 2000 Almost 60 percent of US trade deficit since 2000 was attributable to China's exports. China's expanding trade surplus has rapidly amassed foreign exchange in China's banking system. The People's Bank of China (PBOC) absorbs the dollars earned through exporters by giving out Renminbi (RMB). However, this act has increased RMB liquidity in the market, which likely pushes up commodity and assets inflation. To avoid domestic inflation, PBOC needs to sterilise the increased liquidity by selling bonds to commercial banks or setting a high required reserve ratio (Subacchi 2017: 91). China's foreign reserve was negligible immediately after the establishment of the People's Republic China. As indicated in Table 5.3, foreign reserves were just US$157 million in 1950 and the level remained almost unchanged on the

Table 5.3 China's Foreign Reserves (100 million US dollars)

Year	Foreign reserves
1950	1.57
1960	0.46
1970	0.88
1978	1.67
1983	89.01
1990	110.93
1995	735.97
2000	1655.74
2005	8188.72
2006	10663.44
2007	15282.49
2008	19460.30
2009	23991.52
2010	28473.38
2011	31811.48
2012	33115.89
2013	38213.15
2014	38430.18
2015	33303.62
2016	30105.17
2017	31399.49

Source: State Administration of Foreign Exchange. Available at: www.safe.gov.cn/en/2018/0408/1426.html (Accessed on 15 January 2019)

eve of open door policy at US$167 million in 1978. However, after about a decade of opening up, China's foreign reserves experienced an impressive jump to US$11.09 billion. The rising trend of foreign reserves has continued, and it reached US$165.57 billion in 2000, which represents a growth of 13.9 times. From 2000 to 2008, China used about 64 percent of its trade surplus with the US to buy US treasury bonds and the debt of government chartered organisations such as Fannie Mae (Table 5.4). With rising trade surplus with the US, China's hoarding of treasury bonds grew correspondingly. On the eve of 2008 GFC, China's holding of foreign reserves growth hit a historic high of 43.3 percent in 2007. Central leaders expressed concern over the default and exchange rate risks embedded in mounting foreign reserves, with the dominance of US dollars. Premier Wen Jiabao explicitly stated his concern over China's substantial holding of US Treasury bonds at the end of the National People's Congress in 2009. Wen said:

> We have lent a huge amount of money to the U.S. Of course we are concerned about the safety of our assets, to be honest, I am definitely a little worried.[9]

He even demanded "guarantee safety" from the Obama administration. China took immediate action of selling US$32.4 billion US Treasury bonds after Wen's speech (Branigan and Stewart 2010). In addition, the Chinese government and enterprises became sceptical of the exchange rate risk inherent in the holding of a substantial amount of US debt. Any appreciation of RMB and/or depreciation of US$ means a reduction in value of China's hard earned foreign exchange. Further, as mentioned previously, with amassed foreign reserves, PBOC issues bills to absorb the increased liquidity in the market (i.e., sterilisation) to avoid inflationary pressure. Nevertheless, the costs of sterilisation are always higher than the returns earned from the US Treasuries. For instance, the return of a one-year US Treasury bill was 0.11 percent in August 2014 while the rate offered by PBOC for a one-year bill was 3.7 percent at the same time (Subacchi 2017: 94).

Table 5.4 China's Utilisation of Foreign Exchange Earning from US Trade Surplus 2000–2008

	US$ (billion)	Percentage
Debt of government chartered organisations (e.g., Fannie Mae)	474	33.3
US Treasuries	439	30.8
Investment in real estate and other companies in the US	400	28.1
Stock in US companies	96	6.7
Corporate bonds	16	1.1
Total	1,425	100

Source: Lilly (2009: 2)

Foreign reserves accumulation and its associated sterilisation insert considerable financial pressure on the central bank. More importantly, the Chinese leaders had developed a view that increasing hoarding of foreign reserve and purchase of US bonds did not serve the best interest of China's long-term development. An international norm of adequate foreign reserve holding is equal to a country's outstanding short-term debt or 3-4 months of the value of imports. China's foreign reserves amounted to US$165.6 billion in 2000, which amply fulfilled both conditions. China's short-term foreign loans and the value of 4 months' imports were US$13.1 billion and US$75.0 billion respectively in 2000.[10] The amount of foreign reserves was more than enough to buffer potential external shocks. The holding of excess reserves prompted central leaders to acquire overseas companies that could secure China's energy and raw materials sources as well as transferring advanced technology and business models to Chinese enterprises. This "going out" strategy provided more concrete benefits for China's long-term growth and development than holding excessive reserves and US Treasury bonds.

The amount of overseas direct investment (ODI) was negligible before 2000. Since China's announcement of the "going out" strategy in 2000, ODI has picked up its growth momentum. Table 5.5 reveals that ODI started with a small base of US$2.5 billion and skyrocketed to 55.91 in 2008. Immediate after the GFC, the figures experienced a meagre growth of 1.1 percent, which reflected China's cautious approach to capital outflow in the aftermath of the crisis. Since

Table 5.5 China's Overseas Direct Investment (ODI)

Year	ODI (US$ billion)	Growth (%)
2002	2.50	
2003	2.86	14.4
2004	5.50	92.3
2005	12.26	122.9
2006	17.63	43.8
2007	26.51	50.4
2008	55.91	110.9
2009	56.53	1.1
2010	68.81	21.7
2011	74.65	8.5
2012	87.80	17.6
2013	107.84	22.8
2014	123.12	14.2
2015	145.67	18.3
2016	196.15	34.7
2017	158.29	(19.3)

Source: Huang and Wikes (2011); *China Statistical Yearbook 2005, 2007, 2009, 2011, 2013, 2015, 2017, 2018*. Available at: www.stats.gov.cn/english/statisticaldata/annualdata/ (Accessed on 20 January 2019)

Note
Figures from 2002 to 2005 include only non-financial overseas direct investment, while figures from 2006 onward include all industries.

then, China's ODI growth has demonstrated a more stable double-digit growth till 2017. China's ODI has fallen sharply since Beijing in late 2016 implemented strict controls on capital outflow to avoid massive capital flight (Cheng 2018). ODI in less strategic areas such as hotel, property, sports and entertainment has been limited by the central government, which resulted in the first-ever negative growth of 19.3 percent in 2017. Trade war broke out in 2018 and further reduced China's ODI as developed countries, in particular the US, have been increasingly reluctant to allow China acquisition of technology and energy firms that have direct bearing on national security. The growth of non-financial ODI grew only marginally at 0.3 percent in 2018.

China's high profile acquisitions have drawn the US and European countries' attention and concern about China's control on some of their key enterprises. During the initial years of China's outbound merger and acquisition (M&As), Germany's small and medium-sized manufacturing firms were the major targets of China's acquisition as the manufacturing technology and high standards of quality assurance obtained from these German firms were well suited for Chinese firms' industry upgrade. Some salient examples include the purchase of German machinery maker Putzmeiser by Sany, the purchase of solar panel manufacturer Sunways by LDK Solars and the acquisition of Kiekert by Hebei Lingyun. (Shambaugh 2013: 182). Overseas M&A by Chinese firms grew remarkably over the past decade and reached its record high of 173 M&A with a total amount of US$128.7 billion in 2016. It not only broke China's yearly record but also topped the US as the largest global acquirer of overseas companies (Shepard 2016). The pattern of China's overseas M&A has undergone recognisable changes. Before 2013, SOEs dominated most of the M&A to acquire energy and commodities companies such as iron ores in Australia, energy producers from Canada and copper mines in Africa. Since 2013, government-backed buyers have mainly acquired internet and software companies, which became the third major sector for China's acquisition in 2016, just behind chemicals and property companies (Table 5.6) while the M&A

Table 5.6 Sectoral Distribution of China's M&A (US$ billion)

Sector	2012	2016
Traditional Energy*	30.0	2.8
Finance	1.40	18.2
Property	0.6	28.5
Mining	2.3	5.4
Chemicals	2.0	47.6
Internet/Software	0.24	26.6
Utilities	1.5	22.5
Logistics	0.32	23.1

Source: Bloomberg (2018)

Note
* Traditional energy covers coal, oil, gas and services and pipelines.

in traditional energy has shown a drastic decline. This stark change reflects China's robust intention to upgrade its technology in manufacturing and service industries. China's rapid expansion of acquisition in high-tech industry has increased the US and European countries' scrutiny on China's cross-border deals. The Committee on Foreign Investment in the US has banned some transactions in the technology sector and is cautious of any potential M&A that could affect national security. In Europe, China's takeover of robot maker Kuka AG drew opposition from the politicians, and the UK government has devised new policies to review large acquisitions in sensitive industries (Bloomberg 2018).

From rule follower to rule setter: China's admission to the World Trade Organization

Parallel to the "going out" strategy, China had made gigantic efforts to bargain for admission into the World Trade Organization (WTO). China was a member of General Agreement of Tariffs and Trade (GATT) – the predecessor of WTO – but not a member of WTO prior to 2001. China joined GATT in 1947, and the nationalist government signed the agreement. However, two years after joining the GATT, the nationalist government retreated to Taiwan and withdrew its membership. Eight years after its implementation of open door policy in 1978, China tried to resume its GATT membership in 1986 and a lengthy and arduous journey of negotiation began (Boden 2012: 13). GATT was transformed into WTO in 1995 to cover issues not just on commodity trade but also on service trade and intellectual property. After 15 years of negotiation, China was formally granted a full membership to the WTO in 2001. The long process of bargaining resulted in China's unprecedented and dramatic concessions in tariff reduction and further opening up to foreign investors. The average tariffs would be reduced below 10 percent by 2005. A tariff-rate quota system was introduced to bring the tariff rate for key agricultural commodities, such as wheat, almost to zero for a significant volume of imports. All quotas and licenses that restricted the flow of imports would be gradually eliminated. Key service sectors such as telecommunications, distribution, banking, insurance, asset management and securities would be opened up further to foreign direct investment. Further, China agreed to abide by international standards in the protection of intellectual property (Lardy 2001).[11] China also concurred to amend existing laws to facilitate fulfilment of the admission conditions. All of these changes would create short- to medium-term uncertainties in the Chinese economies, which would also destabilise the society. With the paramount goal of maintaining economic and social stability, why was China willing to concede substantially and face the uncertainties ahead to obtain a membership of the WTO?

The first obvious motivation for entering the WTO was to free China from annual negotiation with the US to seek normal trade relations (NTR), also known as the Most Favored Nation Clause (MFN), which gives China equal trading privileges with any other US trade partners. China had been granted NTR since 1980, but needed annual review and endorsement by the US Congress

(Nolt 1999). The annual review of NTR was always tied with China's commitments to improve human rights conditions. China could avoid the troublesome review and negotiation after obtaining the WTO membership, which allowed China to trade with member countries on an equal footing basis. Chinese leaders were intensely concerned with this consideration when Western countries imposed sanctions on China after the June Fourth Incidence in 1989 (Saich 2002: 4). If China was outside the system, it may encounter a lot of bilateral trade sanctions, which would cause China sizable economic costs. After being admitted to the WTO, any sanctions against China had to be endorsed by the WTO.

Related to the previous point, China had regularly faced dumping[12] accusation by western countries. Indeed, China has been the number one target of anti-dumping cases. From January 1995 to June 2008, 640 anti-dumping cases had been filed against China's exports, which constituted about 20 percent of the world total. The United States, European Union, Japan, India, and Argentina initiated the most anti-dumping cases against China. Products often involved in these cases include base metal, chemical, machinery and electrical appliances and textiles, accounting for 70 percent of all the cases (Le and Tong 2009: 1). If a dumping case is established, the importing countries will either impose a hefty penalty or punitive tariffs. Before entering the WTO, China, for most of the cases, accepted the penalty or punitive tariffs instead of going through legal procedures to argue against the accusation as the lawsuit could be very lengthy and exorbitant. After obtaining the full membership to WTO, China could make use of the WTO tribunal mechanism to settle trade disputes, which was less costly and more impartial from the perspective of China.

Third, of paramount importance, China could lift its influence over the global political economy with its admission into WTO. After less than 2 decades of opening up, China had already become one of the top 10 trading countries. In the 1990s, China was the second largest FDI recipient in the world, just after the US. It is noteworthy that China was the largest provider of ODI among developing countries in 1995 (Lardy 2001). China's exponential growth in trade and ODI changed the scene of developing countries' reliance on Western countries for market and foreign investment. On Chinese side, it was eager to take up a leading role in collaborating with developing countries to bargain with developed countries, through which China could further its footprint and influence in global governance. To illustrate, China, together with other developing countries including Brazil, South Africa and India, bargained with developed countries in the WTO in the 2000s on important issues such as abolition of subsidies to farmers in developed countries and slowing down the pace of opening up financial markets in developing countries (Hung 2017: 142). The presence of China in the bargaining camp of developing countries noticeably strengthened its negotiating positions. China and other developing countries have long been raising concern over the disproportionate influence of some leading countries in the West, particularly the US, in the international economic governance system. Advanced Western countries have a dominant influence within international economic institutions such as the International Monetary Fund and WTO. Chinese leaders believed that admission to the WTO would enable China to be a "rule setter" rather than just a "rule follower" in global governance and to establish more balanced international institutions.

Fourth, China's eagerness to join the WTO was largely pushed by reform leaders, such as the former Premier Zhu Rongji, who made admission to the WTO a national goal, because of which China had to reform its financial and trade policies to align with international norms and regulations to satisfy admission requirements. Zhu used external pressure to clear the resistance against further market reforms imposed by the conservative elements in the party. When Zhu Rongji visited the US in April 1999, he explicitly stated at his joint press conference with President Clinton that "the competition arising (from WTO membership) will also promote a more rapid and more healthy development of China's national economy".[13] WTO admission entrusted reformist leaders with a legitimate reason to deepen market reform and forge further integration into the global economy.

Last but not least, China expected that entering the WTO would expand its overseas market and that the gradual opening up of the service sector would attract more FDI. Economic growth could be pushed up by 2 percentage points, which would generate 10 to 15 million jobs. This additional growth and employment creation were especially important for China after the Asian Financial Crisis in 1997. China needed new growth sources to counterweigh potential economic downturn (Saich 2002: 5). As a huge manufacturing exporting country, Chinese leaders realised the importance of securing a stable supply of parts, raw materials and energy. Accession to the WTO increased China's economic tie with member countries, which could enlarge its sources of energy and factor inputs in the supply chain.

The previous factors largely explain China's substantial concessions to the WTO accession, though China foresaw potential negative impacts on its rather protected industries and service sectors. However, beyond China's expectation, the predicted negative economic impacts have not taken place after noticeable tariff reduction and opening up of the domestic market. Both imports and exports continue to balloon, and more importantly, net exports rose considerably and reached a historic high of 20868.4 billion yuan in 2008 before the GFC. Export growth constantly outpaced import growth during the post-WTO period. Exports experienced some slowdown after the 2008 GFC, but picked up momentum again in 2010. Net exports grew further to hit a new height of 36830.7 billion yuan in 2015. This implies that China's products maintain its competitiveness in an international market, which is more than adequate to counterweigh rising imports after WTO accession. Similar positive effects happened in realised FDI. Over 16 years, from 2002 to 2017, FDI demonstrated notable growth except for 4 years of slight negative growth, ranging from 0.2 to 3.7 percent. That said, China has been cautious about opening up strategic areas such as finance, telecommunications, energy and national defence, regarding which China has national security concerns. Foreign investors have been facing restrictions on controlling ownership of Chinese enterprises through equity caps, limited voting rights and participation on companies' board of directors.

China's Catalogue for the Guidance of Foreign Investment in Industries, or Foreign Investment Catalogue (FIC), governs the market access of FDI. The economic sectors open to FDI are categorised into "encouraged", "restricted" or "prohibited". In both the encouraged and restricted categories, the FIC outlines industry sectors that are completely liberalised and those that are open to foreign investment but subject to equity caps, joint ventures requirements and Chinese national leadership requirements. For example, in the oil and natural gas exploration and development industry, foreign investment is required to take the form of equity joint ventures and cooperative joint ventures. In the accounting and auditing sectors, the chief partner of a firm must be a Chinese national. In some sectors such as construction and operation of civilian airports, construction and operation of nuclear power plants and even establishment and operation of cinemas, the Chinese partners must maintain control of the enterprise (Export.com 2017). Though the Chinese government lessened some restrictions on foreign investment in the agriculture, mining and infrastructure sectors in July 2018, restrictions on sensitive sectors including finance, insurance and automobiles remain. The real effects of the relaxation remain to be seen (Wong 2018). China's restrictive FDI policies in contrast to its active overseas M&A have sown the seeds of a hostile economic and trade relationship with the advanced countries, particularly the US and some EU countries.

Belt-and-road initiatives: from integrating to leading

China's "going out" strategy, together with the notable development in trade, FDI and ODI did away with China's worry and reservation regarding market liberalisation. With accumulated experience in the global economy and strikingly escalated state power, President Xi Jinping propounded his vision of a "New Silk Road" when he delivered a speech at the Nazarbayev University in Astana, Kazakhstan in September 2013. In the following month, Xi advocated his notion of a "Maritime Silk Road" in Indonesia. The "New Silk Road" and "Maritime Silk Road" are later concretised as the Silk Road Economic Belt (land route) and the 21st Century Maritime Silk Road (sea route), which constitute the Belt and Road Initiative (BRI). The BRI connects countries in Asia, Europe and Africa along six routes: (1) the New Eurasia Land Bridge Economic Corridor; (2) the China-Mongolia-Russia Economic Corridor; (3) the China-Central Asia-West Asia Economic Corridor; (4) the China-Indochina Peninsula Economic Corridor; (5) the China-Pakistan Economic Corridor and (6) the Bangladesh-China-India-Myanmar Economic Corridor. The grand plan covers 60 percent of the world's population living in 60-plus countries, 30 percent the global GDP and 35 percent of world trade. According to the official documents, cooperation under the BRI encompasses 5 major areas: policy co-ordination, facilities connectivity, unimpeded trade, financial integration and people-to-people bonds. The cooperation mechanism of the BRI rests on the principles of joint development through bilateral and multilateral co-operation to promote regional and inter-regional integration of the development of the countries along the route.[14]

To kick off the BRI, a US$40 billion Silk Road Fund was established in December 2014 to finance the BRI projects, with its main investment in infrastructure, resources and industrial and financial co-operation. The Fund was set up as a limited liability company in December 2014 with its founding shareholders including China's State Administration of Foreign Exchange, the China Investment Corp, the Export-Import Bank of China and the China Development Bank. On 14 May 2017, President Xi Jinping delivered a keynote speech at the opening ceremony of the "Belt and Road Forum for International Co-operation" and announced that China would contribute an additional 100 billion yuan to the Fund.[15] Another financing source for BRI projects is the Asian Infrastructure Investment Bank which is a multinational financial institution founded in January 2016 and headquartered in Beijing to finance the huge infrastructure needs across Asia and countries along the BRI regions. AIIB focuses on financing projects in energy and power, transportation and telecommunications, rural infrastructure and agriculture development, water supply and sanitation, environmental protection and urban development and logistics. As of February 2019, AIIB has 70 approved members and 23 prospective members and has financed 35 projects with total funding amounting to US$7.5 billion.[16]

The BRI, in parallel with Silk Road Fund and AIIB, brings China to a new height of the "going out" strategy and marks a clear departure from the strategy of "maintaining a low profile" (*taoguang yanghui*) advocated by Deng Xiaoping that when dealing with diplomatic and global affairs China should "observe the situation calmly. Stand firm in our position. Respond cautiously. Conceal our capabilities and await an opportune moment. Never claim leadership. Take some action". (*lengjing guancha, wenzhu zhenjiao, chenzhuo yingfu, taoguang yanghui, juebu dangtou, yousuo zuowei*) (Garver 2006: 98)[17] What made Xi adopt a strategy that shook the fundamental principle of Deng Xiaoping, the paramount reform leader? Xi's move was incentivised by a bundle of politico-economic factors developed since his inception of power in late 2012.

First, after assuming leadership, Xi repeatedly highlighted the importance of China's rejuvenation, and he coined the conception "Chinese Dream" which entails the multi-target mission of doubling China's GDP during the period 2010–2020, raising the welfare of the people and making China stronger both domestically and diplomatically. The very first statement demonstrating Xi's gesture of highlighting China's new diplomatic role in the world was made during his visit to Washington DC in 2012. He described the relationship between China and the US as a "new type of relationship among major countries" (*xinxing daguo guanxi*) He explicitly stated in his remarks at the Politburo in December 2014, "make China's voice heard, and inject more Chinese elements into international rules". (Economy 2018: 186, 190) Xi's intention to exert more influence in the global political arena through the BRI is also a response to US President Barrack Obama's "rebalance to Asia" strategy advocated in 2011, which covers 4 major elements: (1) greatly engage China; (2) balance the first element with a strong alliance with Japan; (3) address the North Korean problem and (4) review free-trade agreements (Cha 2016). Xi's BRI is to counterweigh Obama's influence resulting from "rebalance to Asia" and elevate China's influence in shaping the economic and political order of the Asian-Pacific region.

Second, as discussed earlier, the slowdown of the Chinese economy since 2010 drove the central leaders to source a new growth engine for the economy. The countries along the BRI region consist of numerous emerging economies, which provide huge markets for China's exports. These potential markets are especially important for China as it faces increasing trade protection from the US. Apart from external trade, BRI provides an option for China to absorb its overcapacity. As examined in last chapter, in response to the downside economic pressure brought about by the outbreak of the GFC in 2008, the central government initiated a 4-trillion yuan stimulus package which prompted rapid credit expansion. The 2008 stimulus package intensified the already pressing problem of excess capacity. Local governments injected capital in investment projects through local government financial platforms to boost economic rebound. Excessive capacity is exceptionally serious in steel, cement, flat glass and electrolytic aluminium production. It is foreseeable that Central Asia, the Middle East and sub-Saharan Africa need investments in infrastructure on a massive scale in order to speed up economic development. In Asia alone, the Asia Development Bank (ADB) estimates that the demand for infrastructure investment will be up to $1.7 trillion every year until 2025 (Hewko 2017). Infrastructure investment along the countries of the BRI helps to reduce the size of China's excess capacity.

Third, China makes use of BRI to ensure its energy security. With its rapid economic growth over the past 4 decades, China has become one of the major energy consumption countries. By 2040, China's share of global energy demand is expected to rise to 24 percent. Over this period, natural gas demand will double from 6 to 13 percent, while the share of renewable resources is expected to rise from 3 to 18 percent. China's dependence for oil imports will rise from 63 to 72 percent, while the figure for gas imports will grow from 34 to 43 percent. China perceives its increasing reliance on oil and gas imports as a potential national security threat, particularly the import by sea route. It is estimated that 80 percent of China's crude oil import passes through the Strait of Malacca (Len 2018). BRI is used to diversify its import sources of energy and to explore alternative supply routes, including overland transit pipelines to avoid the possible risk of sea blockage. China can access new energy sources in Pakistan and Central Asia through the China-Pakistan Economic Corridor to diversify energy access and avoid volatility in the Middle East (Viehe, Gunasekaran and Downing 2015).

Fourth, BRI can serve as a channel to foster RMB internationalisation. The current use of RMB outside China is still limited. RMB only accounted for 2.5 percent of all international payments recorded by SWIFT,[18] in contrast to 43.3 percent for the US dollar and 28.7 percent for the euro. Further, about 70 percent of the international transactions involving the RMB were between Hong Kong and the mainland. If Hong Kong is excluded, RMB only accounts for 0.8% of global SWIFT payments (Graceffo 2017). However, it is predicted that through increased bilateral trade between China and countries along the BRI regions, RMB will be more widely used as settlement currency. The volume of bilateral trade between China and these countries rose from US$877.2 billion in 2012 to reach US$995.5 billion in 2015 (Xinhua 2016). The BRI also furthers RMB outflows through the capital account. RMB-denominated ODI entered 49 countries in the BRI regions, with investment amounting to US$14.8 billion in 2015, which registered a 18.2 percent growth from 2014 (Liu et al. 2017: 7). In addition, it is expected that BRI will heighten the role of RMB as an investment and reserve currency – a key feature of any global currency. Demand for RMB-denominated investment products has been increasing in BRI countries. These countries have demonstrated increased willingness to use RMB as a reserve asset (Peng and Liu 2016). This provides an opportunity to increase the scale and circulation of RMB in the BRI region.

It is undeniable that China's capital flowing into the infrastructure projects in the BRI countries best caters to the capital need in the region. Notwithstanding, some countries worry that China's loans and assistance to these developing countries would largely enhance China's presence and influence in these countries, which may shake the geopolitical balance in the BRI regions. Recent evidence suggests that this worry may not be overstated. In 2017, Sri Lanka was unable to repay its debt to its Chinese partners. Sri Lanka finally handed over the strategic port of Hambantota to China on a 99-year lease. The deal was severely criticised by domestic critics saying that it threatens the country's sovereignty (Schultz 2017). Zambia, following the footsteps of Sri Lanka, had to relinquish control of its international airport and a state power company to China in 2018. In addition, Tajik was willing to surrender its control over some 1,158 square kilometres of disputed territory close to its border with China's troubled Northwestern province of Xinjiang to China. In exchange, China agreed to write off an undisclosed amount of Tajik debt (Dorsey 2018). Increasing resistance against BRI has been observed across the region. In 2018, protests against forced resettlement of eight Nepali villages pressured the CWE Investment Corporation, a subsidiary of China Three Gorges, to consider cancelling a hydropower project. Malaysian Prime Minister Mahathir Mohamad has put a halt to a total of US$26 billion in Chinese-funded projects since his successful election in May 2018. Further, Myanmar has been negotiating to scale down markedly its Chinese-funded port project on the Bay of Bengal from $7.3 billion to $1.3 billion to avoid overborrowing (Chaudhury 2018).

BRI is one of China's most significant national development strategies in the 21st century, which was motivated by multi-dimensional political economy considerations. China's goal is much more than realising economic benefits. Rather, it aims to enhance its leading role in global development and governance as well as ensure national security amid dynamic geopolitics. It is China's grand plan to balance the US's global politics and hegemony, at least in the BRI regions. Whether BRI can successfully and smoothly be implemented rests on the mutual trust among participating countries, which in turn depends on an acceptable distribution of mutual benefits among countries. Even more important is that China has to build trust among participating countries that it would not make use of financial assistance and lending to jeopardise any country's sovereignty. To build trust in the region is by no means easy given the fact that some of the BRI countries are allies of the US and some, such as Russia and India, are potential rivals of China (Cheng 2016: 311). Besides political tension, the success of the BRI faces two other major challenges. There has been so far no coordination mechanism among BRI countries (Huang 2016: 320). Collaboration between China and these countries is largely achieved by bilateral negotiations. Lack of policy coordination framework in the BRI regions would mean very high transaction costs for bilateral and multilateral negotiations. It is especially true as each country has its own investment policies, financial regulations and legal framework. Second, China's financial sector has already extended substantial loans to finance infrastructure projects after the 2008 GFC to boom the downsizing economy. As examined in a previous chapter, some of these projects are not profitable, which hampers their repayability. Both NPLs amounts and ratios have been rising in recent years. Further extension of overseas loans may make China's financial sector more vulnerable to risks as the returns on the BRI projects are uncertain and default risks are possible (Varma, Paracuelles and Chan 2018). Both returns and cost recovery on infrastructure projects are, in general, relatively low. By the end of 2016, 89 percent of loans to BRI projects were financed by the 2 Chinese policy banks (the China Development Bank and the China Export-Import Bank) or from the big 4 state-owned commercial banks. Loans offered by the Silk Road Fund, the Asian Infrastructure Investment Bank (AIIB) and the New Development Bank (NDB) operated by the BRICS countries[19] account for less than 10 percent of the total (EURObiz 2019). This financing pattern implies that China's exposure to financial risks is proportionally higher.

Conclusion

Shambaugh (2013: 9) describes China's global presence as a "pattern of breadth but not depth, presence but not influence". However, China's development since 2013 seems to render Shambaugh's view invalid. China as the world's second largest economy, largest exporter and second largest importer could be a stabiliser, like what happened after the 2008 GFC, but it could also be a major destabilising factor as its economy has been heading towards a slowdown since 2010. The growth figure for the fourth quarter of 2018 went further downward to 6.4 percent from 6.5 percent in the third quarter. Import values soared 16.1 percent in 2017 but were followed by a decline of 7.6 percent in 2018 (Roach 2019). Any fluctuations in China's macroeconomy will have direct bearing on the stability of the global economy. Advanced countries, particularly the US, have been facing a paradox: a rapidly rising Chinese economy will threaten the economic and even political hegemony of the West, but China's economic slowdown will mean a weakening global demand and shrinking ODI, which will adversely affect the advanced countries' economy. No matter how the West perceives the rise of the Chinese economy, China has become a determining factor for global economic stability. That said, the "going out" strategy and the high profile BRI have raised politico-economic concern of not just the Western countries but also the BRI countries. China's expanding global footprint will emphatically encounter resistance from countries who perceive China's rise as a threat both economically and politically. Whether China can integrate further into the global economy and even take a leading role in international collaboration depends on China's ability to demonstrate mutually beneficial cooperation with partner countries, its commitment to issues of global governance and its enhancement of China's soft power in the global arena.

Notes

1 Data derived from Investopedia (2018a).
2 Data derived from The Guardian (2013).
3 For a snapshot of China's open economic zones and coastal cities, see "Opening to the Outside World", *China in Brief*. Available at: www.china.org.cn/e-china/openingup/sez.htm (Accessed on 31 December 2018)
4 See Chai (1997: 161).
5 In 1989, Hong Kong (including Macau), Taiwan and Japan, shared 84.3 percent of FDI in China while the US shared only 7.6 percent. See Chai (1997: 161).
6 Calculated based on the data from Table 17–3 and Table 17–12 of *China's Statistical Yearbook 1999*. Available at: www.stats.gov.cn/english/statisticaldata/yearlydata/YB1999e/index1.htm (Accessed on 10 February 2019) and Table 11–3 and Table 11–10 of *China's Statistical Yearbook 2018*. Available at: www.stats.gov.cn/tjsj/ndsj/2018/indexeh.htm (Accessed on 10 February 2019)
7 Jiang Zemin served as General Secretary of the Communist Party of China from 1989 to 2002, as Chairman of the Central Military Commission from 1989 to 2004 and as President of the People's Republic of China from 1993 to 2003.
8 For a discussion on the origin of the "going out" policy, please see Shambaugh (2013: 174–176).
9 Quote from Faiola (2009).
10 Data from Table 8.21 and 17.3 of *China's Statistical Yearbook 2001*. Available at: www.stats.gov.cn/english/statisticaldata/yearlydata/YB2001e/ml/indexE.htm (Accessed on 18 January 2018)
11 For a detailed discussion of China's concessions to the WTO, please see Lardy (2002: 63–105).
12 Dumping refers to the pricing strategy wherein a manufacturer lowers the price of a good entering a foreign market to a level that is lower than the price paid by domestic customers in the exporting country. Dumping is regarded as an unfair trade practice as the government may subsidise the exporting manufacturer so that it can sell the products below production costs. For further details, see Investopedia (2018b).
13 Quote from Lardy (2001).
14 The background information is mainly derived from Hong Kong Trade Development Council (2017).
15 For details of the Silk Road Fund, see www.silkroadfund.com.cn/enweb/23773/index.html (Accessed on 17 February 2019)
16 Data from official website of AIIB. Available at: www.aiib.org/en/about-aiib/who-we-are/third-anniversary/index.html (Accessed on 17 February 2019)
17 Quoted from Economy (2018: 188).
18 The Society for Worldwide Interbank Financial Telecommunication (SWIFT) provides a network that allows information exchange of financial transactions among financial institutions worldwide.
19 The BRICS countries refer to Brazil, Russia, India, China and South Africa.

References

Bloomberg (2018) 'China Deal Watch.' Available at: www.bloomberg.com/graphics/2016-china-deals/ (Accessed on 15 February 2019).

Boden, G. (2012) 'China's Accession to the WTO: Economic Benefits,' *The Park Place Economist*, Vol. 20. Available at: http://digitalcommons.iwu.edu/parkplace/vol20/iss1/8 (Accessed on 23 January 2019).

Branigan, T. and Stewart, H. (2010) 'China Sells $34.2bn of US Treasury Bonds,' *The Guardian*, 17 February. Available at: www.theguardian.com/business/2010/feb/17/china-sells-us-treasury-bonds (Accessed on 18 January 2019).

Buckley, P. J., Clegg, J. and Wang, C. (2002) 'The Impact of Inward FDI on the Performance of Chinese Manufacturing Firms,' *Journal of International Business Studies*, Vol. 33, No. 4, pp. 637–655.

Cha, V. (2016) 'The Unfinished Legacy of Obama's Pivot to Asia,' *Foreign Policy*, 6 September. Available at: https://foreignpolicy.com/2016/09/06/the-unfinished-legacy-of-obamas-pivot-to-asia/ (Accessed on 18 February 2019).

Chai, J. C. H. (1983) 'China's Open-Door Strategy: A Preliminary Assessment with Special Reference to the Foreign Trade Sector,' in Yoo, S-H. (ed.) *Political Leadership and Economic Development: Korea and China*, Seoul: The Institute for Sino-Soviet Studies, Hanyang University, pp. 104–132.

Chai, J. C. H. (1997) *China: Transition to a Market Economy*, Oxford: Clarendon Press.

Chaudhury, D. R. (2018) 'China Admits Challenges in BRI Amid Pushback,' *The Economics Times*, 24 September. Available at: https://economictimes.indiatimes.com/news/defence/china-admits-challenges-in-bri-amid-pushback/articleshow/65928923.cms (Accessed on 18 February 2019).

Cheng, E. (2018) 'China's Overseas Investment Drops in 2017 for the First Time on Record,' *CNBC*, 28 September. Available at: www.cnbc.com/2018/09/28/chinas-overseas-investment-drops-for-the-first-time-on-record.html (Accessed on 20 January 2019).

Cheng, L. K. (2016) 'Three Questions on China's "Belt and Road Initiatives",' *China Economic Review*, Vol. 40, pp. 309–313.

Chi, P. S. K. (1994) 'Hong Kong and Taiwan Enterprises in Mainland China: Acceleration of Economic Transformation and Development?' Paper presented at the *International Symposium China: A New Growth Centre in the World Economy*, Duisburg, Germany, July.

Dorsey, J. M. (2018) 'China Struggles with Belt and Road Pushback,' *BESA Center Perspectives Paper*, No. 965, 3 October. Available at: https://besacenter.org/perspectives-papers/china-belt-road-pushback/ (Accessed on 18 February 2019).

Economy, E. C. (2018) *The Third Revolution: Xi Jinping and the New Chinese State*, New York: Oxford University Press.

EURObiz (2019) 'The Belt and Road Initiative: Scope of Projects and Financing Issues,' *Journal of the European Union Chamber of Commerce in China*. Available at: www.eurobiz.com.cn/the-belt-road-initiative-scope-of-projects-and-financing-issues/ (Available on 18 February 2019).

Export.com (2017) 'China – 1- Openness to, & Restrictions Upon Foreign Investment.' Available at: www.export.gov/article?id=China-1-Openness-to-Restrictions-Upon-Foreign-Investment (Accessed on 9 February 2019).

Faiola, A. (2009) 'China Worried About U.S. Debt,' *Washington Post*, 14 March. Available at: www.washingtonpost.com/wp-dyn/content/article/2009/03/13/AR2009031300703.html?noredirect=on (Accessed on 18 January 2019).

Garver, J. (2006) *China and Iran*, Seattle: University of Washington Press.

Graceffo, A. (2017) 'The Chinese Yuan (RMB) as a Hard Currency,' *Foreign Policy Journal*. Available at: www.foreignpolicyjournal.com/2017/04/14/the-chinese-yuan-rmb-as-a-hard-currency/ (Accessed on 6 May 2018).

The Guardian (2013) 'China Surpasses US as World's Largest Trading Nation.' Available at: www.theguardian.com/business/2014/jan/10/china-surpasses-us-world-largest-trading-nation (Accessed on 17 December 2018).

Hewko, J. (2017) 'How Much Does It Cost to Power the World's Fastest Growing Economies?' *International Trade Forum*. Available at: www.tradeforum.org/article/How-much-does-it-cost-to-power-the-worlds-fastest-growing-economies/ (Accessed on 2 May 2018).

Hiemenz, U. (1990) 'Foreign Direct Investment and Capital Formation in China Since 1979: Implications for Economic Development,' in Cassel, D. and Heiduck, G. (eds.) *China's Contemporary Economics Reforms as a Development Strategy*, Baden-Baden: Nomos Publisher, pp. 85–104.

Hong Kong Trade Development Council (HKTDC) (2017) 'Belt and Road Initiative.' Available at: http://china-trade-research.hktdc.com/business-news/article/The-Belt-and-Road Initiative/The-Belt-and-Road-Initiative/obor/en/1/1X3CGF6L/1X0A36B7.htm (Accessed on 11 April 2018).

Huan, G. (1986) 'China's Open Door Policy 1979–1984,' *Journal of International Affairs*, Vol. 39, January, pp. 1–18.

Huang, W. and Wikes, A. (2011) 'Analysis of China's Overseas Investment Policies,' *Center for International Forestry Research, Working Paper*, No. 79. Available at: www.cifor.org/publications/pdf_files/WPapers/WP-79CIFOR.pdf (Accessed on 20 January 2019).

Huang, Y. (2016) 'Understanding China's Belt and Road Initiative: Motivation, Framework and Assessment,' *China Economic Review*, Vol. 40, pp. 314–321.

Hung, H. (2017) *The China Boom: Why China Will Not Rule the World*, New York: Columbia University Press.

Investopedia (2018a) 'What Country Is the World's Largest Export,' 21 October. Available at: www.investopedia.com/ask/answers/011915/what-country-worlds-largest-exporter-goods.asp (Accessed on 17 December 2018).

Investopedia (2018b) 'Dumping,' 31 January. Available at: www.investopedia.com/terms/d/dumping.asp (Accessed on 23 January 2019).

KPMG (2016) 'China ODI Surpassed FDI for the First Time in 2015,' 29 September. Available at: https://home.kpmg.com/cn/en/home/insights/2016/09/china-odi-exceeded-fdi-2015-private-sector.html (Accessed on 17 December 2018).

Kueh, Y. Y. (1992) 'Foreign Investment and Economic Change in China,' *China Quarterly*, No. 131, pp. 637–690.

Lardy, N. R. (2001) 'Issues in China's WTO Accession,' *Brookings, Testimony*, 9 May. Available at: www.brookings.edu/testimonies/issues-in-chinas-wto-accession/ (Accessed on 20 January 2019).

Lardy, N. R. (2002) *Integrating China into the Global Economy*, Washington, DC: The Brookings Institution.

Le, T. T. V. and Tong, S. Y. (2009) 'China and Anti-Dumping Regulations, Practices and Responses,' *EAI Working Paper*, No. 149. Available at: www.eai.nus.edu.sg/publications/files/EWP149.pdf (Accessed on 23 January 2019).

Len, C. (2018) 'Belt and Road Initiative: Beijing's Ambition to Be a Player in Global Energy Governance,' *China Policy Institute Analysis*. Available at: https://

cpianalysis.org/2018/03/27/belt-and-road-initiative-beijings-ambition-to-be-a-major-player-in-global-energy-governance/ (Accessed on 1 May 2018).

Lilly, S. (2009) 'Should We Be Grateful to China for Buying U.S. Treasuries?' *Centre for American Progress*. Available at: https://cdn.americanprogress.org/wp-content/uploads/issues/2009/04/pdf/lilly_china_report.pdf (Accessed on 8 January 2019).

Liu, D., Gao, H., Oxenford, M., Xu, Q., Song, S., Subacchi, P. and Li, Y. (2017) 'The "Belt and Road" Initiative and the London Market – The Next Steps in Renminbi Internationalization – Part 1: The View from Beijing,' *Research Paper*, Chatham House, The Royal Institute of International Affairs. Available at: www.chathamhouse.org/sites/files/chathamhouse/publications/research/2017-01-17-belt-road-renminbi-internationalization-liu-gao-xu-li-song.pdf (Accessed on 2 May 2018).

Nolt, J. H. (1999) 'China in the WTO: The Debate,' *Foreign Policy in Focus*, 1 December. Available at: https://fpif.org/china_in_the_wto_the_debate/ (22 January 2019).

Peng, H. and Liu, Z. (2016) 'The Belt and Road Initiative Promotes Renminbi Internationalization,' *People's Daily*, 31 May. Available at: http://opinion.people.com.cn/n1/2016/0531/c1003-28394302.html [in Chinese]. (Accessed on 6 May 2018).

Pomfret, R. (1991) *Investing in China: Ten Years of the Open Door Policy*, Hemel Hempstead: Harvester Wheatsheaf.

Roach, S. S. (2019) 'Warnings from the Global Trade Cycle,' *Project Syndicate*, 28 January. Available at: www.project-syndicate.org/commentary/global-trade-slowdown-weakening-economic-conditions-by-stephen-s-roach-2019-01?utm_source=Project+Syndicate+Newsletter&utm_campaign=0fba69ee69-sunday_newsletter_3_2_2019&utm_medium=email&utm_term=0_73bad5b7d8-0fba69ee69-93737041 (Accessed on 4 February 2019).

Saich, T. (2002) 'China as Member of the WTO: Political and Social Questions.' Available at: https://sites.hks.harvard.edu/fs/asaich/China%20and%20the%20WTO.pdf (Accessed on 24 January 2019).

Schultz, K. (2017) 'Sri Lanka, Struggling with Debt, Hands a Major Port to China,' *The New York Times*, 12 December. Available at: www.nytimes.com/2017/12/12/world/asia/sri-lanka-china-port.html (Accessed on 17 February 2019).

Shambaugh, D. (2013) *China Goes Global: The Partial Power*, New York: Oxford University Press.

Shepard, W. (2016) 'China Hits Record High M&A Investment in Western Firms,' *Forbes*, 10 September. Available at: www.forbes.com/sites/wadeshepard/2016/09/10/from-made-in-china-to-owned-by-china-chinese-enterprises-buying-up-western-companies-at-record-pace/#40a5cb635d87 (Accessed on 15 February 2019).

Subacchi, P. (2017) *The People's Money: How China Is Building a Global Currency*, New York: Columbia University Press.

Varma, S., Paracuelles, E. and Chan, C. (2018) 'The Belt and Road Initiative: Globalization, China Style,' *Nomura, Focus Thinking*, April. Available at: www.nomuraconnects.com/focused-thinking-posts/the-belt-and-road-initiative-globalisation-china-style/ (Accessed on 18 February 2019).

Viehe, A., Gunasekaran, A. and Downing, H. (2015) 'Understanding China's Belt and Road Initiatives: Opportunities and Risks,' *Foreign Policy and Security*. Available at: www.americanprogress.org/issues/security/reports/2015/09/22/121628/ understanding-chinas-belt-and-road-initiative/ (Accessed on 1 May 2018).

Wong, D. (2018) 'How to Read China's 2018 Negative List,' *China Briefing*, 7 July. Available at: www.china-briefing.com/news/how-to-read-chinas-2018-negative-list/ (Accessed on 9 February 2019).

World Bank (1988) *China: External Trade and Capital*, Washington, DC: World Bank.

Xinhua (2016) 'News Analysis: China's Yuan Heads for Global Currency Status,' 23 September. Available at: http://news.xinhuanet.com/english/2016--09/23/c_135708854.htm. (Accessed on 3 May 2018).

6 Population growth and human capital investment

Hindrance to growth?

Introduction

The Heckscher-Ohlin model (H-O model) states that a country can acquire comparative advantage in producing a good requiring a factor input that the country has in abundant supply. Put it straightforwardly, if a country is endowed with a plentiful supply of labour, the labour cost will naturally be lower relative to other countries with less labour supply. Then this country will possess the comparative advantage in producing labour-intensive product. The H-O model best explains China's comparative advantage of producing labour-intensive products, which had been very competitive in the international market in the 1980s and 1990s. China's export-oriented strategy adopted after the reform has contributed substantially to its economic growth and employment creation as discussed in the previous chapter. However, this chapter expounded that China's cost advantage in labour intensive products has encountered emerging challenges as its natural growth rate of population has been shrinking since the late 1990s. The so called population dividend gradually fades away as real wage has demonstrated persistent increase in the past two decades. In face of declining population and labour force, China needs to swiftly enhance its labour productivity in order to sustain economic growth. Nevertheless, labour productivity has also exhibited a waning trend since the 2008 GFC. To jump out of the low productivity trap, new policy initiatives are urgently needed to lift human capital through investment in education and appropriate on-the-job training.

Population ageing and labour force: the core issues

During the initial period of reform, China was endowed with a huge population of 54.17 million in 1949 and 97.54 million in 1979, registering a spectacular growth of 80.1 percent, which generated an abundant supply of labour for labour-intensive production. The labour pool was also contributed by China's rural surplus labour migrating to urban areas to provide a low-cost input for the manufacturing sector. This labour transfer enabled China to utilise its comparative advantage to boom the industrial production and export sector. Data of the 2010 census indicates that about 221 million rural workers had migrated to cities to fill job vacancies (National Bureau of Statistics of China 2011). However, China's comparative advantage in labour-intensive production has been hampered by two salient facts. First, the amount of rural surplus labour has been shrinking from 120 million in 1997 to about 25 million in 2015 (Purdy, Li and Light 2014: 4), which indicates that the size of surplus labour migrating to the urban sector's labour market has been dwindling considerably over the past two decades. Second, since the implementation of the one-child policy in 1979, birth rate had still risen for the subsequent years and peaked at 23.33 percent in 1987 (Table 6.1). Nevertheless, the birth rate has been diminishing since then and reached a new low of 10.94 in 2018, representing a noticeable drop of 12.39 percentage points. With a relatively stable death rate ranging from 6.21 to 7.16 percent, the natural growth rate of population in China had diminished from its historic high of 16.61 in 1987 to 9.14 percent in 1998 (Table 6.1), which was the first ever single-digit growth since the enactment of one-child policy. The falling trend has lasted for the past three decades, and the natural growth rate recorded an unprecedented slow growth of 3.81 percent in 2018.

Waning population growth has at least two implications. First, since the slowing birth rate accompanied with improving medical services, population ageing has been noticeable. China's life expectancy experienced a remarkable rise from 67.8 in 1981 to 76.6 in 2018[1] while the median age rose from 21.7 in 1980 to 37 in 2015 (Statista 2019a). The figure is predicted to grow further to 40.6 in 2025. Forecasts also indicate that China's elderly population aged at and above 60 will increase from 240 million in 2018 to 400 million in 2035 (ABC News 2019). Population ageing coupled with decreasing birth rate implies that the future younger generation needs to spend more resources to support the dependent aged population. China's "old dependency ratio" (ODR), which measures the ratio of population aged 65 or above to population aged between 15 and 64, grew relatively slowly from 8.0 percent in 1982 to 9.9 percent in 2000, representing a rise of 1.9 percentage points over a period of 18 years, but the ratio has soared since then and climbed to a record high of 15.9 percent, recording a jump of 6.0 percentage points in 17 years (Table 6.2). The ratio is prone to rise further in the coming decades. Provided that the younger generation is productive and the growth of real income is higher than the growth of the aged population, it would otherwise insert heavy fiscal pressure on providing services and support for the livelihood for the aged. Actually, the problem became evident when pension expenses rose 11.6 percent to 2.58 trillion yuan in 2016, which forced the use of government coffer to cover a shortfall of 429.1 billion yuan, according to the data from the Ministry of Finance. The shortfall could reach 890 billion yuan in 2020 as estimated by the National Academy of Economic Strategy in Beijing (The Straits Times 2018). Second, labour force has been dwindling since the mid-1980s. As indicated in Table 6.3, among the 28 years since 1991, the labour force experienced a growth of less than one percent for 17 years, and the problem of falling labour force has been remarkably apparent in recent years, with two consecutive years of negative growth in 2017 and 2018. Diminishing labour force unavoidably leads to rising wages (Table 6.6), which adversely affects the

Table 6.1 China's Birth Rate, Death Rate and Natural Growth Rate of Population 1978–2018 (percent)

Year	Birth rate	Death rate	Natural growth rate of population
1978	18.25	6.25	12.0
1979	17.82	6.21	11.61
1980	18.21	6.34	11.87
1981	20.91	6.36	14.55
1982	22.28	6.60	15.68
1983	20.19	6.90	13.29
1984	19.90	6.82	13.08
1985	21.04	6.78	14.26
1986	22.43	6.86	15.57
1987	23.33	6.72	16.61
1988	22.37	6.64	15.73
1989	21.58	6.54	15.04
1990	21.06	6.67	14.39
1991	19.68	6.70	12.98
1992	18.24	6.64	11.60
1993	18.09	6.54	11.45
1994	17.70	6.49	11.21
1995	17.12	6.57	10.55
1996	16.98	6.56	10.42
1997	16.57	6.51	10.06
1998	15.64	6.50	9.14
1999	14.64	6.46	8.18
2000	14.03	6.45	7.58
2001	13.38	6.43	6.95
2002	12.86	6.41	6.45
2003	12.41	6.40	6.01
2004	12.29	6.42	5.87
2005	12.40	6.51	5.89
2006	12.09	6.81	5.28
2007	12.10	6.93	5.17
2008	12.14	7.06	5.08
2009	11.95	7.08	4.87
2010	11.90	7.11	4.79
2011	11.93	7.14	4.79
2012	12.10	7.15	4.95
2013	12.08	7.16	4.92
2014	12.37	7.16	5.21
2015	12.07	7.11	4.96
2016	12.95	7.09	5.86
2017	12.43	7.11	5.32
2018	10.94	7.13	3.81

Source: China Statistical Yearbook 2018, Table 2.2. Available at: www.stats.gov.cn/tjsj/ndsj/2018/indexeh.htm (accessed on 22 February 2019); China Statistical Yearbook 2001, Table 4.2. Available at: www.stats.gov.cn/english/statisticaldata/yearlydata/YB2001e/ml/indexE.htm (accessed on 22 February 2019); China Internet Watch (2019)

Table 6.2 Old Dependency Ratio (ODR) 1982–2017

Year	ODR (percent)
1982	8.0
1990	8.3
1995	9.2
2000	9.9
2005	10.7
2010	11.9
2011	12.3
2012	12.7
2013	13.1
2014	13.7
2015	14.3
2016	15.7
2017	15.9

Source: China Statistical Yearbook 2018: Table 2.5. Available at: www.stats.gov.cn/tjsj/ndsj/2018/indexeh.htm (Accessed on 3 March 2019)

competitiveness of China's products in the international market. The Ministry of Human Resources and Social Security estimated that the labour force would undergo continuous decline and reach 700 million in 2050, which is about the level in 1997 (Wu 2016). It is foreseeable that labour shortage and rising wages will become increasingly prominent in the coming 2 decades.

Central leaders have been well aware of the problem of depopulation and have tried to relax the one-child policy in 2013 for couples: if either one was a single child, the couple was allowed to have two babies. To act further, the central government abolished its decades long one-child policy in 2016,[2] with an aim to revert the shrinking trend of labour force. However, the policy has not incentivized couples to give birth to more babies. There are some obvious reasons for the low inclination to have a second child. According to a survey done by the China Youth Daily, 84.9 percent of respondents indicated that they were worried about the financial pressure of raising a second child (Liu 2015). It is especially true in big cities such as Beijing and Shanghai where the cost of housing and education is comparatively higher. The survey found that couples who are wealthy enough to bring up a second child are usually aged over 40, which is not most suitable for giving birth. Instead, young couples prefer having "a better child" to "more children". According to the 2009 urban household survey, a one-child household in China spends an average of 10.6 percent of its total income on education, whereas a household with twins spends 17.3 percent. It is estimated that as China has more two-children families, the aggregate saving rate in China will fall by 7 to 10 percentage points from 2009 to 2019. This presents a dilemma. Encouraging higher birth rate may mean less education investment per child, which could lead to a lower level of human capital per capita. Actually, the survey reveals that the average twin receives far less support after age 15 than the average only child,

Table 6.3 China's Labour Force 1978–2018 (10,000 persons)

Year	Labour force*	Growth rate
1978	40682	–
1979	41592	2.24
1980	42903	3.15
1981	44165	2.94
1982	45674	3.42
1983	46707	2.26
1984	48433	3.70
1985	50112	3.47
1986	51546	2.86
1987	53060	2.94
1988	54630	2.96
1989	55707	1.97
1990**	64483	15.75
1991	65399	1.42
1992	66184	1.20
1993	67033	1.28
1994	67879	1.26
1995	68737	1.26
1996	69665	1.35
1997	70580	1.31
1998	71407	1.17
1999	71983	0.81
2000	73992	2.79
2001	73884	-0.15
2002	74492	0.82
2003	74911	0.56
2004	75290	0.51
2005	76120	1.10
2006	76315	0.26
2007	76531	0.28
2008	77046	0.67
2009	77510	0.60
2010	78388	1.13
2011	78579	0.24
2012	78894	0.40
2013	79300	0.51
2014	79690	0.49
2015	80091	0.50
2016	80694	0.75
2017	80686	-0.01
2018	80216	-0.58

Source: China Statistical Yearbook (2001: 108, 2005: 117, 2011: 112, 2015: Table 4.1, 2018: Table 4.1); Bloomberg (2019a)

Notes
* Labour force refers to the population aged at or above 16 who are participating in or willing to participate in economic activities.
** Data on economically active population from 1990 to 2000 are estimated on the basis of the 2000 National Population Census and the annual Sample Survey on Labour Force. Therefore, figures since 1990 are not strictly comparable with those from 1978 to 1989.

Table 6.4 Sex Ratio for Population Aged 0–4

Year	Sex ratio (female = 100)
1980	106.4
1990	108.5
2000	113.5
2010	116.7
2017	114.5

Source: Calculated based on the data from China Statistical Yearbook 2018: Table 2.9. Available at: www.stats.gov.cn/tjsj/ndsj/2018/indexeh.htm (accessed on 4 March 2019); China Power Team (2016)

resulting in clear differences in education attainment. Twins are 40 percent more likely to go to a vocational high school than only children (Jin 2016). On top of economic consideration, this generation of young couples, unlike their parents, does not perceive having a child as must for a family, which reflects a change in social value. Further, the implementation of the one child policy prior to 2016 has generated an unintended outcome of sex ratio imbalance. Table 6.4 shows that the sex ratio for males and females aged 0–4 has demonstrated steady rise from 106.4 in 1980 to 114.5 in 2017. It is difficult to collect hard evidence on gender-selective abortion, but adoption figures suggest that parents tend to give up their female children to adoption agencies. Between 1999 and 2013, Americans adopted 71,632 children from China, of which nearly 90 percent were female (China Power Team 2016). Sex ratio imbalance reduces the number of women of childbearing age (15–49). There were 380 million women of child-bearing age in 2010, which shrank to 346 million in 2018 (Global Times 2018). Most probably, this declining trend will continue during the 13th Five-Year Plan (2016–20). The number of childbearing-aged women will diminish by 5 million a year, which will further lower the fertility rate (Mu 2018). This unintended repercussion of the one-child policy, combined with rising economic costs of raising children, makes population rebound difficult.

Labour productivity and wage growth: a further impediment

As discussed earlier, the abolition of the one-child policy seems not very motivating for couples to have more children. After a slight rebound from 12.07 in 2015 to 12.95 in 2016, the birth rate dropped again to 12.43 in 2017 and diminished further to a historic low of 10.94 in 2018 (Table 6.1). Correspondingly, labour force has entered a period of slow growth since 2011, with an annual growth rate less than 0.5 percentage point. The contribution of the labour force to output growth can be decomposed into two components: the quantity of labour and the marginal product of labour. If the labour force is unlikely to rebound in the coming two decades, to counterweigh the impact of sinking labour force, labour productivity, defined as real output per worker, must be raised to sustain output (i.e., economic) growth. Seminal work by Schultz (1961) emphasizes the importance of human capital as a contributor to productivity and economic growth. Human capital can be broadly defined as "the knowledge, skills, competencies and attributes embodied in individuals that facilitate the creation of personal, social and economic well-being' (Keeley 2007). Whalley and Zhao (2010) make use Schultz's concept to develop a human capital measure and evaluate the contribution of human capital to China's economic growth. The results indicate that human capital plays an important part in China's economic growth. It is estimated that human capital contributes 38.12 percent of economic growth during the period 1978–2008, and the contribution is even higher for 1999–2008, reaching 39.41 percent, which is probably attributable to accelerated expansion of higher education after 1999. However, while growth rates of GDP demonstrate little change over the period after 1999, total factor productivity (TFP) growth falls from 16.92 percent of growth between 1978 and 2008 to -7.03% between 1999 and 2008 (Table 6.5). TFP measures the proportion of output not explained by the inputs (i.e., capital and labour) used for production.[3] Negative TFP growth suggests that the efficiency of inputs use has diminished or worsened misallocation of physical and human capital. It can also be caused by stagnant growth in technology and production knowhow. Recent statistics seem to echo this point. As mentioned earlier, to sustain China's long term growth, a decreasing workforce has to be compensated by enhanced labour productivity. However, statistics exhibits that labour productivity has been dwindling since the 2008 GFC. Labour productivity growth (LPG) fell from the high point of 10.24 percent in 2010 to 6.85 percent in 2017 (Table 6.6). If efficiency of labour use does not have any marked change and the real GDP maintains its diminishing trend, LPG would probably taper off further in the coming two decades (Table 6.7).

Decreasing LPG does not necessarily imply vanishing competitiveness of Chinese products if labour productivity growth (LPG) is higher than real wage growth (RWG). Notwithstanding, among the 10 years from 2008 to 2017, there are only 3 years that LPG is higher than RWG by a very thin margin (Table 6.6). As analysed earlier, the shrinking trend of labour force will continue due to ongoing decline in population growth. Amid declining economic growth, China's unemployment rate maintains a stable level, with an average of 4.09 percent from 2002 to 2018. The unemployment rate even shows a falling trend in recent years,

Table 6.5 Contribution to GDP Growth (%)

	1978–2008	1978–1999	1999–2008
Physical capital stock	44.96%	36.35	67.62
Human capital stock	38.12%	37.00%	39.41%
Total factor productivity	16.92%	26.65%	–7.03%

Source: Whalley and Zhao (2010)

Table 6.6 China's Labour Productivity and Real Wage Growth 2008–2018

Year	Labour Productivity Growth* (LPG)	Real Wage Growth (RWG)	LPG–RWG
2008	9.30	10.7	−1.4
2009	9.02	12.6	−3.58
2010	10.24	9.8	0.44
2011	9.09	8.6	0.49
2012	7.46	9.0	−1.54
2013	7.38	7.3	0.08
2014	6.93	7.2	−0.27
2015	6.65	8.5	−1.85
2016	6.49	6.7	−0.21
2017	6.85	8.2	−1.35

Source: CEIC (2018); China Statistical Yearbook 2014 (Table 4.11) Available at: www.stats.gov.cn/tjsj/ndsj/2014/indexeh.htm (accessed on 1 March 2019); China Statistical Yearbook 2018 (Table 4.12). Available at: www.stats.gov.cn/tjsj/ndsj/2018/indexeh.htm (accessed on 1 March 2019)

Notes
* Labour productivity is calculated by dividing the real GDP by number of workers.
** Estimated by the author, based on the data from Conference Board (2018). The estimate here is higher than that in Table 6.2 because the author uses the actual growth rate (i.e., 6.6 percent) of China's GDP in 2018 while Conference Board (2018) uses an estimated growth of 4 percent of GDP for estimation.

Table 6.7 Forecast of Average Annual Growth of Labour Productivity by Period

Period	Average annual growth of labour productivity (%)
1995–2010	8.9
2011–2015	8.3
2016–2020	7.1
2021–2025	6.2
2026–2030	5.5

Source: Statista (2019b)

with a gradual decline from 4.05 in 2015 to 3.80 in 2018.[4] Though no comprehensive data are available to illustrate the tight labour market, anecdotal evidence indicates that labour shortage exists in some localities. A study done to survey 20 factories in Dongguan, Guangdong, a major manufacturing base in China, in 2019 reveals that factories have encountered difficulties in recruiting workers. Some of the factories have to offer a wage increase from 9 to 20 percent for new recruits and some go directly to remote villages to tag new labour sources (Bloomberg 2019b). It is thus plausible to predict that RWG will continue to outpace LPG especially in labour intensive production, which implies that the negative impact brought by increasing RWG could not be offset by increasing labour productivity.

In relative terms, China's LPG remains strong and is the highest among advanced countries and BRICS countries, except India, as indicated in Table 6.8. However, China's competitive edge in labour costs has been fading, when labour productivity is taken into account. China's average hourly wages escalated for about 3 times from 2005 to 2016 and reached US$3.6 per hour, according to a study by Euromonitor (China Economic Review 2017). It is estimated that the hourly wage moved up further to US$4.2 in 2018.[5] Compared with US's hourly wage of US$21.6,[6] China's hourly wage is only 19.4 percent of that of the US, but at the time, China's labour productivity was only 21.9 percent of that of the US. It reveals that China does not possess a marked advantage over the US in terms of labour costs if labour productivity is considered as well. Among the BRICS countries, Brazil and South Africa have a higher labour productivity than China, but hourly wages fell from $2.90 to $2.70 in Brazil and from $4.30 to $3.60 in South Africa between 2005 and 2016. India's labour productivity is about 66.7 percent of that of China, but India's hourly wage is just a meager US$0.7, which is about 19.4 percent of China's level. (China Economic Review 2019). Taking into account both hourly wage and labour productivity, China's competitiveness has been less impressive particularly when wage level is expected to rise, and labour productivity has been exhibiting a waning trend.

The way out of population constraint: a quantitative and qualitative approach

As discussed earlier, real output growth is contributed to by expansion of the labour force (quantitative dimension) and/or rise of labour productivity (qualitative dimension). From a quantitative perspective, growth of labour force is directly related to population growth, which is in turn dependent on raising the fertility rate. Some delegates of the 13th National People's Congress (NPC) submitted proposals advocating abandonment of the decades long policy of family planning, which has been implemented since the late 1970s to restrict the birth

Table 6.8 Labour Productivity Growth in Advanced and BRICS Countries 2018

Country	Labour productivity growth	Labour productivity relative to US (US = 100)
China	4.3	21.9
US	1.5	100
UK	0.8	71.6
Germany	1.4	75.0
Japan	0.9	64.1
India	5.2	14.6
Russia	0.9	45.9
Brazil	−0.2	24.4
South Africa	0.2	34.4

Source: Conference Board (2018)

rate (Stanway 2019). The central government has viewed family planning as a vital policy to improve people's material wellbeing and poverty reduction. The proposed abolition of family planning signifies a complete policy turnaround. Nonetheless, even without family planning, studies show that "fertility desire" in China is only about 1.6 to 1.8, far lower than replacement fertility rate of 2.1.[7] Worse still, the actual fertility rate is much lower than the desired fertility rate. The fifth national census in 2000 unveiled that China's total fertility rate was only 1.22 and fell further to 1.18 in the sixth national census in 2010. Such a low fertility rate it naturally leads to depopulation. Though the fertility rate rose to 1.62 in 2016, it is largely below the world average of 2.439 and is the lowest among all BRICS countries (Table 6.9). As Mu (2018) points out, women's "fertility desire" has shifted from being eager "to give birth" to "don't want to" or "can't afford to" give birth. It partially explains why the abolition of the one-child policy has not effectively boosted the fertility rate. Relative to this change in "fertility desire", the abolition of the one-child policy comes too late to revert the trend of shrinking population. That said, government policies are still desperately needed to raise population growth, which may upturn the labour force in 2035–2040. This rise is crucial to counterweigh the rapidly ageing population. According to the United Nation's statistics, 9.5 percent of China's population was 65 or above in 2015, but the figure will soar to 27.5 percent in 2050 (China Power Team 2016).

Among the various constraining factors for raising fertility rate is opportunity cost, more specifically time cost, of raising a child. The time utilised for raising a child can be very plentiful. The income foregone for giving birth and raising a child could be very substantial, in particular for those middle- and high-income parents. China can learn from the experience in France, which achieved a fertility rate of 1.96 in 2016 that is closer to the optimal replacement rate of 2.1 percent, compared with a fertility rate of 1.8 in both the US and UK, 1.5 in Germany and 1.44 in Japan (World Bank 2017). In France, women are entitled 16 weeks of full pay maternity leave and men are allowed 11 days paternity leave with full pay. The amount of paid leave will increase when a woman gives birth to more children. France not only allows for paid maternity and paternity leave but also creates a less costly and more family friendly environment as well as pro-child policies for

Table 6.9 Fertility Rates in BRICS Countries 2016

Country	Fertility rate
World	2.44
China	1.62
India	2.33
Russia	1.75
Brazil	1.73
South Africa	2.46

Source: World Bank (2017)

raising children. The government has sponsored the provision of wide-ranging child-care services, including public day care, subsidized private day care, part-time babysitter and company day care. France has earmarked a budget of almost 3 percent of the GDP each year for these supportive measures for parents (Smith 2015; Croxell 2015). To further alleviate prospective parents' burden and concern, China needs to enhance the quality and scope of its subsidized education especially for higher education, medical services and public services in general. Actually, the Chinese government has taken some initiatives in changing the tax policy to alleviate the financial burden on parents. With effect on 1 January 2019, an amount of RMB12,000 will be deducted each year from the parent's taxable income for the education of each child (Kaizen CPA Limited 2019). This is a desirable but limited step. Tax breaks should be given to parents with newborn babies and tax deduction should be increased for couples with more children. Tax deductions should be increased every year for each child, preferably progressive increase, to cope with rising expenditure on education when the children grow up. However, incentive and support policies for raising children are not commonly effective around the world. Taking Japan as example, Japan has one of the most generous supportive policies for childbearing women in Asia. The government provides a 420,000 yen baby bonus, 14 weeks of maternity leave allowance amounting to 67 percent of the mother's monthly salary and child leave allowance of up to 50 percent of the mother's salary for 10.5 months if mothers need to take leave to look after their children (Minajp.com 2016). With such generous policies, Japan's fertility rate, 1.44 in 2016, remains one of the lowest in Asia. It illustrates that there are other factors, such as the declining population at childbearing age, that constrain the rise of fertility rate. The change in social value also plays a significant role in low fertility rate as mentioned earlier. After decades of social and economic transformation, the new generation does not perceive having children as a "must" or an important part of marriage, unlike their parents' generation. They put more emphasis on their own satisfaction, lifestyle and leisure instead of raising children (DW News 2019). While it is considerably difficult to raise fertility rate and population in short term, it is more feasible to raise retirement age to slow down the shrinking labour force. Currently, male workers in China are required to retire at 60 while female worker at 55. Thanks to the improvement of medical services, workers at retirement age are still physically fit for their current and other posts. Extending the retirement age to 65 for both male and female workers will not only increase labour supply but also slow down the pace of the rising dependency population. It indirectly attenuates the degree of pension shortfall mentioned earlier. Rising retirement age is only a partial solution; the long term solution unavoidably rests on population and labour productivity growth.

The response to the new policy allowing couples to have two children has been modest, and the effects of proposed pro-child measures are uncertain. The more immediate and practical solution to the declining labour force is to elevate labour productivity. Nevertheless, recent labour productivity, as examined earlier, has exhibited a deteriorating trend, which deserves immediate attention. Labour productivity demonstrates a promising growth prior to 2010, which was attributable to a number of factors. First, huge amount of surplus labour moving from low-value-added agricultural activities to high-value-added industrial and service sectors remarkably escalates the output value per migrant worker. Second, over the past two decades, private enterprises (PEs) have accomplished an important mission of absorbing the layoffs from downsized SOEs and generating new jobs for the labour force. The number of workers employed by PEs in urban areas skyrocketed from 45.81 million in 2007 to 75.57 million in 2012, and soared to 120.83 in 2016. In contrast, employment in SOE has shrunk from 64.24 to 61.7 million workers in 2007 and 2016 respectively. Taking a broader perspective, the state sector only created 14.9 percent of urban employment, and the non-state sector created about 85.1 percent of urban employment in 2016. The transfer of redundant labour with very low marginal products from the sector to the more efficiently operated private sector has raised the productivity of the transferred workers. The previous two factors indicate that the rise of labour productivity in the 1980s and 1990s was largely contributed by the reallocation of labour force from low-value-added sectors to high-value-added sectors. Apart from labour reallocation, rapid expansion of education since 1976 has also played an essential role in improving labour productivity by nourishing the labour force with basic literacy and work skills, which are conducive to the development of manufacturing and service industries. The amount of schooling for the age group 25–64 rose from 4.3 years in 1980 to 9.6 years in 2015 (Li et al. 2017: 27). Last but not least, the enhancement of labour productivity in the first two decades of reform is partially ascribable to the huge inflow of FDI, which brought physical capital (machinery and equipment), human capital (training) and managerial skills that generated enormous positive impact on labour productivity.[8]

What makes China's labour productivity slow down? One obvious explanation is that labour productivity was at very low level during the initiative years of economic reform. With a low base, the favourable factors just mentioned would probably cause a big jump in productivity growth. When labour productivity rises to a much higher level, with the same amount of real output growth, the growth rate will become smaller. Though this explanation is by no means invalid, there are some real factors which cause bottlenecks for labour productivity growth.

First, China's labour market is separated by the *hukou* system (i.e., household registration system). From 1950 to 1980, a rural resident could only live in and work in his/her registered location with minimal mobility. Though the system was relaxed in the early 1990s, which allowed rural residents to move around different localities and even migrate to urban areas to work, their administrative restrictions remain unchanged. That means their social, medical and education registration is still attached to their registered localities. The *hukou* system separates two distinctive groups of rural and urban residents whose social, medical and education provision have been in stark contrast. Rural residents, particularly in poor and remote areas, receive a much lower quality and provision of social services and education opportunities. In 2015, only 11.3 percent of rural workers aged 25–64 received senior secondary school education while 44.1 percent of urban workers in the same age group obtained senior secondary education (Li et al. 2017). It is noteworthy that rural workers still occupied about 45.3 percent of China's labour force in 2017.[9] A large number of rural workers has migrated to urban areas to work. It is estimated that there were 287 million migrant workers in China in 2017, which was about 30 percent of the total working population. Most of these workers are unskilled and semi-skilled labour due to their low education attainment and lack of training. About 70 percent of migrant workers receive junior secondary school education or below (National Bureau of Statistics 2018). That said, migrant workers have provided a huge pool of labour force to boost China's spectacular growth over the last four decades. However, migrant workers' *hukou* registration makes their children unable to enroll in formal schools and receive social and medical services in the cities on par with the urban residents. The number of children of migrant workers has remained at a level around 100 million since 2005. According to the *Annual Survey of Migrant Workers 2017*, most of the migrant workers indicate that high fees, difficult access to education and lack of childcare are the biggest challenges facing them (National Bureau of Statistics 2018). Rural residents, rural workers, migrant workers and their children have long lagged behind their urban counterparts in terms of quantity and quality of education, social support and medical services, but they constitute a potential pool of labour force to compensate for the declining labour force. The lack of education and training of migrant workers and their next generation limit the growth of labour productivity. If their education and training can be enhanced to a level closer to that of urban residents, their labour productivity will likely be lifted. Of migrant workers aged 16–40, 52.4 percent are still highly trainable either in formal education or on-the-job training. They may not fill the high-end posts, such as professional and managerial posts, in the cities, but they are perfectly fit for filling the gap of labour shortage in semi-skilled and technician posts in manufacturing industries.

Second, the labour force has been much educated in recent years and almost half of the newly increased labour force has received university education, which in principle should foster labour productivity. Nonetheless, skills mismatch has become more prominent over the past years. There is a gap between the skills and knowledge obtained by the graduates from universities and those needed by labour market especially in those high-end industries. It explains why the number of university graduates increases but does not correlate with an increase in real output per graduate. Data shows that high-skilled talents needed for industrial upgrade and professional sectors only account for 4 percent of China's labor market, common-skilled labor force 20 percent and unskilled labour 76 percent (Wu 2016). A survey of 2,361 employers covering 4,017,026 employees reveals that companies encounter difficulties in recruiting professionals to fill the posts of senior management in sales, marketing, research and development, engineering, accounting and finance, operations, technical, human resources and IT (Hays 2019). These posts are those high-value-added positions in the market. If a new labour force is incapable of filling these posts, it will certainly impede China's economic upgrade. Table 6.10 illustrates that employment rate of university graduates has gradually diminished

Table 6.10 Employment Rate of University Graduates and Vocational College Graduates 2013–2017 (percent)

Year	Bachelor	Vocational college graduate
2013	91.8	90.9
2014	92.6	91.5
2015	92.2	91.2
2016	91.8	91.5
2017	91.6	92.1

Source: Statista (2019c)

since 2014 while the employment rate of vocational college graduates has demonstrated a more stable trend with slight increase in 2016 and 2017. These figures may reflect that the current skills acquired by university graduates may not fit the market demand for graduates who could serve the upgrading economy. Skills mismatch hampers the efficient use of human capital. Increasing amounts of resources have been diverted to train university students, but the positive impact on labour productivity growth is not that obvious. Emphasis must be put on the skill sets needed in the market and the proper training in the universities.

Conclusion

The current population problem is ironically due to the very successful implementation of one child-policy adopted four decades ago when such a policy was needed to curb excessive population growth to ensure households' material wellbeing. A belated relaxation of the one-child policy has makes it difficult, if not impossible, to revert the trend of declining birth rate that has taken place since the 1990s. Shrinking population, falling labour force and population ageing constitute a constraining factor for China's sustained growth. Combined with rising wage and waning labour productivity growth, central leaders' policy initiatives are badly needed to enhance China's labour productivity to offset the negative impact of depopulation. The Chinese government needs to tap the rural labour force and migrant workers as well as their next generation and equip them with appropriate education and on-the-job training to upgrade them to be skilled labourers and sophisticated technicians to support industrial upgrade. In the domain of higher education, prompt assessment is needed to look into what skill sets and knowledge are pertinent to China's economic upgrading. The persistence of skills mismatch reflects the inefficient use of human capital investment. As China gradually develops away from labour-intensive production to high-value-added production and services, such as ICT and innovation industries, the quality of human capital is of primary importance. China's future development could be sustained if the rise of labour productivity outpaces the decline in labour force. Upgrading human capital for rural workers and migrant workers as well as reducing the skills mismatch in higher education are the vital clues to success.

Notes

1 Data from China Statistical Yearbook 2018, Table 2–4. Available at: www.stats. gov.cn/tjsj/ndsj/2018/indexeh.htm (accessed on 7 March 2019); 'China Life Expectancy, 1951–2018.' Available at: https://knoema.com/atlas/China/topics/ Demographics/Population-forecast/Life-expectancy (Accessed on 7 March 2019).
2 On 29 October 2015, the 18th central committee of the Chinese Communist Party (CPC) issued a communiqué announcing that all Chinese couples will be allowed to have two children. The new policy has been effective from March 2016 after formal endorsement by the National People's Congress (Liu 2015).
3 For a brief discussion on the concept of TFP, see Comin (2006).
4 Data from www.ceicdata.com/en/indicator/china/unemployment-rate and https:// tradingeconomics.com/china/unemployment-rate (Accessed on 9 March 2019).
5 China's hourly wage in 2018 is estimated based on the growth rates derived from Table 6.6.
6 Calculated based on the data from Trading Economics (2019).
7 It refers to any fertility rate below the replacement rate that would cause the population of a certain group of people to decrease over time. If a population's fertility rate falls below the replacement rate, that means that adults fail to produce enough offspring to even replace themselves. The sub-replacement fertility rate is generally considered to be anything below the replacement fertility rate of 2.1 children per woman in developed countries (The Hindu 2019). If each woman gives birth to 2.1 children, it is adequate to sustain the population. The closer a country gets to replacement fertility, the less the country will encounter either a population explosion or a collapse (Smith 2015). The replacement rate varies among different countries. In general, the replacement rate is higher in developing countries where the infant mortality rate is higher than in the developed countries due to medical, hygienic and nutrition reasons.
8 For a thorough discussion on the impacts of FDI on the Chinese economy, please refer to Chapter 5 of this book.
9 Calculated based on the data from *China Statistical Year 2018* (Table 4–1).

References

ABC News (2019) 'China's Ageing Population, Low Birth Rate to Cause "Unstoppable" Population Decline, Experts Say,' 6 January. Available at: www.abc.net. au/news/2019-01-06/chinese-declining-population-going-into-overdrive/ 10687996 (Accessed on 3 March 2019).

Bloomberg (2019a) 'China Sees Fewest Births in 2018 Since Mao's Great Famine.' Available at: www.bloomberg.com/news/articles/2019-01-21/china-sees-fewest-births-in-2018-since-mao-s-great-famine (Accessed on 27 February 2019).

Bloomberg (2019b) 'China's Factories Are Struggling to Hire Enough Workers.' Available at: www.bloomberg.com/news/articles/2019-03-07/what-trade-war-china-s-factory-hub-can-t-hire-enoughworkers?utm_campaign=Marketing_Cloud&utm_medium=email&utm_source=USCBC+News+Overview+3.8.2019&%20 utm_content=https%3a%2f%2fwww.bloomberg.com%2fnews%2farticles%2f2019-03-07%2fwhat-trade-war-china-s-factory-hub-can-t-hire-enough-workers (Accessed on 9 March 2019).

CEIC (2018) 'China Labour Productivity Growth.' Available at: www.ceicdata.com/ en/indicator/china/labour-productivity-growth (Accessed on 20 February 2019).

China Economic Review (2017) 'Chinese Wages Higher than Brazil, Mexico,' 27 February. Available at: https://chinaeconomicreview.com/chinese-wages-higher-brazil-mexico/ (Accessed on 10 March 2019).

China Internet Watch (2019) 'China's Population Growth and Birth Rate Reached a Shocking Low in 2018,' 23 January. Available at: www.chinainternetwatch.com/28107/population-2018/ (Accessed on 22 February 2019).

China Power Team (2016) 'Does China Have an Aging Problem?' *China Power*, 15 February. Updated August 11, 2017. Available at: https://chinapower.csis.org/aging-problem/ (Accessed on 3 March 2019).

China Statistical Yearbook 2001, Beijing: Zhongguo Tongji Chubanshe.

China Statistical Yearbook 2005, Beijing: Zhongguo Tongji Chubanshe.

China Statistical Yearbook 2011, Beijing: Zhongguo Tongji Chubanshe.

China Statistical Yearbook 2015. Available at: http://www.stats.gov.cn/tjsj/ndsj/2015/indexeh.htm (Accessed on 11 November 2019).

China Statistical Yearbook 2018. Available at: http://www.stats.gov.cn/tjsj/ndsj/2018/indexeh.htm (Accessed on 11 November 2019).

China Statistical Yearbook 2018. Available at: http://www.stats.gov.cn/tjsj/ndsj/2018/indexeh.htm (Accessed on 11 November 2019)

Comin, D. (2006) 'Total Factor Productivity.' Available at: www.people.hbs.edu/dcomin/def.pdf (Accessed on 9 March 2019).

Conference Board (2018) 'Total Economy Database – Key Findings.' Available at: www.conference-board.org/data/economydatabase/ (Accessed on 21 February 2019).

Croxell, A. (2015) 'France vs U.S. – Paid Maternity and Paternity Leave,' *Peacock Plume*, 11 October. Available at: http://peacockplume.fr/opinions/france/france-vs-us-paid-maternity-and-paternity-leave (Accessed on 17 March 2019).

DW News (2019) 'China's Birth Rate Falls to Historic Low,' 21 January. Available at: www.dw.com/en/chinas-birth-rate-falls-to-historic-low/a-47166326 (Accessed on 16 March).

Global Times (2018) 'China Records 7m Fewer Childbearing-Age Women than Previous Year,' 25 July. Available at: www.globaltimes.cn/content/1112354.shtml (Accessed on 4 March 2019).

Hays (2019) 'China's Tight Talent Market: The Skills Shortage May Hinder Growth Warns Hays.' Available at: www.hays.cn/en/press-releases/HAYS_248696 (Accessed on 17 March 2019).

The Hindu (2019) 'What Is Sub-Replacement Fertility in Demography,' 28 February. Available at: www.thehindu.com/opinion/op-ed/what-is-sub-replacement-fertility-in-demography/article26390014.ece (Accessed on 15 March 2019).

Jin, K. (2016) 'Why the End of the One-Child Policy Is a Major Opportunity for China,' *World Economic Forum*, 6 January. Available at: www.weforum.org/agenda/2016/01/why-the-end-of-the-one-child-policy-is-a-major-opportunity-for-china (Accessed on 3 March 2019).

Kaizen CPA Limited (2019) 'China Interim Measure for Individual Income Tax Itemised Additional Deductions 2019 (Consultation Draft).' Available at: www.bycpa.com/download/china/China%20Interim%20Measures%20for%20Individual%20Income%20Tax%20Itemised%20Additional%20Deductions%202019.pdf (Accessed on 16 March 2019).

Keeley, B. (2007) *Human Capital, How What You Know Shapes Your Life*, Paris: OECD Insights.

Li, H., Loyalka, P., Rozelle, S. and Wu, B. (2017) 'Human Capital and China's Future Growth,' *Journal of Economic Perspectives*, Vol. 31, No. 1, pp. 25–48.

Liu, L. (2015) 'Abolishing China's One-Child Policy Won't Help,' *East Asia Forum*, 20 November. Available at: www.eastasiaforum.org/2015/11/20/abolishing-chinas-one-child-policy-wont-help/ (Accessed on 3 March 2019).

Minajp.com (2016) 'Maternity Leave Benefit in Japan: What Country Has the Best Benefits.' Available at: https://minajp.com/maternity-leave-benefits-145 (Accessed on 16 March 2018).

Mu, G. (2018) 'China's Worrying Decline in Birth Rate,' *The Straits Times*, 24 January. Available at: www.straitstimes.com/asia/east-asia/chinas-worrying-decline-in-birth-rate-china-daily-columnist (Accessed on 4 March 2019).

National Bureau of Statistics (2018) 'Annual Survey of Migrant Worker 2017,' 27 April. Available at: www.stats.gov.cn/tjsj/zxfb/201804/t20180427_1596389.html (Accessed on 17 March 2019).

National Bureau of Statistics of China (2011) 'Communiqué of the National Bureau of Statistics of People's Republic of China on Major Figures of the 2010 Population Census [1] (No. 1).' Available at: www.stats.gov.cn/english/NewsEvents/201104/t20110428_26449.html (Accessed on 1 March 2019).

Purdy, M., Li, G. and Light, D. (2014) 'Beyond Capital and Labor: The View from China's Productivity Frontier,' *Outlook*, No. 1. Available at: www.accenture.com/t20150522T061601Z__w__/us-en/_acnmedia/Accenture/Conversion-Assets/Outlook/Documents/1/Accenture-Outlook-Beyond-Capital-And-Labor-The-View-From-China-Productivity-Frontier.pdf#zoom=50 (Accessed on 21 February 2019).

Schultz, T. W. (1961) 'Investment in Human Capital,' *The American Economics Review*, Vol. 51, No. 1, pp. 1–17.

Smith, N. (2015) 'How to Boost America's Fertility Rate,' *Chicago Tribune*, 4 March. Available at: www.chicagotribune.com/news/opinion/commentary/chi-american-birth-fertility-rates-20150304-story.html (Accessed on 16 March 2019).

Stanway, D. (2019) 'China Lawmakers Urge Freeing Up Family Planning as Birth Rates Plunge,' *Reuters*, 12 March. Available at: www.reuters.com/article/us-china-parliament-population/china-lawmakers-urge-freeing-up-family-planning-as-birth-rates-plunge-idUSKBN1QT0SM (Accessed on 15 2019).

Statista (2019a) 'Median Age of the Population in China from 1950 to 2100 (in Years).' Available at: www.statista.com/statistics/232265/mean-age-of-the-chinese-population/ (Accessed on 7 March 2019).

Statista (2019b) 'Forecast of Average Annual Growth of Labour Productivity.' Available at: www.statista.com/statistics/278400/projected-labor-productivity-growth-in-china/ (Accessed on 27 February 2019).

Statista (2019c) 'Employment Rate of University Graduates in China from 2008 to 2017.' Available at: www.statista.com/statistics/280947/employment-rate-of-university-graduates-in-china/ (Accessed on 17 March 2019).

The Straits Times (2018) 'China's Next Debt Bomb Is an Ageing Population,' 6 February. Available at: www.straitstimes.com/asia/east-asia/chinas-next-debt-bomb-is-an-ageing-population (Accessed on 3 March 2019).

Trading Economics (2019) 'United States Average Hourly Wages in Manufacturing.' Available at: https://tradingeconomics.com/united-states/wages-in-manufacturing (Accessed on 11 March 2019).

Whalley, J. and Zhao, X. (2010) 'The Contribution of Human Capital to China's Economic Growth,' *Working Paper 16592*, National Bureau of Economic Research, Cambridge, MA.

World Bank (2017) 'Fertility Rate, Total (Births per Woman).' Available at: https://data.worldbank.org/indicator/SP.DYN.TFRT.IN (Accessed on 15 March 2019).

Wu, Y. (2016) 'China's Labor Market: Shrinking Workforce, Rising Wages,' *China Daily*, 21 December. Available at: www.chinadaily.com.cn/china/2016-11/21/content_27444998.htm (Accessed on 3 March 2019).

7 A change in development model

A key to sustained success

After four decades of staggering growth, China has reached the level of an upper-middle-income country. China's GDP per capita reached US\$9,517.8 in 2018 and the figure hit a much higher level at US\$18,120, measured in purchasing power parity (PPP).[1] China has lifted 800 million people out of poverty over the past four decades. The remaining poverty population was only about 16.6 million in 2018, representing a meager 1.19 percent of total population.[2] China's Human Development Index (HDI), a measure of quality of human development and wellbeing, has risen steadily from 0.5 in 1990 to 0.752 in 2018, which is slightly higher than the world average of 0.728.[3] No single country in the world has accomplished economic progress comparable to China's astonishing achievements in the 20th and 21st centuries so far. Four decades of reform have transformed China from one of the poorest countries to the second largest economy in the world with an upper-middle income level and from a closed economy to a key player in the global economy. These spectacular results indicate that China's market reforms, open door policy and the investment-led growth model that underpinned this extraordinary progress have served China well with indubitable success. Nonetheless, some strains associated with the export-oriented and investment-led strategy have become evident. On its way to being one of the world's high-income and advanced economies, China has nevertheless encountered declining growth since 2007, with a historic high of 14.2 percent to a unprecedented low of 6.6 percent in 2018.[4] A decade of continued decline in growth suggests more than cyclical adjustments. The shrinking growth behind embeds a number of structural bottlenecks, such as depopulation, dwindling labour force, diminishing labour productivity and waning investment efficiency, which impede China's sustained growth. This chapter will first sketch China's growth and development strategies in the 1980s and 1990s. It will then examine the growth bottlenecks surfacing in the 2000s and assesses the Chinese government's attempt to overcome the growth hurdles. The remaining discussion will focus on what structural adjustments China needs to go through in order to enter another phase of stable and sustained growth.

From plan to market, and opening up[5]

The inauguration of China's economic reform started with institutional changes in the countryside in the late 1970s and implementation of open-door policy in the early 1980s. Though the reforms in the late 1970s lacked a comprehensive blueprint, the rural reform and open-door policy were by no means coincidental. The series of reforms was driven by the devastated economic conditions inherited from the pre-reform era and the political changes, mainly the death of Mao Zedong and fall of the Gang of Four, in the late 1970s. This institutional overhaul signified China's transformation from collective farming to household farming (i.e., the Household Responsibility System, HRS), which provided a much stronger effort-and-reward link than that under the commune system implemented before the reform. Farmers were provided with material incentives to work and invest in their allotted land, which resulted in an enormous rise in household income and efficiency. Externally, China opened up to the outside world in the early 1980s by swift trade expansion and utilisation of foreign direct investment (FDI) through the establishment of Special Economic Zones (SEZs) and coastal open cities. Export-oriented strategy earned China rapid accumulation of foreign exchange, which financed China's rising imports after reform. The massive inflow of FDI bestowed China with technology, equipment and managerial knowhow, which laid the foundation for building modern corporations in China over the past decades.

The initial success of rural reform and open door policy motivated central leaders to reform the state-owned enterprises (SOEs) to enhance workers' and managers' work incentives by instituting a contract responsibility system (CRS) in 1987, which was similar to the nature of the HRS in agriculture. This system required SOEs to reach a number of profit, innovation and efficiency goals. Once the assigned targets were fulfilled, the enterprises were allowed to retain the remaining profits. The CRS tried to incentivise enterprises to better utilise their resources and diminish the problem of soft budget constraint. Nevertheless, the effectiveness of using CRS to boost enterprises' incentives seemed less apparent than that of the HRS in agriculture as the process of production in industrial enterprises was much more complex than that of agriculture. A high level of division of labour was required in industrial production, which made it difficult to reward each worker according to productivity and efforts rendered. The effort-and-reward link in industrial production, particularly at the workers' level, was looser than that in agriculture. Further, the problem of soft budget constraint has still been prevalent as the central government does not want to see the SOEs fail to fulfill the state production targets and ensures its dominant control of large SOEs in strategic sectors such as communication, energy, finance and national defence, through which warranting its control over the whole economy and national security. Of equal importance, central leaders have been reluctant to lay off SOE workers to maintain socio-political stability. Amid these strategic considerations, the Chinese government has been channeling adequate fiscal and financial resources to keep the loss-making SOEs and state projects afloat. Credit and capital expansion constituted one of cornerstones to sustain growth in China in the 1980s and 1990s. Nonetheless, such strategy instigated a far-reaching unintended repercussion of piling up substantial non-performing loans, which brought the state-owned commercial banks (SOCBs) to the verge of insolvency in the 1990s. Deteriorating balance sheets of the commercial banks worsened the fragility of the banking sector and heightened financial instability, which pushed central leaders to implement an institutional overhaul of the SOCBs by commercializing their operation in 1994. The 1997 Asian Financial Crisis further pressed the government to inject huge amounts of capital, about US$402 billion, to recapitalize the ailing banks during the period 1998–2006. Though the banking reform in the 1990s was not a complete success, it has improved the operational efficiency of the commercial banks, and more significantly, it mitigated the chance of running into a financial crisis prior to the emergence of 2008 Global Financial Crisis (GFC).

In a nutshell, there was no roadmap for the first phase of economic reform in the 1980s. Deng adopted a pragmatic and gradual approach of "crossing the river by feeling the stones". The source of growth mainly came from the pragmatic institutional reform that unleashed production and investment incentives. The open door policy allows China to produce and export based on comparative advantage, which proves to be successful in terms of income growth, employment creation and accumulation of foreign exchange. Opening up to the outside world also furnishes China with massive influx of capital and embedded technology and managerial knowhow. In the mid-1990s to early 2000s, China made strenuous efforts to integrate further into the global economy by embarking on a new journey of "going out" and joining the WTO, with an aim to reach a wider global market and augment its leading role in global affairs. However, the advantages that propelled China's double-digit growth rates in the first three decades of the reform era have gradually faded. Rising labour costs, diminishing capital efficiency and labour productivity and rising competition from neighbouring emerging economies have constrained China's long-term growth. By the later years of the Hu-Wen administration, China was struggling to maintain a growth rate of 8 percent, which later turned out to be unattainable. Since Xi Jinping's ascension to top leadership, he has been fully aware of the urgency of inaugurating structural reforms to revitalise productivity.

The emergence of growth bottlenecks

Chapter 6 illustrates that China's growth before the 2008 GFC depended heavily on physical and human capital. Physical capital contributed 44.96 percent of GDP growth during 1978–2008, and the percentage soared to 67.62 percent during 1999–2008 while contribution by human capital stock was 38.12 percent and 39.41 percent for the same periods respectively (Whalley and Zhao 2010). The investment-led growth model does not undergo much fundamental change, though central leaders have indicated their intention to transform China's growth model from investment-led to productivity-led. Nonetheless, the 2008 GFC has once again put China into the trap of fostering its growth by credit expansion to finance infrastructure and real estate projects. Table 7.1 reveals that total investment in fixed assets (TIFA) has been rising continuously and its growth reached its peak in 2009, with 29.95 percent, immediately after the 2008 GFC. Though the growth rate has shown steady decline since 2014 after the Chinese

Table 7.1 Total Investment in Fixed Assets (TIFA) 1995–2017 (100 million yuan)

Year	TIFA	Growth (%)	TIFA/GDP
1995	20019.3	22.29	0.33
1996	22913.5	14.46	0.32
1997	24941.1	8.85	0.31
1998	28406.2	13.89	0.33
1999	29854.7	5.10	0.33
2000	32917.7	10.26	0.33
2001	37213.5	13.05	0.34
2002	43499.9	16.89	0.36
2003	55566.6	27.74	0.40
2004	70477.4	26.83	0.44
2005	88773.6	25.96	0.47
2006	109998.2	23.91	0.50
2007	137323.9	24.84	0.51
2008	172828.4	25.85	0.54
2009	224598.8	29.95	0.64
2010	251683.8	12.06	0.61
2011	311485.1	23.76	0.64
2012	374694.7	20.29	0.69
2013	446294.1	19.11	0.75
2014	512020.7	14.73	0.80
2015	561999.8	9.76	0.82
2016	606465.7	7.91	0.82
2017	641238.4	5.73	0.78

Source: *China Statistical Yearbook 1995*, Beijing: China Statistical Publishing House, p. 137; *China Statistical Yearbook 2014* (Table 10.2). Available at: www.stats.gov.cn/tjsj/ndsj/2014/indexeh.htm (accessed on 15 April 2019); *China Statistical Yearbook 2018* (Table 10.2). Available at: www.stats.gov.cn/tjsj/ndsj/2018/indexeh.htm (accessed on 15 April 2019); GDP figures are derived from Table 5.2 of this book

government's repeated claim of deleveraging, the average growth of TIFA was 17.53 percent during 1995–2017, which was much higher than the GDP growth rate over the same period. Of vital importance, the TIFA/GDP ratio has been ever increasing, which exhibits the fact that increasing amount of capital investment is needed to generate one unit of GDP. Bear in mind that the labour force increased from 687.37 million in 1995 to 806.86 million in 2017, registering an average annual growth of 0.75 percent.[6] A rising TIFA/GDP ratio with increasing labour force reveals shrinking efficiency of factor inputs. Rising debt-to-GDP ratio over the past decade reconfirms the phenomenon of diminishing efficiency of capital- and credit-driven growth models. The ratio soared from 144 percent in 2006 to 255 percent in 2017 (Table 7.2), which was higher than major developed countries such as the US, the UK and Germany, except Japan. It is not just the high percentage but also the pace of credit expansion that deserves greater concern. The ratio skyrocketed 111 percentage points in 12 years, and there are several points worth noting. First, immediately after the GFC, China's debt-to-GDP ratio rose dramatically from 141 percent in 2008 to 179 percent in

Table 7.2 Debt-to-GDP Ratio 2006–2017 (percent)

	2006	2007	2008	2009	2010	2011	2012	2013	2014	2015	2016	2017
Corp*	107	97	96	120	121	120	131	141	150	163	166	160
Govt	26	29	27	35	34	34	34	37	40	42	45	47
HH	11	19	18	24	27	28	30	33	36	39	44	48
Total	144	145	141	179	182	182	195	211	226	244	255	255

Source: Bank for International Settlements, quoted from China Power Team (2017)

* Corp = Corporate debt; Govt = Government debt; HH = Household debt

2009, which shows Beijing's great concern of ensuring growth and stability. Second, the higher the ratio is, the lower the efficiency it indicates. It also suggests that the output generated may not be adequate to repay the interest, not to mention the principal. It inevitably causes rising NPLs. Output expansion is built at the expense of escalating fragility of the financial sector. Third, looking into the composition of the debt, corporate debt has displayed slower growth, but household debt has demonstrated the fastest growth in recent years. Of mounting concern is that rapid expansion of household loans, mainly mortgage loans, in recent years does not contribute much to a promising GDP growth, which undermines the strategy of consumption-led growth advocated by the central leaders.

Wu (2014) analyses China's Total Factor Productivity (TFP), a broad measure of an economy's productivity with given factor inputs, such as labour and capital. The study estimates that China's TFP growth after the global financial crisis declined from an average of 3.3 percent from 2001–2007 to -0.9 percent from 2007–2012. These results indicate that the credit expansion after the financial crisis had successfully boosted growth, but the growth was attributable to increase in factor inputs rather than the rise in factor productivity. A further study by Wu (2016) indicates that the trend of tapering TFP has continued after 2012. Wu's analyses are consistent with the previous exposition that GDP growth in the past decades was a result of injecting more factor inputs (i.e., physical capital and labour), rather the efficiency improvement of factor use and technological enhancement. These findings are in line with an earlier empirical study by Whalley and Zhao (2010) discussed earlier. All these empirical findings, together with the rising TIFA/GDP ratio and debt/GDP ratio, robustly reveal that credit- and capital-driven growth have enabled China to maintain impressive growth during the reform era. However, the waning efficiency in capital and investment in recent years has rung the alarm that the seemingly workable growth model has gradually been losing its impetus when more credits are needed to generate one unit of GDP (i.e., output). Another main pillar of China's growth model is the reliance on low costs of labour and natural resources, but these comparative advantages have been undermined by neighbouring emerging economies such as Vietnam and Indonesia. China needs to reengineer its growth model to capture potential productivity gain to avoid falling into the "middle-income trap", which refers to the phenomenon where when a majority of the developing countries reach a level of middle income at around US$16,000-US$17,000 in PPP terms, they tend to lose their growth momentum caused by rising costs, ageing population, shrinking productivity and stagnant technological change.[7]

A "new 4-trillion yuan stimulus package" in 2019: return to an old model?

Over the past decades, in particular after the 2008 GFC, the Chinese government has initiated stimulus measures, mainly monetary and fiscal expansion, to boost the economy during economic downturn. The Chinese government that relies largely on economic growth and stability to maintain its legitimacy cannot allow a major decline. The stimulus packages put forward in 2008 were effective, at least in the short term, to bring about a swift rebound of the economy. It conveys an important lesson to central leaders that as long as the magnitude of monetary easing and fiscal expansion increase faster than GDP growth, the economy will likely be kept buoyant. Beijing has been fully cognisant of the possible repercussions of stimulus package such as accumulated NPLs and building up of overcapacity, as discussed in Chapter 4. However, when China faces an unprecedented decelerating growth of 6.6 percent in 2018, which is the lowest pace since 1990, China responds with its longstanding practice of credit easing. In January 2019, total social financing (TSF), the broadest measure of financing growth in China, reached an all-time high of 4.6 trillion yuan, a 52 percent jump from January 2018, the second highest record since data have been available. TSF in January alone is equal to 24 percent of all financing in 2018. Even if Beijing restrains credit growth for the rest of the year, though unlikely, the rapid expansion of TSF will probably keep overall credit growth higher than in 2018. Although credit growth was considerably slowed down in February, new TSF for the first two months of 2019 is still 25 percent higher than the same period in 2018 (Balding 2019).

In face of the critical years ahead, Chinese Premier Li Keqiang delivered the annual Work Report on 5 March 2019 to focus again on maintaining growth and creating employment. The employment rate is always one of the major concerns of central leaders. The annual Work Report has put particular emphasis on employment creation, which is of paramount importance for maintaining social stability. It is planned to increase 11 million new urban jobs in 2019 and keep urban unemployment rate below 4.5 percent (Koty 2019a; Chen 2019). To achieve the target, the Work Report unveiled new initiatives to lighten the burdens for businesses, including a massive cut in costs for businesses by nearly 2 trillion yuan (US$298.3 billion). Major reduction items include tax exemption and reduction of corporate income tax (CIT) and reduction of value-added tax (VAT), with preferential reductions targeted to small and micro businesses.[8] State-owned commercial banks are instructed to increase 30 percent of loans to small and micro businesses to ease their problems of loan financing (Ecns.cn 2019). Apart from tax reduction and easing loans, a substantial 2.6 trillion yuan of infrastructure investment will be kick started in 2019, with 800 billion yuan in railway construction and 1.8 trillion yuan in road construction and waterway projects. The investment will start with some major water conservancy projects and the planning and construction of the Sichuan-Tibet Railway (Xinhua 2019a). Combining the 2 trillion yuan of tax and cost reduction with the 2.6 trillion yuan of infrastructure investment, the magnitude of this "New 4-Trillion Yuan Stimulus Package" (the New Package hereafter) is even stronger than the 2008 stimulus package. There is a noteworthy difference of the New Package from the 2008 package in that it initiates massive tax reduction to allow more investment funds retained by the enterprises, especially the small and micro businesses. The central government also recognizes the need to extend ample loanable funds to private small enterprises, which are a main source of employment creation and economic growth. The government has adopted a more targeted approach when compared to the stimulus package in 2008. As examined in Chapter 4, the central government only financed 30 percent (i.e., 1.2 trillion yuan) of the stimulus programme in 2008, and local governments financed the remaining balance (i.e., 2.8 trillion yuan). Facing the investment targets delegated from the central government, local governments were active in setting up more local government financial platforms (LGFPs) to enlarge the fund pool for local projects. Local officials are keen to work in response to the stimulus package handed down from the central government as working in conformity with central policy, improvement in local infrastructure and rise in income are important appraisal criteria for local officials. Like what happened in 2008, the central coffer only covers 577.6 billion yuan of the infrastructure investment, and the remaining shortfall will be financed by other sources including private capital (Xinhua 2019b). Though the central government has not specified whether the local governments will engage in financing the infrastructure projects, it has already been announced that local governments' special bond issuance quota will be raised from 1.35 trillion yuan to 2.15 trillion yuan in 2019 (Koty 2019a), which could be a preamble for local governments' participation in the stimulus projects. According to the statistics released by the Ministry of Finance (MOF), local governments have already issued a total of 1.18 trillion yuan of bonds in the first quarter of 2019 to ensure adequate funding to finance targeted projects. Central authorities also raised the quota for local government debt to 3.08 trillion yuan for the whole year of 2019 (Xinhuanet 2019). To avoid repeating the unintended repercussions of the 2008 stimulus package, Li has explicitly pointed out that: "Facing new circumstances and developments, we were firm in choosing not to adopt a deluge of strong stimulus policies".[9] However, from the magnitude of the current stimulus package, it appears that Beijing foresees a deep and prolonged downturn. When shrinking growth and unemployment reach the central government's critical point, Beijing will probably allow a larger scale of stimulus programme, like what happened in 2008.

The pattern of economic downturn followed by a stimulus package has almost become a policy rule. The only difference lies on the magnitude of the stimulus package, which depends on the anticipated severity of the downturn. This countercyclical policy measure has been particularly obvious since the 2008 GFC. After a massive stimulus programme implemented in 2008, China's impressive rebound was accompanied by mounting NPLs and overcapacity, which motivates central leaders to embark on a new round of reforms in 2013 to transform China's investment-led growth towards a more sustainable and decelerated growth through upgrading the economy. Beijing is inclined to accept a more moderate growth to allow more time to undertake structural reforms. Nevertheless, when the property market had declined for five consecutive months since May 2014, the Chinese government started to be concerned about the property-led downturn, given the fact that GDP growth was 7.3 percent in the third quarter of 2014, representing the lowest growth since 1990, and the property sector shared about 16 percent of GDP in 2013 (Anderlini 2014). In response, the central bank reduced down payment and mortgage interest rates for second-home buyers in September 2014. One year later, down payment requirements for first-time home buyers were reduced from 30 percent to 25 percent. However, the monetary easing did not achieve the desired effect as growth rates fell below the target for two consecutive years, in 2014 and 2015. To attenuate the mounting risks ahead, the percentage of down payments was further decreased to 20 percent for both first and second home buyers in February 2016 (Hsu 2016) and the central banks encouraged commercial banks to increase loans to boost the ailing property sector (Zhou 2019). This series of monetary easing reverts the previous efforts of deleveraging credit growth and clearly illustrates the central government's obvious priority on stability over structural reforms when central leaders face policy dilemma. Before the 2008 GFC, China's economy had already been heavily relying on capital investment to fuel economic growth. Since then, China has not shown signs of deviating from its previous growth strategy and had even gone further in accelerating credit to maintain economic growth.

It is indubitable that China has plenty of tools, monetary, fiscal and regulatory, to fine tune the economy, but these tools are effective to correct the economy under short term cyclical fluctuation and have limited impacts on long term growth. Likewise, the Chinese government and many of China's observers repeatedly highlight the importance of promoting consumption to boost the economy. Rising consumption would stimulate production and investment, but the impacts are on the aggregate demand side. Pushing consumption to boom the economy in the Keynesian sense is demand management addressing short term cyclical fluctuations caused by inadequate aggregate demand. That said, promoting consumption may effectively lower the pace of economic deceleration in the short term; it permits more time for central leaders to undertake structural reforms. However, a consumption-led growth strategy will probably confront a number of constraints in the years ahead. First, there is no clear sign that the economy will experience a noticeable rebound. It will certainly put downward pressure on household income and consumption. Data indicates that households have further depressed their consumption, particularly for durable goods. Car sales have dropped for 7 consecutive months since January 2019. Total car sales recorded a decline of 15.8 percent in 2018, with just 2.37 million vehicles sold (Tudose 2019). Mobile phone sales experienced an even bigger decline of 19.9 percent on a year-on-year basis (Jing 2019). Second, the rapid rise of mortgage loans has pressed down the household budget available for retail consumption. In 2009, 71 percent of total loans were corporate loans, and 18 percent were mortgage loans while the percentage of corporate loans dropped to 60 percent and mortgage loans expanded to 27 percent in the first half of 2018 (Gopalan 2019). Expenditure on housing, in terms of either rental or mortgage repayment, is the biggest spending item for China's households, which occupies about 20 percent of household spending. The figure reaches 30 percent in first tier cities such as Beijing and Shanghai (Qi et al. 2019). Though the Chinese leaders have recurrently indicated their intention to boost domestic consumption, annual growth of retail sales have demonstrated ongoing decline after reaching a peak at 23.3 percent in 2010 and hit a new low of 8.5 percent in 2018 (Table 7.3). The growth is expected to be on the downside in the coming years amid weakening economic growth.

Though the waning growth may reflect the damage inflicted by the trade war with the US and the shaky global market, the fundamental causes stem from the structural issues embedded in China's growth strategy. To boost China to enter another phase of sustained growth, the Chinese government needs not just to accept a decelerated growth, which is a sign of a maturing economy that grows with an enlarged base. Similar decelerated growth is found in other advanced countries like the US, Germany and Japan. Nevertheless, of vital importance is that China incept de facto structural reform to rejuvenate the growth sources. Boosting aggregate demand, such as consumption and investment, stimulates growth in the short run. Long run economic growth depends primarily on the quantity and efficient use of capital, labour, technology and institutional changes. China is no exception. Putting together the growth bottlenecks analysed earlier, several policies can be conducive to easing the structural constraints on growth in the long run.

First, capital efficiency can be enhanced if more financial resources (i.e., credits) are channeled to private enterprises (PEs). As illustrated in Chapter 3, the dynamic private sector is much more efficient than strongly government-backed

Table 7.3 Annual Growth of Retail Sales 2009–2018 (percent)

Year	Annual growth of retail sales (%)
2009	15.5
2010	23.3
2011	17.1
2012	14.3
2013	13.1
2014	12.0
2015	10.7
2016	10.4
2017	10.3
2018	8.5

Source: Statista (2019); China Internet Watch (2019c)

SOEs. The profitability of SOEs was only about 27.4 percent of that of the PEs in 2016. It implies that, with a given amount of credits, PEs can generate more returns on capital than SOEs. Guo Shuqing, Chairman of the China Banking and Insurance Regulatory Committee, actually proposed in late 2018 that 50 percent of new loans should be diverted to PEs over the next 3 years. However, the response from the market was lukewarm. Commercial banks have reservations in extending loans to PEs, for potential risks are involved as banks have inadequate information to evaluate the credit risk of PEs systematically. Commercial banks' reluctance to offer loans to private sector lending is reinforced by venerable preferences for lending to SOEs, lack of collateral of PEs and insufficient net interest margins to compensate for the additional risks associated with lending to PEs (Rhodium Group 2019).

Second, given depopulation and dwindling labour force, it is unlikely that there are short term policies to revert the trend. To counterweigh diminishing labour force, the Chinese government must raise not just the years of schooling but also the quality of education at all levels and on-the-job training. As analysed in Chapter 6, China does not only need high-tech and high-end personnel, it needs to fill the talent gap of technicians and skilled workers who are urgently needed for China's industrial upgrade. Actually, Premier Li Keqiang has raised in his *Report on the Work of the Government* in March 2019 that China will reemphasize and improve vocational education to address the shortage of highly-skilled workers. More financial assistance will be offered to students of vocational college. The government even plans to transform a number of regular undergraduate institutions into applied colleges that offer more vocation-oriented training (Li 2019). Appropriate human capital investment is pivotal in reversing the tapering growth of labour productivity.[10]

Third, with the given amount of factor inputs, technological innovation is essential to elevate China's TFP, which gauges the efficiency of the factor use. China's technology level and scientific research capability have demonstrated a spectacular rise since the mid-2000s by various quantitative measures. China's Research and Development (R&D) expenditure reached a historic high of 1.76 trillion yuan, approximately US$254 million, which was 2.1 percent of China's GDP in 2017 (Caixin 2018). China has been only second to the US in terms of spending in R&D. According to China's State Intellectual Property Office (SIPO), the number of patents filed by China was 825,136 in 2013 and soared remarkably to 1.7 million in 2018 (Sneddon 2015; Xinhua 2019b). In the dimension of research capability and output, Xie and Freeman (2019) conduct an extensive research of China's scientific research papers, including those written in Chinese and English with and without being indexed in a citation database. It is found that China accounted for 36 percent of 2016 global scientific articles and 37 percent of global citations to scientific articles published in 2013. Xie and Freeman argue that with shares of articles and citations more than twice its share of global population or GDP, China has achieved a comparative advantage in scientific knowledge creation. It is expected that these kinds of research findings will generate a lot of debate, but one thing that is clear:

China has climbed swiftly up the ladder of scientific research and technological innovation. Notwithstanding, there is another side to these eye-catching figures. For instance, among the patents registered in the US in 2018, the US took the lead of having registered 143,000 US patents, followed by Japan in second place with 48,300 patents, followed by South Korea with 20,200 and Germany with 14,800. China took fifth with 12,589 US patents (Manners 2019), which was in stark contrast with the number of China's local patent registrations that accomplished a new high of 1.7 million in 2018 (Xinhua 2019b). A better measure of invention is the triadic patent registration, which requires the joint recognition in the largest global technology markets: the Japan Patent Office (JPO), the United States Patent and Trademark Office (USPTO) and the European Patent Office (EPO). Joint registration ensures broader intellectual property protection and recognition worldwide. The US has registered at least 10,000 triadic patents granted each year since 1990. It was not until 2013 that China had about 2,000 triadic patents granted every year (China Power Team 2016). The huge disparity between the number of local and overseas patents may imply that quite a proportion of China's patents do not meet the patent registration standards overseas (Kelion 2016). China is good at innovating upon existing technology through licensing, merging and acquisition. China's patents focus on improving product design and quality, enhancing speed or making it more user-friendly, instead of creating a scientific breakthrough that can generate a brand new product or industry. Smartphone producer Xiaomi is a typical example. Its production technology is not indigenously developed, but it has a huge customer base that provides useful feedback to Xiaomi to improve its operating system to work faster and smoother. Xiaomi updated its operating system 52 times in 2014 (Economy 2018: 124–125). China's technological progress has been remarkable over the past decade, but the TFP has not shown a corresponding upsurge, which implies that more needs to be done to raise innovation that is conducive to productivity gain. As mentioned earlier, China has taken the lead, only second to the US, in R&D spending, but its share in GDP remains at around 2.11 percent in 2016, compared to 4.25 percent in Israel, 4.24 in South Korea, 3.15 in Japan, 2.94 in Germany and 2.74 in the US (World Bank 2019). China's financial resources in both private and public sectors are capable of channeling more funding to upgrade the patent quality on top of boosting patent quantity. Pertaining to the patent quality, China has to fill its talent gap. According to the 2017–2018 World Economic Forum's Global Competitiveness Report, China was ranked 28 in innovation and 47 in higher education. The rankings are not low when compared with other developing countries, but these rankings imply that China needs to enrich its talent pool if it targets developing an innovative economy in the years to come. About 4 million students have studied overseas since 1987, but only 1.2 million graduates returned (Economy 2018: 137–138). The Chinese government should improve further not just the monetary reward but also the research and living environment to attract overseas talents and Chinese graduates trained overseas back to the mainland. Further, the central government released the blueprint of the grand development plan of Guangdong-Hong Kong-Macao

Greater Bay Area (GBA) on 18 February 2019, which encompasses Hong Kong, Macao, Shenzhen, Zhuhai, Guangzhou and 6 other Guangdong cities to form a sizable economic bay area with 56,500 km^2 and total GDP of US$1.58 trillion in 2017 (Cheung and Tsang 2019).[11] China should promptly initiate concrete policies to facilitate R&D collaborations between Hong Kong and Shenzhen to utilise the prominent research capability of universities in Hong Kong[12] and the substantial experiences of giant tech firms in Shenzhen, such as Huawei, Tencent, ZTE, BYD and BGI, in converting research into marketable products at competitive prices. The other Guangdong cities, such as Dongguan and Zhuhai, have already accumulated ample experience and mature skills to assemble high-tech products. If the grand plan is successfully implemented, GBA will probably become an innovation and high-value-added bay area for the whole country.

Last but never least, efficiency-enhancing institutional reforms are needed to unleash potential productivity. Internally, preferential treatment towards the state sectors should be further peeled off to force SOEs to operate according to market discipline. Compared to private enterprises, SOEs still enjoy relatively easy access to bank loans. SOE obtained about 55 percent of the total corporate loans in 2016 but only produced 22 percent of GDP (Chow and Anderson 2017: 2). In connection to SOEs reform, banks should mainly shoulder the responsibility of channeling loanable funds to finance creditworthy projects rather than serving as the central government's leveraging tool at the time of economic downturn. It is evidenced that China has successfully made use of the banking sector to stabilise the economy in times of turbulence. However, it at the same times shrinks capital efficiency, which ends up with utilising more loanable funds to create fewer outputs. Short-term stabilization is achieved at the expense of long-term growth and efficiency. To enhance the efficiency of China's loanable market, the central government needs to devise a gradual exit from the banking sector to wind down its influence on state banks' loan decisions. Externally, China needs to open up further its protected sectors, such as finance, telecommunication and energy, to foreign investment. It not only creates a more competitive environment to push up the efficiency of local enterprises but also makes an important gesture indicating that China is a fair player in the global economy. It is crucial to build China's soft power and earn trust among both developed and developing countries, which is critical for the smooth progression of China's BRI and China's intention to expand its global politico-economic leadership.

Conclusion

The Chinese economic development over the past four decades reveals that it possesses a steep learning curve. The remarkable achievement started with bottom-up institutional reforms, which unleashed households' and enterprises' incentives to work and invest. Opening up to the outside world since the 1980s has enabled China to capture the world market by utilising its comparative advantage in production. Continued learning from and integrating into the global economy has bestowed China with plentiful business and technological knowhow, apart from the sizable FDI. Nevertheless, the decades-long reliance on export-oriented and investment-led growth has gradually lost impetus as evidenced by shrinking growth in labour productivity and capital efficiency as well as declining TFP. All these structural bottlenecks are reflected in the dwindling growth since 2007. Unceasing decline over more than a decade is far more than a cyclical adjustment but rather a result of China's inadequacy of structural reforms. Central leaders are caught in a dilemma of maintaining growth and implementing de facto structural reforms. Under the Xi-Li administration, it is apparent that rebalancing and restructuring are still subordinate to growth and stability. The central government is willing to trade greater debt for higher growth. Beijing's emphasis is on growth and stability rather than rebalancing and restructuring, in particular when facing economic downturn. The Chinese economy has ample resilience and enormous potential to unleash accumulated wealth, extensive global presence and a strong and practical government with its huge domestic market. It is very unlikely that China will encounter a "hard landing" in the coming decade, even if China fails to implement its structural reforms. That said, the longer China keeps the status quo of its growth model, the higher the probability China will encounter the "middle-income trap". Chinese leaders have shown clear signs of accepting a slower growth in the years ahead, but the essence lies in de facto structural reforms that are conducive to the enhancement of labour productivity, capital efficiency, technological innovation and further market reforms. If China maintains its investment-led growth model without addressing the issue of efficient use of factor inputs and resources at large, China will not get out of the trap of gradually declining growth.

Notes

1 GDP per capita is calculated based on the GDP data from China Internet Watch (2019a, 2019b). GDP per capita at purchasing power parity is derived from CEIC (2019).
2 Calculated based on the data from Executive Intelligence Review (2019).
3 HDI is composite measure of human development and wellbeing by gauging the level of gross national income (GNI) per capita, life expectancy and number of years of schooling. For further elaboration of the index, please refer to *Human Development Reports*. Available at: www.hdr.undp.org/en/humandev (Accessed on 1 April 2019).
4 Data from *Statistical Year Book of China 2018*, Table 3–4. Available at: www. stats.gov.cn/tjsj/ndsj/2018/indexeh.htm (Accessed on 1 April 2019); CNBC (2019).
5 For a detailed discussion of different stages of economic reform, please see Chapter 1.
6 Calculated based on the data from Table 6.3 in Chapter 6 of this book.
7 China's relevance to the middle-income trap will be further discussed in the next chapter.
8 For details of CIT and VAT exemption and reduction, see Koty (2019a, 2019b).
9 See Fifield (2019) and Li (2019).
10 For a detailed discussion of the issue of human capital, please refer to Chapter 6 of this book.

11 See www.bayarea.gov.hk/en/home/index.html (Accessed on 29 April 2019) for further details of GBA.
12 With a population size of only about 7.4 million and 11 universities, 4 universities in Hong Kong were ranked top 50 universities and 7 were categorized as "very high" research output by the QS World University Ranking in 2018. See www.topuniversities.com/universities/lingnan-university-hong-kong (Accessed on 28 April 2019). For a brief background of the five tech giants in Shenzhen, please see He (2018).

References

Anderlini, J. (2014) 'China Property Decline Continues,' *Financial Times*, 24 October. Available at: www.google.com/amp/s/amp.ft.com/content/2af87f46-5b3a-11e4-a674-00144feab7de (Accessed on 11 April 2019).

Balding, C. (2019) 'What's Causing China's Economic Slowdown,' *Foreign Affairs*, 11 March. Available at: www.foreignaffairs.com/articles/china/2019-03-11/whats-causing-chinas-economic-slowdown (Accessed on 5 April 2019).

Caixin (2018) 'Chart of the Day: Another Record Year for China R&D Spending,' 10 October. Available at: www.caixinglobal.com/2018-10-10/chart-of-the-day-another-record-year-for-china-rd-spending-101333479.html (Accessed on 22 April 2019).

CEIC (2019) 'China Forecast: GDP PPP Per Capita.' Available at: www.ceicdata.com/en/indicator/china/forecast-gdp-ppp-per-capita (Accessed on 1 April 2019).

Chen, L. (2019) 'Jobs, Jobs, Jobs: China Focuses on Quality of Life as Trade War and Lower Growth Take Toll,' *South China Morning Post*, 5 March. Available at: www.scmp.com/news/china/politics/article/2188745/jobs-jobs-jobs-china-focuses-quality-life-trade-war-and-lower (Accessed on 6 April 2019).

Cheung, T. and Tsang, D. (2019) 'Blueprint for China's "Greater Bay Area" Project Covering Hong Kong, Macau and 9 Guangdong Cities Set to Be Revealed on Monday at the Earliest,' *South China Morning Post*, 18 February. Available at: www.google.com/amp/s/amp.scmp.com/news/hong-kong/hong-kong-economy/article/2186528/blueprint-chinas-greater-bay-area-project-hong-kong (Accessed on 28 April 2019).

China Internet Watch (2019a) 'China's GDP Growth 2018; Consumption Expenditure Contributed 76.2%,' 23 January. Available at: www.chinainternetwatch.com/28096/gdp-2018/ (Accessed on 1 April 2019).

China Internet Watch (2019b) 'China's Population Growth and Birth Rate Reached a Shocking Low in 2018,' 23 January. Available at: www.chinainternetwatch.com/28107/population-2018/ (Accessed on 1 April 2019).

China Internet Watch (2019c) 'China Retail Market to Exceed US$5.6 Trillion by 2019,' 7 February. Available at: www.chinainternetwatch.com/28213/retail-2019-forecast/ (Accessed on 13 April 2019).

China Power Team (2016) 'Are Patents Indicative of Chinese Innovation?' *China Power*, 15 February. Updated 18 December 2018. Available at: https://chinapower.csis.org/patents/ (Accessed on 22 April 2019).

China Power Team (2017) 'Does China Face a Looming Debt Crisis?' *China Power*, 7 September. Updated 28 February 2019. Available at: https://chinapower.csis.org/china-face-looming-debt-crisis/ (Accessed on 17 April 2019).

Chow, M. and Anderson, H. (2017) 'Tackling China's Debt Mountain Needs More Than SOE Reform,' *Market Bulletin*, JP Morgan.

CNBC (2019) 'China's Economy Grew 6.6% in 2018, the Lowest Pace in 28 Years,' 20 January. Available at: www.cnbc.com/2019/01/21/china-2018-gdp-china-reports-economic-growth-for-fourth-quarter-year.html (Accessed on 1 April 2019).

Ecns.cn (2019) 'China to Increase Small Business Loans by 30 pct in 2019,' 5 March. Available at: www.ecns.cn/news/2019-03-05/detail-ifzezqac5083813.shtml (Accessed on 6 April 2019).

Economy, E. C. (2018) *The Third Revolution: Xi Jinping and the New Chinese State*, New York: Oxford University Press.

Executive Intelligence Review (2019) 'The True Magnitude of China's Poverty Reduction Achievements and Plans,' 10 March. Available at: https://larouchepub.com/pr/2019/190310_china_out_poverty.html (Accessed on 1 April 2019).

Fifield, A. (2019) 'China's Communist Party Is Battening Down the Hatches as the Economy Slows,' *The Washington Post*, 5 March. Available at: www.washingtonpost.com/world/asia_pacific/chinas-communist-party-is-battening-down-the-hatches-as-the-economy-slows/2019/03/05/22516e98-3f1f-11e9-a44b-42f4df262a4c_story.html?utm_term=.1c2c7a4a2c6b (Accessed on 7 April 2019).

Gopalan, N. (2019) 'Home Truths Are Holding Back China's Consumers,' *Bloomberg*, 22 January. Available at: www.bloomberg.com/opinion/articles/2019-01-22/china-s-rising-consumer-debt-is-weighing-on-spending (Accessed on 14 April 2019).

He, H. (2018) 'Top 5 Tech Giants Who Shape Shenzhen, "China's Silicon Valley",' *South China Morning Post*, 12 December. Available at: www.google.com/amp/s/amp.scmp.com/lifestyle/technology/enterprises/article/1765430/top-5-tech-giants-who-shape-shenzhen-chinas-silicon (Accessed on 29 April 2019).

Hsu, S. (2016) 'China's Housing Bubble Is Finally Here – As Expected,' *Forbes*, 11 October. Available at: www.forbes.com/sites/sarahsu/2016/10/11/chinas-housing-bubble-is-finally-here-as-expected/#6875a0e160e6 (Accessed on 11 April 2019).

Jing, M. (2019) 'China Economy Enjoys "Good Start" to 2019 Despite Slumping Car and Mobile Phone Sales,' *South China Morning Post*, 12 March. Available at: www.scmp.com/economy/china-economy/article/3001325/china-enjoys-good-start-2019-despite-slumping-car-and-mobile (Accessed on 12 April 2019).

Kelion, L. (2016) 'China Breaks Patent Application Record,' *BBC News*, 24 November. Available at: www.bbc.com/news/technology-38082210 (Accessed on 22 April 2019).

Koty, A. C. (2019a) 'China's 2019 Work Report: Growth Target, Tax Cuts Announced,' *China Briefing*, 6 March. Available at: www.china-briefing.com/news/chinas-2019-work-report-growth-target-tax-cuts/ (Accessed on 6 April 2019).

Koty, A. C. (2019b) 'China Extends Tax Relief, Incentives for Small and Micro Businesses,' *China Briefing*, 22 January. Available at: www.china-briefing.com/news/china-extends-tax-relief-incentives-small-micro-businesses/ (Accessed on 6 April 2019).

Li, K. (2019) 'Report on the Work of the Government,' delivered at the Second Session of the 13th National People's Congress of the People's Republic of China, 5 March. Available at: www.wsj.com/public/resources/documents/2019NPCWorkReportEN.pdf?mod=article_inline (Accessed on 7 April 2019).

Manners, D. (2019) 'China Accelerating Patent Activity,' *Electronics Weekly.com*, 8 January. Available at: www.electronicsweekly.com/news/business/china-accelerating-patent-activity-2019-01/ (Accessed on 22 April 2019).

Qi, L., Zhu, G., Zhu, L., Kubota, Y., Li, S. and Moss, T. (2019) 'Chinese Consumers Tighten Their Belts and the World Feels the Squeeze,' *The Wall Street Journal*, 3 January. Available at: www.wsj.com/articles/chinese-consumers-curb-spending-likely-deepening-slowdown-11546526257 (Accessed on 14 April 2019).

Rhodium Group (2019) 'Financial System: Financial System Policy Reform,' *The China DashBoard*. Available at: https://chinadashboard.asiasociety.org/winter-2019/page/financial-system (Accessed on 13 April 2019).

Sneddon, M. (2015) 'Inside Views: A Look at the Huge Upswing in China Patent Filing,' *Intellectual Property Watch*, 22 April. Available at: www.ip-watch.org/2015/04/22/a-look-at-the-huge-upswing-in-china-patent-filings/ (Accessed on 23 April 2019).

Statista (2019) 'Annual Growth of Total Retail Sales in China from 2009 to 2019.' Available at: www.statista.com/statistics/373934/china-retail-sales-growth/ (Accessed on 13 April 2019).

Tudose, S. (2019) 'Car Sales Decline in China for Seventh Straight Month,' *Carscoop*, 19 February. Available at: www.carscoops.com/2019/02/car-sales-decline-china-seventh-straight-month/ (Accessed on 12 April 2019).

Whalley, J. and Zhao, X. (2010) 'The Contribution of Human Capital to China's Economic Growth,' *Working Paper 16592*, National Bureau of Economic Research, Cambridge, MA.

World Bank (2019) 'Research and Development Expenditure (% of GDP).' Available at: https://data.worldbank.org/indicator/GB.XPD.RSDV.GD.ZS (Accessed on 23 April 2019).

Wu, H. X. (2014) 'Re-estimating Chinese Productivity,' *China Center Special Briefing Paper*. Available at: www.conference-board.org/publications/publicationdetail.cfm?publicationid=2780

Wu, H. X. (2016) 'What's Behind China's Productivity Slowdown?' *East Asia Forum*, 9 August. Available at: www.eastasiaforum.org/2016/08/09/whats-behind-chinas-productivity-slowdown/ (Accessed on 14 April 2019).

Xie, Q. and Freeman, R. B. (2019) 'Bigger Than You Thought: China's Contribution to Scientific Publication and Its Impact,' *China & World Economy*, Vol. 27, No. 1, pp. 1–27. Available at: https://economics.harvard.edu/files/economics/files/freeman-and-xie_bigger_than_you_thought_chinas_contribution_journal_china_and_world_economy_jan2019.pdf (Accessed on 21 April 2019).

Xinhua (2019a) 'China to Expand Infrastructure Investment in 2019,' 5 March. Available at: http://english.gov.cn/premier/news/2019/03/05/content_2814 76549687152.htm (Accessed on 6 April 2019).

Xinhua (2019b) 'China Sees More Invention Patents in 2018,' 8 January. Available at: www.china.org.cn/business/2019-01/08/content_74351010.htm (Accessed on 22 April 2019).

Xinhuanet (2019) 'Local Gov'ts Step Up Bond Issuance to Finance Major Projects,' 16 April. Available at: www.xinhuanet.com/english/2019-04/16/c_137982237. htm?utm_campaign=Marketing_Cloud&utm_medium=email&utm_source=USCB C+News+Overview+4.16.2019&%20utm_content=http%3a%2f%2fwww.xinhuanet. com%2fenglish%2f2019-04%2f16%2fc_137982237.htm (Accessed on 17 April 2019).

Zhou, H. (2019) 'For China, Tax Cuts May Work Where Its 4 Trillion Yuan Stimulus Failed – by Boosting the Economy Without Creating More Debt,' *South China Morning Post*, 2 January. Available at: www.scmp.com/comment/insight-opinion/united-states/article/2180254/china-tax-cuts-may-work-where-its-4-trillion (Accessed on 6 April 2019).

8 Conclusion

Transformation and challenges of a rising economic power: from rapid growth to sustained growth

The spectacular success of the Chinese economy is beyond argument. The initial achievement is attributable to the institutional changes that allow a continual flow of rural surplus labour from the countryside to the cities, which enables China to utilise its abundant labour supply to produce and export goods according to its comparative advantage. Combined with the open-door policy that attracts huge inflow of capital, embedded technology and managerial knowhow, China has embarked on an unprecedented path of rapid economic growth. In the 1980s and early 1990s, labour moved from low-value-added sector (agricultural sector) to high-value-added sector (industrial and service sectors) boosted both economic growth and total factor productivity (TFP). Infrastructure investment by local and central government has added momentum to substantiate four decades of staggering growth. However, growth bottlenecks started to emerge in the mid-1990s. Mounting non-performing loans (NPLs) motivated central leaders to implement banking reform in 1994 but with limited results; it pushed central leaders to inject huge capital into the banking sector to improve state-owned commercial banks' (SOCBs) balance sheet. However, the improved balance sheets faced another challenge when the central government initiated the "4-trillion-stimulus package" in 2008 to buffer the economic downturn caused by the global financial crisis (GFC). Rapid credit expansion to finance projects of low return gave rise of another round of rising NPLs and, more importantly, entered a phase of decelerated growth. Central leaders have been fully aware of the inherited structural problem, and thus President Xi Jinping put forward the notion of 'New Normal' and implemented supply-side reforms. Beijing explicitly accepted a lower growth with an aim to allow more time for structural economic reforms. While heading in the right direction towards quality growth, decelerating growth amid trade war with the US and an unstable global market induced the Chinese government to put forward a "New 4-trillion-Stimulus Package" in 2019 to stabilize growth and maintain employment. This move gives robust evidence that central government will not surrender its all-important goal of stability in growth and employment. However, the reluctance to accept further decelerated growth will only delay the necessary structural reforms. New stimulus programmes may generate a quick fix to slow down growth deceleration in the short term, but is deemed to be ineffective to cure the structural problems of declining labour and capital productivity, extending loans to sectors of low return, rising costs of production and failure to generate inclusive growth. The longer the central government drags on the needed reforms, the more severe the problems amassed. To embark China on another journey of sustained growth, central leaders must initiate de facto structural reforms that transform the Chinese economy from investment-led growth to productivity-led growth. It is equally important that China make its growth inclusive as long term growth would be unlikely if the benefits of economic growth are hugely unevenly distributed. Last but not least, sustained growth must be environmentally sustainable or the deteriorating environment will gradually erode the improved livelihood brought about by the four decades of economic reforms. Continued environmental degradation will also entail rising resource costs facing the next generation.

The middle-income trap: is there a way out?

Empirically, less developed countries (LDCs) tend to grow faster than developed countries (DCs) largely because once the LDCs can attract FDI and technological transfer from the DCs; they can grow faster by imitation rather than invention, that is the so called advantage of backwardness. In addition, LDCs are in general endowed with abundant labour and some other inputs such as raw materials and energy sources, which furnish the LDCs with comparative advantage in producing labour-intensive or raw material-intensive products. However, it does not guarantee that all LDCs can catch up with DCs in terms of per capita income. Instead, World Bank's empirical analysis indicates that most middle-income countries in 1960 remained so in 2008 after years of attempt to catch up. Among 101 middle-income countries in 1960, only 13 countries jumped out of the middle-income trap and reached the level of a high-income country in 2008 (World Bank 2013: 12).[1] Most economies in Latin America and the Middle East have been trapped in middle-income for three main reasons. First, before reaching middle-income, the LDCs utilise the surplus labour, mainly from the countryside, for manufacturing production. They have an unblemished competitive edge over the DCs in terms of labour cost. However, after periods of industrial expansion and economic growth, the surplus labour shrinks, wages rise and competitiveness fades. The comparative advantage in labour-intensive production is further jeopardised by a falling fertility rate and waning labour force. Second, labour productivity gain, reflected by a rise in TFP, at the initial stage of economic growth was attributable to sectoral reallocation of factor inputs. Factors such as labour moved from the low-value-added sector (agriculture in the countryside) to the high-value-added sector (manufacturing and service sectors in urban areas). However, when the manufacturing sector grew to a mature stage and the development of the high- value-added service sector lagged behind, factors reallocation was impeded. Third, imported technology and equipment at the early stage of economic growth, embedded in FDI, resulted in technology catch-up and rise in labour productivity as workers had better technology and equipment to work with. Nonetheless, the initial productivity gain was eventually exhausted as the DCs would not continuously supply up-to-date, not to mention cutting-edge, technology to these middle-income countries. If these countries could not increase productivity through their own technological innovation, they would finally fall into the technology and productivity trap if they relied predominantly on imported technology.

China stands at a critical transition to its future growth. Analyses in preceding chapters have pinpointed the growth bottlenecks facing China, which are very much converged with those facing the Latin American and Middle East countries trapped in middle-income. China has entered a stage of slowing growth. Whether China can rejuvenate its growth depends primarily on its ability to create high-value-added products and services, which in turn rests on lowering the costs of production and/or raising output value per worker. Reducing costs seems a less plausible option for China as its labour cost and raw materials costs have been losing their competitive edge compared to other Asian countries, including Burma, Bangladesh, Cambodia and Vietnam. The remaining feasible option lies in raising the labour productivity, the output value per labour hour, which equals the price times the quantity of output. The price of the product in the market is determined principally by demand and supply. Put straightforwardly, a product can yield a higher price if its design, quality and functionality can outperform other competitors. Enhancement in human capital and technological innovation are of the essence of product design and quality improvement and industrial upgrade at large. The case of Finland is illustrative. Finland has injected huge investment in research and development (R&D), almost 4 percent of GDP, with the lead of the Finnish National Technology Agency to develop high technology, in particular the ICT (information communication technology) sector. The Nokia business conglomerate has successfully transformed into a global leader of household electronics. Finland's ICT products, led by Nokia, contributed about 20 percent of Finland's TFP growth in the 1990s (Lin 2012: 218). South Korea is another example showcasing how investment in human capital brings sustained growth. Since the 1980s, Korea's government began to strategically invest in human capital development, research and technological innovation. Korean households also devoted much of their resources to education of their next generation, which boosted rapid expansion in education. The number of students in higher education soared from 539,000 in 1980 to 3.3 million in 2015 according to UNESCO data (Mani and Trines 2018). The descriptive and empirical analysis by Lee (1997) indicates that Korea has accomplished an extraordinary record of high and sustained economic growth and human development during the period of 1962–1992. The analysis illustrates that economic growth and human development have been closely connected and interacted with each other throughout periods of high economic growth. Lee's study further reveals that human capital enhancement not only directly contributes to economic growth but also fuels output growth indirectly as the abundant well-educated labour force has been capable of absorbing advanced technology from DCs and has laid a solid foundation for its R&D development in subsequent periods.

Apart from industrial upgrade through technological innovation and human capital advancement, China should further expand its service sector, especially the high-value-added services such financial, business-supporting and medical services, that are hugely demanded by a swelling middle class and entrepreneurs in China. China has had the largest pool of middle-class in the world since 2015, with 109 million in China and 105 million in the US (The Telegraph 2015).[2] Data over the past decades suggests that there is an increasingly close relationship between the service sector development and economic growth. In 1997, service sector accounted for 69 percent of GDP, and the figure climbed steadily to 74 percent in 2015 in high-income countries. The increasing share of services in GDP was even more noticeable in low- and middle-income countries, where it bounded from 48 percent in 1997 to 57 percent in 2015 (Buckley and Majumdar 2018). Notwithstanding, services in China shared only 34.5 percent of China's GDP in 1997 and 53.7 in 2015.[3] These figures reveal that China's service sector development lags behind the average of the low- and middle-income countries, not to mention the high-income countries. China needs to develop a high-value-added service sector that allows factors reallocation from the manufacturing sector to the service sector to yield higher value, which in turn bolsters economic growth. In a nutshell, an upgraded industrial sector and expansion of the high-value-added service sector are vital for China to avoid the middle-income trap.

Inclusive growth

Economic growth and improvement of people's livelihood are critical cornerstones of China's ruling party's legitimacy. Beijing needs to solicit support not just from the middle class and the entrepreneurs but also the majority of the ordinary households. Deng Xiaoping's notion of 'letting some people get rich first' was appropriate and understandable at the initial stage of reform. China could not risk a comprehensive reform implemented over the whole country when it first attempted institutional reforms. The outcomes were highly unpredictable. Some experimental steps need to be taken as it was not certain whether the reforms would make some people get wealthy first or end up with a mess and failure. No matter what the outcome would be, such a gradual approach minimized the risks and costs of economic reform in the 1980s. The noticeable economic growth during the reform period proves that the reforms were very successful in lifting income and people's livelihood, as some economists and policy makers predicted that income inequality would increase at the onset of economic reform. When growth becomes extensive across different sectors, the income gap will be narrowed gradually. Contrary to the prediction, it turns out that some people do get rich first at a very fast pace, but the economic fruits have not spread evenly over the whole country. The Gini Coefficient,[4] a statistical measure used to gauge income distribution, rose continuously from 0.3 in 1980 to 0.41 in 2000, which is regarded as a warning level by the United Nations. It reached its historic high of 0.491 in 2008 and then started to decline (Table 8.1).

Table 8.1 China's Gini Coefficient 1980–2017

1980	0.30[a]
1990	0.35[b]
2000	0.41[c]
2004	0.473[d]
2005	0.485
2006	0.487
2007	0.484
2008	0.491
2009	0.49
2010	0.481
2011	0.477
2012	0.474
2013	0.473
2014	0.469
2015	0.462
2016	0.465
2017	0.467

Source: [a,c]Yu and Xiang (2014); [b]Jain-Chandra (2018); data from 2004 onwards is derived from National Bureau of Statistics of China; figures of 2004 and 2005 are quoted from Shambaugh (2016) and data from 2006 onwards is quoted from CEIC (2019)

The Coefficient hit a record low of 0.462 in 2015, but it exhibited a rebound in 2016 and 2017. Despite the up and down, China's Gini Coefficient has never been below the warning level of 0.4 since 2000. The reasons for China's widening income gap are at least threefold. First, income disparity is primarily caused by China's rural-urban divide. Agricultural products are, in general, low value-added while manufacturing products and services in the urban sector are more high value-added. It naturally follows that rural dwellers receive lower income than their urban counterparts. However, of more importance is that labour mobility from rural to urban areas has been impeded by the *hukou* system (household registration system). Not all surplus labour in the countryside can move freely to the cities, as the costs of migration could be prohibitive. They have to consider costs of living, such as housing and education, in the cities, as the migrant workers are their families are not entitled to enjoy the social and public services and benefits like their urban counterparts. This institutional barrier restricts labour mobility, which hinders wage convergence. Table 8.2 demonstrates that the ratio of disposable income of urban households to rural households. (Yu/Yr) was 2.57 in 1978 and the gap had diminished to 1.86 in 1985, attributable to the rapid rise of rural household income resulting from early reforms in the countryside implemented since the late 1970s. With the urban reforms and an open door policy that benefits the urban households more, the urban-rural income ratio has been rising since 1990, and the ratio remained above 3.0 across many years in the 2000s. Though the gap has shown sign of narrowing, it remains substantial and the ratio in 2017 only reached back to the level in 1995. Second, pertinent to the previous point, residents in rural and low-income areas have less access to higher

Table 8.2 Urban-Rural Disposable Income Gap 1978–2017

Year	Yu (yuan)	Yr (yuan)	Yu/Yr
1978	343.4	133.6	2.57
1980	477.6	191.3	2.50
1985	739.1	397.6	1.86
1990	1510.2	686.3	2.20
1995	4283.0	1577.7	2.71
2000	6255.7	2282.1	2.74
2001	6824.0	2406.9	2.84
2002	7652.4	2528.9	3.03
2003	8405.5	2690.3	3.12
2004	9334.8	3026.6	3.08
2005	10382.3	3370.2	3.08
2006	11619.7	3731.0	3.11
2007	13602.5	4327.0	3.14
2008	15549.4	4998.8	3.11
2009	16900.5	5435.1	3.11
2010	18779.1	6272.4	2.99
2011	21426.9	7393.9	2.90
2012	24126.7	8389.3	2.88
2013	26467.0	9429.6	2.81
2014	28843.9	10488.9	2.75
2015	31194.8	11421.7	2.73
2016	33616.2	12363.4	2.72
2017	36396.2	13432.4	2.71

Source: *China Statistical Yearbook 2018*, Table 6.16. Available at: www.stats.gov.cn/tjsj/ndsj/2018/indexeh.htm (Accessed on 13 May 2019)

Notes
Yu = Disposable income of urban households;
Yr = Disposable income of rural households.

education, which undermines their human capital enhancement and makes them uncompetitive in an economy heading to industrial upgrade and technology-based development. Access to higher-level education has thrived since 1980. There were about 8 million university graduates in China in 2017, registering a spectacular jump of 10 times compared to more than two decades ago. However, a huge gap in tertiary education between wealthy and poor regions has prevailed. To illustrate, the percentage of college-age population enrolled in tertiary institutions in 2017 was 70 percent, 60 percent and 55 percent in Shanghai, Beijing and Tianjin respectively while the comparable figures in relatively low-income Gansu, Yunnan and Guangxi were 22 percent, 20 percent and 19 percent respectively (Trivedi 2018). Unequal access to education instigates a skill and knowledge gap, which underpins ongoing income disparity. Third, rising income inequality is also attributable to the government's long-standing development policies that tilt to coastal, more developed regions over less developed inland regions (Kuo 2014). Favourable policies attracting FDI first started with the four Special Economic

Zones (SEZs) in Guangdong and Fujian and later extended to the eastern coastal cities. The recent development plans of the Greater Bay Area and Yangtze River Delta Integration Plan do not show any sign of deviating from the preferential policies towards coastal and delta regions. Though the central government has initiated policies to rectify development imbalance among the eastern, central and western regions, with the Western Development Strategy endorsed by the central government in March 1999 to boost investment in infrastructure development and natural resources exploitation (Huang, Ma and Sullivan 2010), it is evidenced in Table 8.3 that while the Western Development Strategy generated some positive impacts on narrowing the income gap between eastern and central/western regions between 2005 and 2010, both Ye/Yc and Ye/Yw exhibited a declining ratio. The ratios rebounded in 2013 but have not indicated marked improvement since then. Prevailing regional development disparity has hindered the efforts to alleviate income inequality.

The problem of inequality has slightly improved, with the Gini Coefficient falling over the past decade but still above the warning level of 0.4. The urban-rural gap has been narrowed since 2007 after the government's series of policies, such as abolition of agricultural tax and increased investment in agriculture and infrastructure, implemented in the countryside to alleviate the burden and raise the income of rural residents.[5] However, the Gini Coefficient rebounded in two consecutive years in 2016 and 2017. Further, the urban-rural gap remains noticeable, and the gap is much more pronounced if we take into account the difference in quality and quantity of provision of public and social services, such as education and medical services, between urban and rural areas. Aside from urban-rural disparity, the regional development gap has not shown significant changes. Though the western regions have recorded an average annual GDP growth rate of 8.9 percent, 1.8 percentage points higher than the national growth rate (Li 2019), the per capita disposable income ratio in Eastern, Central and Western regions has remained almost at the same level since 2013, which implies that

Table 8.3 Per Capita Disposable Income Ratio in Eastern, Central and Western Regions

	2005	*2010*	*2013*	*2014*	*2015*	*2016*	*2017*
Ye/Yc	1.53	1.46	1.55	1.54	1.53	1.53	1.53
Ye/Yw	1.62	1.55	1.70	1.69	1.67	1.67	1.66

Sources: Calculated based on the data from *China Statistical Yearbook 2014*, Table 6.6 and 6.13. Available at: www.stats.gov.cn/tjsj/ndsj/2014/indexeh.htm and www.stats.gov.cn/tjsj/ndsj/2014/indexeh.htm (accessed on 14 May 2019); *China Statistical Yearbook 2018*, Table 6.3. Available at: www.stats.gov.cn/tjsj/ndsj/2018/indexeh.htm (Accessed on 14 May 2019)

Notes
Ye/Yc = Per capita disposable income in eastern region divided by per capita disposable income in central region;
Ye/Yw = Per capita disposable income in eastern region divided by per capita disposable income in western region.

benefits of faster economic growth have not filtered down to household level. All indicators point to the fact that income inequality still matters in China. From a global perspective, China is ranked high on the list of countries with substantial income inequality, just behind some of the worst cases such as South Africa, Namibia, Brazil and Botswana.[6] Despite persistent inequality, studies indicate that income disparity does not cause apparent social unrest. Based on extensive survey, Whyte (2010) concludes that inequality issues do not cause widespread discontent and social unrest across the country. A more recent study by Xie (2016) also argues with survey evidence that Chinese people tend to believe that economic growth itself leads to inequality, which is an unavoidable outcome of economic growth and improvement of people's livelihood. However, such conclusion requires further scrutiny. First, it is probable that discontent over inequality will be less widespread when the economy undergoes rapid growth and absolute income of rural and urban residents exhibits marked growth. Given the fact that income growth has dwindled, over the past decade and the low-income households are more adversely affected, discontent may gradually amass. Data reveals that growth of disposable income of China's high-income class was 9.1 percent in 2017 while the respective rates of upper-middle, middle, lower-middle and lower-income classes were 7.7 percent, 7.2 percent, 7.1 percent and 7.5 percent. The income growth rates of the lowest two classes were 2 and 1.6 percentage points lower than that of the high-income group. The income gap may be further widened by the fact that the high-income class possesses proportionally much more assets than the lower-income class. The income growth from assets has risen steadily in recent years and hit 11 percent in 2017, which was the highest growth since 2014 (Harada and Takahashi 2018). The low-income class does not have much assets income to buffer the slowing growth in income from wages under the economic slowdown. Second, when income gap is widened, the high-income class will not increase their marginal propensity to consume (MPC) as they have already fulfilled their basic consumption need. Higher income will probably result in higher wealth accumulation for high-income households. On the contrary, when low-income households face a slower growth in income, their MPC will tend to fall as they prefer hoarding to safeguard uncertainty and potential further income decline in the future. This will at least partially defeat China's original purpose of boosting growth by enhancing consumption. As shown in Table 7.3 in Chapter 7, growth in retail sales has already demonstrated a declining trend since 2010. Raising consumption cannot rely solely on high-income households but rather must depend on the rise of mass consumption of lower-middle and lower-income classes. Third, as pointed out by Lee (1997), Korea's high income growth during the takeoff period was accompanied by equitable income distribution, which enabled the majority of the households to provide education, in particular higher education, for their next generation. It became a leading factor for Korea's spectacular rise in human capital that attributed Korea's rapid income growth. More equal access to education in Korea also plays an important and effective role in avoiding worsening income inequality in the subsequent stages of development.

To address the issue of income inequality, government policies targeting the root of the problem are indispensable. One of the most fundamental cures for inequality is to ensure education equality as income level has a strong correlation with education attainment and on-the-job training. As discussed above, a stark education gap, in particular for higher education, still exists between rural and urban areas as well as between remote and developed areas. All top-notch universities are located in first-tier cities such as Beijing and Shanghai. Secondary students with their urban *hukou* have access to more quality secondary schools and therefore a greater chance of entering the elite universities in the cities. The Chinese government has to increase investment in primary and secondary education in rural and remote areas and subsidise more quality rural students to receive higher education in the cities. This measure enables the students to move from low-paid jobs in the countryside to high productivity and thus high-paid jobs in the cities after graduation. It not only bridges the income gap in the long run but also help alleviate the problem of shortage of skilled labour in urban areas. Pertaining to the urban-rural divide, as discussed above, the Western Development Strategy endorsed in 1999 was the first central programme for China's development of western the region, which injected capital in infrastructure development and natural resource exploitation. The second phase of the development plan started after the 2008 GFC, which called for a new round of liberalization policies to attract FDI. The National Development and Reform Commission (NDRC) modified the Catalogue of Encouraged Industries for Foreign Investment in Central and Western China in 2008 to attract foreign investors to invest in some targeted sectors such as environmentally friendly and energy-efficient industries that took advantage of local resources and utilised the technological knowhow that China lacked. Further, the central government also developed three economic zones with preferential policies in central and western regions, which modeled upon the development zones elsewhere in China (Huang, Ma and Sullivan 2010).[7] The bundle of policies of the Western Development Strategy and the subsequent policy relaxation in 2008 generated limited results as the regional income gap shown in Table 8.3 has not reflected noticeable change. Preferential policies and policy relaxation are not adequate to attract FDI or even local investors. Whether a business will invest in the central and western regions hinges on a bundle of factors such as the availability of a talented labour pool, transportation and logistics networks, and the living environment for foreign investors and their staff. Of primary importance, the cost advantages in central and western regions must not be jeopardized or even outweighed by their less favourable investment environment. Central leaders have to alter their long-lasting policy bias towards the coastal and more developed regions. Apart from enhancing education equity and implementing a more balanced regional development strategy, a more immediate cure for income inequality is to provide more subsidised social services, medical services and education through fiscal transfer from wealthy to poor regions. However, reductions in value-added and personal income taxes and a lowering of the social security contribution rate announced in March 2019 approximately reduces tax income by 2 trillion yuan, which reduces the fiscal income of local governments. Local governments in wealthy provinces and municipalities will be hit hard as big companies and high-paid workers mostly locate in more developed and wealthy regions. Actually, except Jiangxi province and the Xinjiang autonomous region, all other provinces and municipalities have sunk their revenue growth targets for 2019 (Tang and Leng 2019). Squeezed fiscal conditions render fiscal transfer from wealthy to poor regions unlikely.

Environmental bottleneck

Early years of reforms focused on income and employment growth as well as enhancement of living standard. The rapid growth has been achieved by substantial utilisation of capital and resources. Rapid depletion of resources and negligence to protect the environment have accelerated environmental degradation, which has become the paramount concern of central leaders. The reasons behind Beijing's rising concern are at least twofold. First, continued income growth changes people's expectation of quality of life. People have higher expectation of quality of life on top of income growth. The central government understands the importance of managing and fulfilling people's expectations as improved livelihood brought by rising income has increasingly been crowded out by environmental degradation. It is estimated that 5.5 million premature deaths in the world are caused by air pollution. Among the 5.5 million premature deaths, China shares 1.6 million in 2013 (Amos 2016). The exceedingly high level of PM2.5, which are microscopic airborne particles that can be inhaled deep in the lungs, causes serious health damage. PM2.5 is mainly caused by combustion by factories, vehicles and burning of coal and wood. China's emission level of PM2.5 is 48 micrograms per cubic metre of air, more than double the 19 micrograms of the world average of 2,626 cities (Kao 2018). Water pollution has shown some slight but imbalanced progress. In 2017, 77.9 percent of water in sampled sites reached the first three grades, which means that the water was suitable for human contact, demonstrating a small increase of 1.2 percent from 2016. However, there are 27 sites, including Beijing, showing deteriorating water quality. Of the water assessed, 8.3 was Grade 5, which indicates that the water is useless for any purpose. It is still far away from government's target of lowering the percentage of Grade 5 water to 5 percent in 2020 (Standway 2018). The situation for underground water is even worse. A report released in 2016 revealed that 32.9 percent of wells tested across areas mostly in northern and central China had Grade 4 water, meaning that it can only be used for industrial uses. Another 47.3 percent of wells were Grade 5 water quality (i.e., useless level). Only about 20 percent of the well water was suitable for human use (Buckley and Piao 2016). As underground water was one of the main sources of water for rural households, residents in the countryside have been facing more severe water scarcity than their urban counterparts. Worsening environmental conditions threaten people's health, which triggers rising discontent among the public; environmental concern has surpassed illegal land acquisitions to be the main cause of mass social protest and demonstration (Bloomberg 2013). Second, without due care of environmental degradation and rapid depletion of resources, China's growth has actually been abraded by mounting environmental costs. While it is difficult to gauge the real economic costs brought by various kinds of pollution, it is broadly estimated that 3 to 10 percent of China's GDP was dissipated annually by environmental degradation and pollution, through losing of working days, damaging of agricultural products, reduction of tourists and other pollution-related externalities. More specific studies, such as the one conducted by RAND Corporation in 2015, indicate that soil pollution causes damage of about 1.1 percent of China's GDP, and the figure for water pollution is 2.1 percent (Economy 2018: 158). A recent research by Gu et al. (2018) estimates that ground-level ozone (O3) and PM2.5 caused 1.1 million premature deaths and 20 million tonnes of crops, which amount to 267 billion yuan and approximately 0.7 percent of GDP, to be damaged each year. As mentioned above, it is hard to accurately measure the real costs of pollution to the Chinese economy. However, all these figures point to the fact that negative externalities brought by China's intensifying pollution have negated the real growth of China's GDP, which is of rising concern to the central leaders, in particular when China has entered a phase of slowing growth. Rapid depletion of the environment and natural resources unavoidably escalates resource scarcity, which unavoidably raises production costs. Without effectively addressing the pollution problems, China will certainly encounter bottlenecks to sustain its future growth.

At the National People's Congress in 2014, Chinese Premier Li Keqiang declared 'war against pollution', with an action plan stipulating the concrete pollution abatement targets to be achieved in the coming years.[8] Coal consumption has gradually decreased, from 62 percent in 2016 to 60.4 percent in 2017 and further down to 59 percent of China's overall energy consumption in 2018. China will likely reach its target of reducing coal consumption in energy mix to below 58 percent in 2020 while gas, nuclear power and renewable energy combined accounted for 22.1 percent of energy mix in 2018, up 1.3 percentage points from 2017 (China Power Team 2018; Xu, Singh and Jacob-Phillips 2019). However, pollution reduction in other areas such as water pollution has experienced less satisfactory progress, as indicated by the figures shown earlier.[9] One of the major obstacles of realizing the planned targets is that the actual implementation of environmental policies is largely the responsibility of provincial and sub-provincial governments and authorities. Local officials have to meet multiple and sometimes conflicting objectives: maintain social stability by ensuring job creation, maintain desired rates of GDP growth by encouraging investment by new firms and clean up water and air pollution by prohibiting new polluting factories (Webber 2017). It is not surprising that the environmental protection targets have not been put on the top priority of local government officials in particular after the 2008 GFC and the economic slowdown over the past decades. Local government officials weigh the benefits of economic growth higher than the costs of not fulfilling pollution abatement targets. Whether local governments will put pollution abatement on the top of their policy agenda depends largely on the central government's determination to fight pollution. China has a strong central government. If it has strong political will to remedy the rampant pollution problem, it must make reaching the pollution abatement target one of the major assessment criteria for local government officials with a clear stick-and-carrot system. Further, central government's determination to alleviate pollution is of paramount significance as China lacks a mature civil society with unconstrained nongovernmental organizations (NGOs) to put pressure on the government and make it accountable for accomplishing environmental targets (Economy 2018: 184). Without much external pressure, the success of China's 'war on pollution' rests on the central government's policy design and its effective implementation.

In additional to administrative measures, a market-based mechanism is critical to curb pollution from its sources. The environmental tax implemented in 1 January 2019 is a step forward. China abandoned the old system that charged the polluting businesses a local fee, which varied across regions. The new tax will charge the polluting firms under a uniform set of national rules rather than collecting fees at the local level. For instance, firms across the country will face a uniform levy of between 1.2 yuan and 12 yuan for every 0.95 kilogram of nitrogen oxide or sulphur dioxide released by the firms. Preliminary estimates indicate that the new system will increase the payment by the polluting firms by 40 to 300 percent more than the old fee-paying system (Zhang 2017). Whether the new environmental tax is effective to curb pollution at optimal levels depends on appropriate setting of the tax amount to equivalent to, or at least close to, the external costs (i.e., the pollution costs). The tax-included prices have to be reflected in the market and thus the consumers bear the external costs, based on a user-pay principle, which internalises the externalities. As market prices goes up, consumption will fall and so as the pollution level. Another market-based system to tackle the pollution problem is the national emission trading system (ETS) announced by President Xi Jinping in 2015. Under the ETS, the government will set a cap for maximum emissions and then allocate the carbon emission permits to the polluting firms. If a firm emits less than its assigned quota, it can sell the permits on the open market. The ETS is planned to be launched nationwide in 2019. If effectively implemented, the ETS will have reduced carbon dioxides emissions by 27.5 percent by 2030 (Pike and Zhe 2017). However, the system was further refined in 2018 to cover only the energy sector rather than the 8 heavy industries that were originally planned to be covered. This will mean that the new scheme can only cover less than a third of China's emissions (Gan 2018). Of critical importance, the success of the system rests on how the central authorities set the maximum cap of emissions and how to accurately measure the emissions level of each firm. The full effect of ETS is also dependent on the central government's schedule of extending the system to all heavy industries as originally planned. Last but not least, development and use of clean energy, such as renewable and nuclear power, is a crucial long-term solution to the pollution problem. China has endeavoured to reduce coal consumption especially after Xi assumed his leadership, but coal remains a dominant share in China's energy mix. If clean energy generates positive externalities (i.e., external benefits) to the society, the government can subsidise clean energy consumption. So long as the amount of subsidy is equal or close to the magnitude of external benefits, the use of clean energy will be increased to approach the optimal level.

It is worth noting that pollution abatement is not in conflict with economic growth. According to a report by Goldman Sachs, environmental expenditures in the 13th Five-Year Plan (2016–2020) will exceed US$1 trillion, which will provide many opportunities for the firms to develop renewable resources and innovation to protect the environment (Krishnaswamy 2015). China's investment in environmental protection and governance registered a spectacular increase of 43 percent in 2018 (Yuan 2019). Just for the investment in renewable energy, it skyrocketed from US$3 billion in 2005 to US$100 billion in 2015 (Luxton 2016). New jobs created in the renewable energy sector have exceeded those created in the traditional oil and gas sectors (UN News 2019). Environmental business can be a potential sector for development in the coming decades if Beijing continues to maintain environmental protection on the top of the policy agenda. The green economy not only adds momentum to China's future growth but also fosters its transformation from quantity to quality growth.

A final word: an easy recipe, but difficult to cook

Not a small number of China's observers and economists analyse and predict when the Chinese economy will catch up with the US in terms of economic size and technology level. China will likely surpass the US to be the largest economic entity in the world. However, attention placed on the China-US comparison has missed the core issues facing the Chinese economy. Whether China can take the place of the US's economic hegemony is only secondary. What is really worth our concern is whether China can embark on another phase of stable growth after a decade's decelerating growth and what structural adjustments are needed to warrant such growth. The analyses of previous chapters highlight the structural bottlenecks including depopulation, dwindling labour force and productivity as well as diminishing capital efficiency that is closely associated with the partial SOEs and banking reforms. The recipe of further reform is straightforward: raising labour productivity through improved human capital investment, instituting de facto SOEs and banking reforms to raise investment efficiency and restraining from massive stimulus programmes to avoid over-leveraging. Though central leaders are fully aware of the ways of breaking the growth bottleneck, the preceding discussion reveals that the central government is unlikely to abandon the investment-led growth model as it provides effective, though sometimes inefficient, economic levers for the government to achieve its economic targets, given the fact that plausible economic growth is essential to the ruling party's legitimacy. China's sustained growth rests on central leaders' decisive departure from the downturn-stimulus policy pattern, without which growth will gradually decline and the maintenance of growth and employment will be costly. More resources pouring into the economy does not guarantee a proportional rise in output. There is no quick fix. A productivity-led inclusive growth with due concern on environmental protection will be a feasible way out, though China will probably experience some short- and medium-term slowdown and instability. From a global development perspective, China's profound changes and remarkable accomplishments over the past four decades render valuable development experience to other developing countries. Of even more significance are the challenges and bottlenecks that China has encountered during its course of transition, which offer lessons in advance to emerging economies to conceive the possible hurdles and feasible options to overcome them.

Notes

1 The 13 countries/regions are Equatorial Guinea, Greece, Hong Kong SAR, Ireland, Israel, Japan, Mauritius, Portugal, Puerto Rico, Republic of Korea, Singapore, Spain and Taiwan (World Bank 2013: 12).
2 The minimum threshold income of middle class is the double of the annual medium income of the respective country.
3 Data is derived from *China Statistical Yearbook 2016*, Table 3–7. Available at: www.stats.gov.cn/tjsj/ndsj/2016/indexeh.htm (Accessed on 12 May 2019).
4 The Gini Coefficient ranges from 0 to1. The closer the value is to 1, the greater the inequality is.
5 China proposed to build a 'new socialist countryside' (NSC) in the 11th Five-Year Plan (2006–2010) in order to advance rural development and livelihood. For details of the policy initiatives, please refer to Chapter 1 of this book.
6 Please see 'Gini Index (World Bank Estimate).' Available at: https://data.world bank.org/indicator/SI.POV.GINI (Accessed on 16 May 2019).
7 The three regional developments: the Chengdu-Chongqing Economic Zone, Guangxi-Beibu Gulf Economic Zone and Guanzhong-Tianshui Economic Zone.
8 For detailed of the action plan, see www.gov.cn/zwgk/2013-09/12/con tent_2486773.htm (Accessed on 2 June 2019).
9 For a detailed analysis of China's water pollution, see Han, Currell and Cao (2016).

References

Amos, J. (2016) 'Polluted Air Causes 5.5 Million Deaths a Year New Research Says,' *BBC News*, 13 February. Available at: www.bbc.com/news/science-environment-35568249 (Accessed on 25 May 2019).

Bloomberg (2013) 'Chinese Anger Over Pollution Becomes Main Cause of Social Unrest,' *Bloomberg News*, 7 March. Available at: www.bloomberg.com/news/articles/2013-03-06/pollution-passes-land-grievances-as-main-spark-of-china-protests (Accessed on 1 June 2019).

Buckley, C. and Piao, V. (2016) 'Rural Water, Not City Smog, May Be China's Pollution Nightmare,' *The New York Times*, 11 April. Available at: www.nytimes.com/2016/04/12/world/asia/china-underground-water-pollution.html (Accessed on 27 May 2019).

Buckley, P. and Majumdar, R. (2018) 'The Services Powerhouse: Increasingly Vital to World Economic Growth,' *Deloitte Insight*, July. Available at: https://www2.deloitte.com/insights/us/en/economy/issues-by-the-numbers/trade-in-services-economy-growth.html (Accessed on 12 May 2019).

CEIC (2019) 'China Gini Coefficient.' Available at: www.ceicdata.com/en/china/resident-income-distribution/gini-coefficient (Accessed on 13 May 2019).

China Power Team (2018) 'How Is China's Energy Footprint Changing?' *China Power*, 15 February 2016. Updated 13 August. Available at: https://chinapower. csis.org/energy-footprint/ (Accessed on 2 June 2019).

Economy, E. C. (2018) *The Third Revolution: Xi Jinping and the New Chinese State*, New York: Oxford University Press.

Gan, N. (2018) 'Will China's Carbon Trading Scheme Work Without an Emissions Cap?' *South China Morning Post*, 3 January. Available at: www.scmp.com/news/ china/policies-politics/article/2125896/big-black-hole-chinas-carbon-market-ambitions (Accessed on 4 June 2019).

Gu, Y., Wong, T. W., Law, S. C. K., Dong, G. H., Ho, K. F., Yang, Y. and Yim, S. H. L. (2018) 'Impacts of Sectoral Emissions in China and the Implications: Air Quality, Public Health, Crop Production, and Economic Costs,' *Environmental Research Letters*, Vol. 13, No. 8. Available at: https://iopscience.iop.org/ article/10.1088/1748-9326/aad138 (Accessed on 1 June 2019).

Han, D., Currell, M. J. and Cao, G. (2016) 'Deep Challenges for China's War on Water Pollution,' *Environmental Pollution*, Vol. 218, November, pp. 1222–1233. Available at: www.sciencedirect.com/science/article/pii/S0269749116310363 (Accessed on 2 June 2019).

Harada, I. and Takahashi, T. (2018) 'Rising Inequality Imperils China's Push for "Quality" Growth,' *Nikkei Asian Review*, 14 February. Available at: https:// asia.nikkei.com/Economy/Rising-inequality-imperils-China-s-push-for-quality-growth (Accessed on 19 May 2019).

Huang, N., Ma, J. and Sullivan, K. (2010) 'Economic Development Policies for Central and Western China,' *China Business Review*, 1 November. Available at: www.chinabusinessreview.com/economic-development-policies-for-central-and-western-china/ (Accessed on 13 May 2019).

Jain-Chandra, S. (2018) 'Chart of the Week: Inequality in China,' *IMFBlog: Insights & Analysis on Economics and Finance*, 20 September. Available at: https:// blogs.imf.org/2018/09/20/chart-of-the-week-inequality-in-china/?utm_ medium=email&utm_source=govdelivery (Accessed on 13 May 2019).

Kao, E. (2018) 'Air Pollution Is Killing 1 Million People and Costing Chinese Economy 267 Billion Yuan a Year, Research from CUHK Shows,' *South China Morning Post*, 18 October. Available at: www.scmp.com/news/china/science/ article/2166542/air-pollution-killing-1-million-people-and-costing-chinese (Accessed on 25 May 2019).

Krishnaswamy, R. (2015) '7 Factors Shaping China's Energy Future,' *World Economic Forum*, 7 September. Available at: www.weforum.org/agenda/2015/09/7-factors-chinas-energy-future/ (Accessed on 3 June 2019).

Kuo, L. (2014) 'China Is Hiding How Bad Income Inequality Is in the Country,' *Quartz*, 30 April. Available at: https://qz.com/204180/china-is-hiding-how-bad-income-inequality-is-in-the-country/ (Accessed on 13 May 2019).

Lee, J. W. (1997) 'Economic Growth and Human Development in the Republic of Korea, 1945–1992,' *Occasional Paper*, No. 24, K-Developedia. Available at: http://smesindia.net/wp-content/uploads/2013/09/Korea.pdf (Accessed on 11 May 2019).

Li, X. (2019) 'China Eyes New Regional Development Plans to Bolster Growth,' *Xinhuanet*, 26 April. Available at: www.xinhuanet.com/english/2019-04/26/ c_138011843.htm (Accessed on 16 May 2019).

Lin, J. Y. (2012) *The Quest for Prosperity: How Developing Economies Can Take Off*, Princeton, NJ: Princeton University Press.

Luxton, E. (2016) 'China Has Become a Green Energy Superpower. These 5 Charts Show How,' *World Economic Forum*, 25 June. Available at: www.weforum.org/agenda/2016/06/china-green-energy-superpower-charts/ (Accessed on 5 June 2016).

Mani, D. and Trines, S. (2018) 'Education in South Korea,' *World Education News + Review*, 16 October. Available at: https://wenr.wes.org/2018/10/education-in-south-korea (Accessed on 11 May 2019).

Pike, L. and Zhe, Y. (2017) 'Five Things to Know About China's National Carbon Market,' *Chinadialogue*, 19 December. Available at: www.chinadialogue.net/blog/10303-Five-things-to-know-about-China-s-national-carbon-market/en (Accessed on 3 June 2019).

Shambaugh, D. (2016) *China's Future*, Cambridge: Polity Press.

Standway, D. (2018) 'China Regions Face Gap in Enforcing Water Quality Standards,' *Reuters*, 31 May. Available at: www.reuters.com/article/us-china-pollution-water-idUSKCN1IW1BR (Accessed on 27 May 2019).

Tang, F. and Leng, S. (2019) 'China's Tax Cuts Were Meant to Boost Its Slowing Economy, but Will They End Up Hurting Debt-Ridden Regions?' *South China Morning Post*, 11 April. Available at: www.scmp.com/economy/china-economy/article/3005670/chinas-tax-cuts-were-meant-boost-its-slowing-economy-will (Accessed on 24 May 2019).

The Telegraph (2015) 'China's Middle Class Overtakes US as Largest in the World,' 14 October. Available at: www.telegraph.co.uk/finance/china-business/11929794/Chinas-middle-class-overtakes-US-as-largest-in-the-world.html.

Trivedi, A. (2018) 'China's Racing to the Top in Income Inequality,' *Bloomberg*, 23 September. Available at: www.bloomberg.com/opinion/articles/2018-09-23/china-s-racing-to-the-top-in-income-inequality (Accessed on 13 May 2019).

UN News (2019) ' "The Green Economy Is the Future," UN Chief Says in Beijing, Urging Climate Solutions That Strengthen Economies, Protect the Environment,' 27 April. Available at: https://news.un.org/en/story/2019/04/1037461 (Accessed on 5 June 2019).

Webber, M. (2017) 'Tackling China's Water Pollution,' *APPS Policy Forum*, Asia & The Pacific Policy Society, 2 October. Available at: www.policyforum.net/tackling-chinas-water-pollution/ (Accessed on 27 May 2019).

Whyte, M. K. (2010) *The Myth of Social Volcano*, Stanford: Stanford University Press.

World Bank (2013) *China 2030: Building a Modern, Harmonious, and Creative Society*, Washington, DC: World Bank. Available at: http://documents.worldbank.org/curated/en/781101468239669951/China-2030-building-a-modern-harmonious-and-creative-society (Accessed on 5 May 2019).

Xie, Y. (2016) 'Inequality in China,' *Chinese Journal of Sociology*, Vol. 2, No. 3, pp. 327–347. Available at: https://journals.sagepub.com/doi/abs/10.1177/2057150X16654059?journalCode=chsa (Accessed on 18 May 2019).

Xu, M., Singh, S. and Jacob-Phillips, S. (2019) 'China Expects to Hit 2020 Coal Cap Targets; Demand Overshadows: Study,' *Reuters*, 29 May. Available at: www.reuters.com/article/us-china-energy-coal/china-expects-to-hit-2020-coal-cap-targets-demand-overshadows-study-idUSKCN1SZ17M?feedType=RSS&feedName=environmentNews&utm_source=feedburner&utm_medium=feed&utm_campaign=

Feed%3A+reuters%2Fenvironment+%28News+%2F+US+%2F+Environment%29 (Accessed on 2 June 2019).

Yu, X. and Xiang, Z. (2014) 'Income Inequality in Today's China,' *Proceedings of the National Academy of Social Sciences of the United States of America*, 13 March. Available at: www.pnas.org/content/111/19/6928 (Accessed on 12 May 2019).

Yuan, S. (2019) 'Experts Tout Sustainable Development at Forum,' *China Daily*, 4 June. Available at: www.chinadaily.com.cn/cndy/2019-06/04/content_37476931.htm (Accessed on 4 June 2019).

Zhang, M. (2017) 'New Environment Tax Will Hit Businesses in China Hard, Say Experts,' *South China Morning Post*, 3 October. Available: www.scmp.com/business/china-business/article/2113650/new-environment-tax-will-hit-businesses-china-hard-say (Accessed on 3 June 2019).

Index

Note: Page numbers in **bold** indicate a table on the corresponding page. Page numbers followed by 'n' indicate a note.